GYPSY FROM THE FOREST

Gypsy from the Forest

A new biography of the international
evangelist Gipsy Smith (1860–1947)

David Lazell

Gwasg **Bryntirion** Press

Cover design:
burgum boorman ltd.

Published by Gwasg **Bryntirion** Press, Bryntirion
Bridgend, CF31 4DX, Wales, UK
Printed by Creative Print and Design (Wales), Ebbw Vale

Contents

Foreword

Looking to the future, we evangelicals often neglect the lessons of the past, or judge it harshly for failing to attain our own enlightenment. Today, when hundreds of thousands of Romany and other Gypsies on all five continents have joined evangelical Christian churches, why should the life of just one, Rodney Smith, who preached mainly to the gaje (non-Gypsies) under the nickname 'Gipsy Smith', still be important? David Lazell's biography, the fruit of his long-term commitment to 'Gipsy' Smith studies, and evangelical history more generally, shows us why.

Rodney Smith was a man of his own era, but one who, by living its contradictions, transcended his time. A largely self-educated man of 'primitive' religion, he nonetheless pointed more truly to the future than most of the wise of his age, through a spirituality which overleapt cultural barriers. In his writing and in his public appearances, Rodney Smith never took anything but delight in his own Romani ethnicity; but equally he was firm that no one's ethnicity preordains what kind of a person they will be. In our own age, where dethroning racism and ethnic hatred appears almost the first item on any agenda of practical love, the life of Rodney Smith is a parable of the possibility of a mutual joy in, and celebration of, cultural difference which nonetheless never permits cultural boundaries to become prison walls from behind which we dare not advance to seek visions of universal truth.

Perhaps I may be accused of anachronism in using contemporary jargon to project back onto Rodney Smith a theorization of his life that he never could have constructed for himself. His was the gospel of Christ and him crucified for lost sinners. It was preached in the same Eurocentric missionary discourse as Moody and Sankey and Booth; but nonetheless it was still the eternal gospel.

He was not able to do what Romany evangelicals do now, to present the gospel in Romani colours, and build up Romany congregations, which sometimes draw in non-Gypsies who might not have ever been reached from within their own traditions. Gypsy Christians of Rodney Smith's day had to make all the compromises and accommodations necessary to become Gypsy members of non-Gypsy churches; but by doing so they still bore witness to the limitless possibilities of the gospel. It is not surprising therefore that since the 1970s Smith has been rediscovered by the leaders of the Romany evangelicals.

Clement LeCossec, the Breton Assemblies of God pastor, who with the Gypsy convert Mandz Reinhardt, founded the Gypsy evangelical church in 1951, paid his second major missionary visit to Britain in 1975, when the British Gypsies for Christ movement was founded in Cardiff (Acton, 1979:294). As the person who ran the bookstall for the National Gypsy Education Council, I helped him look for copies of Gipsy Smith's autobiography in second-hand bookshops. Since then the price of its various editions has risen at least five-fold. It has never ceased to be an important alternative view of Gypsy life to that presented by the racial-romanticism of the Gypsy Lore Society; it is now coming back into its own as a statement of Christian witness.

The contradictions of being a prominent Christian Gypsy were not, however, lived without pain. Within his own close social circle he faced fierce criticisms both from Gypsies and non-Gypsies: that he had betrayed his own people, and that his personal life fell short of traditional Romany moral standards. It is perhaps worth examining and responding to these criticisms in some detail.

His accuser on the first count is no less than Eunice Evens, the gaji wife of his nephew the Rev. G. Bramwell Evens, a Methodist minister and popular nature broadcaster (under the name 'Romany of the BBC'. She wrote of Rodney and his brothers:

As a family, in one sense they never grew up, for not only did they retain a childlike simplicity and sincerity, but they were very susceptible to big things, especially big crowds. This pride

8

in the crowds which they attracted was a definite failing of theirs, and my husband always considered that, in reports in certain religious weeklies, undue emphasis was laid upon the huge building and masses of people who attended one mission meeting after another. That this had been so was true, but to them 'two or three' being gathered together did not signify success. It must have been difficult too for Cornelius [Rodney's father], too, after his 'conversion', [note the snigger-quotes imposed by Eunice's anti-evangelicalism] not to use his persuasive powers occasionally for his own ends, and it is not surprising that his children enjoyed the material benefits showered on them as a result of their missions' (Evens 1946:239).

Even though she also criticises her own husband for emotionalism and impracticality, Eunice never fails to draw him into these criticisms of Rodney's missions which

often caused disheartenment amongst the clergy and ministers concerned, and dissatisfaction amongst members of the congregation, who were inclined to compare the methods used to the disparagement of those to which they were accustomed. After one of these missions I remember a very conscientious, hard-working young minister coming to see my husband in a state of great mental distress. He was convinced that he was a failure, that he must change his methods or give up his work. My husband, to his surprise, laughed at him and assured him that though his relatives were eminently fitted for mission work, they had neither the training nor the intellectual ability to occupy his pulpit year after year' (Evens, 1946:175).

If, however, Rodney was too ignorant for Eunice, he was also too educated for his Romany critics. In a tape-recorded autobiography Gordon Boswell, a distant relation of Rodney on his mother's side, recounts how as a child his father, Trafalgar Boswell, preached alongside Rodney in Southend, but broke with him when 'he deserted his race of people . . . to go to America and preach the gospel among a different class of people' (Boswell, 1970:53).

9

In 1937, Gordon got the chance to denounce Rodney to his face when with his 'blonde secretary' (later his second wife Mary Alice) he visited Cambridge Midsummer Fair:

You know you've done a terrible thing after you was uplifted by the name of Gypsy. You were a leader among poor people, and you was needed and your teaching and education. You suddently picked your stakes up and you went to America and you massed a great fortune over there. In our estimation you made a fortune. You've come back for a holiday. And the Gypsy people that was old enough to know what you was doing at the time—they thought it was a shameful thing. You must have been money-crazed to do it. You should have been the very man that might have been a turning point in the Gypsies' lives by bringing up with that education that you have got some of it. And I believe you and my father and mother with their good way of living could have been the turning point among a lot of Gypsies to bring them on a level with someone else. But you went to America, you amassed a fortune and evidently you'll probably marry this young lady (Boswell, 1970:54).

What a catalogue of indictment! How could Rodney live with it, and how can David Lazell and I still admire him? Let me deal with these criticisms, one by one, starting with the last, Boswell's implication of impropriety in Smith's having a young woman secretary, and marrying her after the death of his first wife.

On this matter I entirely share Lazell's common-sense view. Nobody, who knew personally Mrs Mary Alice Smith during her marriage or during her long widowhood, has ever suggested that she was anything but a faithful supporter and encourager of her husband. Despite the disparity of age, this was a genuine love match. Rodney Smith's resolute enjoyment of the married state puts one in mind of his defence of his own parents and other older Gypsies' common-law marriages as being like that of Abraham who 'took Sara and she was his wife'. That many great evangelists are magnetically sexually attractive may make us properly cautious; but we should not be provoked either by the prudery of traditional Romani culture, or the cynicism of modern mass media, into seeing it as either surprising or shaming. Those who cannot see the beauty of this marriage are blind to one of God's great gifts.

More substantial is Boswell's accusation that Smith deserted his 'race', which Boswell conflates with the accusation that he deserted the poor. Lazell's account of Smith's ministry in other countries shows how unfair this accusation is. There were poor people a-plenty at his missions in those other countries, and in fact more Gypsies than ever there were in England. And to imagine that evangelists have a primary moral responsibility to their own 'race' shows a great poverty of imagination. The alleged particularism of the contemporary Gypsy evangelicals offends some established churches; but as a gajo myself I can say I have always received the warmest welcome in any Romani congregation I have visited. In fact the leading pastors are conscious of being leaders of their people in the world and in the church as a whole. Like Rodney Smith, they have a renewed vision of a catholic, universal church, of God's love and discipline for his whole creation. If Rodney Smith had stayed preaching a cut-price gospel with Trafalgar Boswell to poor Gypsies in Southend and Tiptree, they would still have been in the same ecclesiastical cul-de-sac, doomed to peter out, misunderstood by Gypsies and non-Gypsies alike. No doubt Gypsies in my own county of Essex were the losers in the short run by Rodney moving to a wider stage the talents that so dazzled the young Gordon Boswell at the turn of the century; but how many were the gainers?

The one point at which Gordon Boswell's accusations coincide with those of Eunice Evens is their censoriousness at Rodney Smith's standard of living. Though both comfortably off themselves, they object to the notion of the evangelist becoming wealthy through the contributions of their audiences. And such charges gain resonance through the antics of some television evangelists today, whose simoniac fleecing of isolated listeners arouses justified outrage. But there simply is no evidence that any of the Smiths set out to exploit people in this way. They did not pile up fortunes; they lived comfortably. The gifts of

11

congregations to preachers are often voluntary and heartfelt, not extorted. Rodney Smith's early break with the Salvation Army came because he refused to return an inscribed watch given to him by his congregation. He felt to do so would be an unjustified insult to the love which prompted the gift; and if we recall Jesus' reaction to those who criticised the woman who poured costly perfume over his feet we may sympathize with him. Inability to accept and enjoy the honest and open generosity of others can be as much a sign of meanness of spirit as rightness with one's own purse. I do not challenge those who feel a personal vocation to asceticism; but such are rarely among those who feel that the Christian religion is in itself incompatible with the enjoyment of God's earthly bounty.

Rodney Smith's early experiences, incidentally, before and after his leaving the Salvation Army, refute Eunice Evens' implication that he could not have pastored a congregation. As Lazell shows, he was a phenomenally successful and much loved pastor in Hanley. He was not in any way an evangelist without experience of, or concern for, the needs of local congregations. Sometimes, however, a return to first principles, the examination by individuals of their own relation with a transcendent God—or the transcendent in any discourse—will shake up the habits of institutional complacency. This does not imply, however, a lack of sympathy with the work of the pastoral institution.

We may question, in fact, how far Eunice Evens is correct in identifying her husband, Bramwell Evens, with the faded nostrums of mid-century theological liberalism. She speaks of his loyalties being divided between the 'abnormal religious atmosphere' (Evens 1946:17) or 'the excessively emotional Evangelistic Meetings of his youth and his natural preference for the ordinary conventional methods of conducting Church Services' (Evens 1946:34). Her biography shows that much as she loved him, she saw their married life as a crusade to organize his undisciplined gifts. She does her best to show appreciation of the gifts of her husband's Romany family; but she leaves the reader in no doubt what an uphill struggle she found it.

Dora Yates, the secretary of the Gypsy Lore Society, told me before her death (on 12th January 1974), what would happen when Eunice and Bramwell visited her. There would be stilted conversation for half an hour. Then Eunice would leave to visit the shops of Liverpool, and Bramwell would visibly relax and start 'rokkering Romany' with her. Perhaps Bramwell's prolonged solitary treks to observe wildlife were his way of dealing with what we now call 'the dilemma of the Romany intellectual'. Perhaps Eunice's tragedy was that she saw the beauty of a wild flower; but could not rest till she had it safely cut in a vase.

In the 1990s there are thousands of Romany intellectuals supporting dozens of tiny magazines which agonize about the problems of being a Romani intellectual. 'Gipsy' Rodney Smith MBE had no such network of communication and mutual support. He did not have the jargon to put on paper the existential dilemmas between being Gypsy and being educated, between being Gypsy and being a preacher, between being a member of the most persecuted of all European ethnic minorities and nonetheless a human being. But he lived those contradictions with grace and courage and faith and openness, and with a sheer gusto that must encourage all marginal individuals everywhere. I write as a Baptist who was the first member of his family, and of his local church ever to go away to college. I write as a sociologist who is usually the only Christian—the only religious person, even—in any gathering of twenty or thirty professional sociologists. I write as an academic whose speciality—Romani Studies—is often seen as, at best eccentric, at worst, a trendy irrelevance. Like David Lazell, I draw inspiration from Rodney Smith, who was able to live out contradictions, through his faith that one day we will see clearly what now we see, as through a glass, darkly. If that makes people see us as childlike, then God grant that with all God's children, we meet him in person when we enter the kingdom of heaven.

References

Acton, Thomas A., 1979 (ed. S. Cranford), *The Gypsy Evangelical Church* in The Ecumenical Review, Vol. 31, No. 3, July, pp.289-95.

Boswell, S. Gordon, 1970, *The Book of Boswell*, London, Gollancz.
Evens, Eunice, 1946, *Through the Years with Romany*, London, University of London Press.

THOMAS ACTON
June 1997

Preface

One of the many stories of 'the old days' relates to a man in a heavy overcoat, and who assumed a seat in the front row, at one of Gipsy's meetings. Gipsy had been speaking for some time, when the man suddenly stood up, carefully removing his overcoat, and smiling, 'Now for some more!'

Most people who heard Gipsy—and for that matter his friend, Peter Mackenzie—were ready to stay for 'some more', in Peter's case even turning back the hands of the balcony clock so that he would calculate he needed to preach for another half hour or so! As prefaces to books are usually written long after the main content is written, authors have the strange sense that they are introducing material not their own. Long hours at the typewriter (or word processor) have receded, new work taken in hand, so that the writer is surprised to behold some of the material which he/she prepared months earlier. So it is here—Gipsy speaks with his own voice in this narrative, and at times to the author as much as to the reader. As he would advise, prepare for some surprises!

My researching into the life of Gipsy Rodney Smith MBE had a modest beginning, in my buying (for ninepence) a copy of the original 1901 autobiography, an ageing green-covered volume among other bric-à-brac, in an old zinc bath-tub outside an antique shop in Bath. I appraised the book especially for its potential for reading onto recording tape for some blind friends; its quality here confirms how excellent a piece of work the original book was, and how close to Gipsy's famous testimony-lecture, 'The Story of My Life'. As that original has recently (1995) been reprinted by Ambassador Productions of Belfast, you may judge for yourself. But, of course, the book told only the first forty years of Gipsy's life, and the friendships I was to make in later years related to my interest in Gipsy Smith's varied and lively ministry through two world wars, and awesome changes in media communication, as well as in the nature of the British Commonwealth of Nations.

My original paperback summary of Gipsy's life, *From The Forest I Came* (1970), was published in Britain and Australia by Concordia Publishing, and in the USA as a Moody paperback. Years after its sell-out, I am still asked for copies, but this new work is not a reissue. Far from it, for in reading the proofs—just a day or two before preparing this preface—I am amazed to discover how different a book it is. A story yes, memories of missions and revival times, true—but arising out of it all, in a way that I had not anticipated, is an exposure of the main issues presented to people of goodwill in our times. For the churches of our day, often struggling to maintain a witness and for that matter their buildings, Gipsy opens out a visionary view of the work. Given his front line service in the First World War—and talks to US servicemen in the Second—Gipsy was bound to follow the counsel of John Wesley— preach as a dying man to dying men. Having seen so much sacrifice and heroism from servicemen, many of them long absent from the churches, he believed that every sincere disciple, every believer in Christ, had to live in a spirit of gratitude. And that, of course, is always close to a spirit of joyfulness, not brought on by religious excitements, but rather in the community life and openness of the people of God. Careful as he was on theological precision, Gipsy would not think much of those who mistake point-scoring for discipleship. 'What we need is to be so showered by the love of God, that it would drench everybody!': that is the sentiment of this book, and I hope that many preachers will find some further 'plums for their cakes' in the material presented here. However, the narrative is designed for all—churchgoers or not—who are trying to make sense of our often spiritually-stifling times.

A word of explanation is needed about the frequent switches in this work from 'Gipsy' to 'Gypsy'. 'Gipsy', which is now archaic, was the word used by Rodney Smith of himself. It was also used when people spoke or wrote of him as Gipsy Smith or the Gipsy. The currently acceptable academic spelling is 'Gypsy'. It is capitalized because it is the proper name of an ethnic group, just as

Welsh is used of the Welsh people, not welsh. Therefore I have used 'Gypsy' throughout where reference is being made to Gypsies as an ethnic group, but I have used 'Gipsy' when referring to Rodney Smith, the name by which he was known to his family.

I have generally preferred to use the word 'Romany' rather than the term 'Romani', because it is better known among the general reading public than 'Romani'.

One final point, as to the element of surprise for the writer. Only in reading the proofs, months after writing the copy, did I realize that the use of mobile YMCA in the First World War, that Gipsy Smith, like other workers and chaplains, could continue a ministry of friendship and assurance. 'Innovations' might have made a good title for the book, for Gipsy Smith was never a man to advise settling down into a rut, even one hallowed by tradition and convention. The wagon moves on, the YMCA hut is replaced, a tree falls, and another grows. Nothing is permanent in this life; Gipsy passed from this world into the presence of his Lord, whilst travelling on the ocean. Building up a good work in the locality is always to be encouraged, but Gipsy added a dimension of pilgrimage to the everyday round of good deeds. A pilgrimage together, not merely in individual terms: the sense of the close-knit family or clan, derived from his Romany origins, was expressed in his talks, as you will read, in terms of a mutual commitment and loving lifestyle among the Christian folk in any particular place. Certainly, a message for our own day.

What a remarkable story it all is! In closing, I must express my thanks to Zillah (Mrs Zillah Palfreman), Romany Watt, and the many others who have encouraged my interest in the old warrior for Christ. Also to the book's editor, David Kingdon, and the staff at Bryntirion, close to my home town of Bridgend, and to Dr Thomas Acton for his foreword. I still receive mail from people interested in the times represented to this book, and a Romany Society (recalling the life and work of Rev. George Bramwell Evens) has been formed. Interest in the traditions of the Romany people has grown a great deal since my researches began, and new concerns for the well-being of travellers are more evident

17

now than for many decades. Could it be that in our own day, another preacher from the forest will come to stir the hearts of the nations?

DAVID LAZELL
April, 1997

Introduction

Gipsy Rodney Smith MBE—hereafter known as 'Gipsy Smith'—came into this world, on the last day of March 1860, on the wings of the 1858–59 revival that came to many churches in the United States and in Great Britain. The Welsh Revival of 1904–05 and the beginnings of modern Pentecostalism, in the Azusa Street Revival in Los Angeles, came at the mid-point of his always busy life. And when Gipsy died, en route to the States in August 1947, a new work of evangelism was soon to begin in Britain and elsewhere with Billy Graham. In his lifetime, Gipsy saw the beginnings of new urban evangelism, through the Methodist Central Missions and the Salvation Army, and in the 1890s he himself was invited to become associated with new inter-church evangelism linked with the National Council Connection of Evangelical Free Churches (NCEFC). Indeed, it was in connexion with this body that Gipsy, with his great helper, Rev. Thomas Law, developed the methods of modern crusade evangelism.

The New Century Campaign, organized by the churches in the face of a great falling-away from the Christian faith, certainly focused on 'great preaching'. But the missions held under the auspicies of the National Council of Evangelical Free Churches, in 1900 and 1901, proved to be a precursor of the great revival of 1904–05 that burst upon the Principality of Wales. Associated especially with the tireless labours of Evan Roberts—'the boy preacher', as he was known (though in his mid twenties and over six feet tall!)—the revival spread far beyond Wales, bringing many young men into the ministry. Certainly, the missions held by Gipsy helped to prepare for the Revival, though the churches in Wales often failed to follow the counsel of the experienced Free Church missioners, who advised careful follow-up and teaching of converts.

Following the traumas of the First World War (1914–18), a catastrophe that robbed so many churches of their youth and potential leadership, Gipsy challenged the churches afresh to live out the gospel they preached. Someone commented to the present writer, a decade or so ago, that congregations in the USA and Britain 'took it from Gipsy because they knew he lived it out himself'. He was a 'pentecostal' preacher, even though his main work lay within the traditional denominations. Gipsy did not say much about 'speaking in tongues', an issue which has come into prominence in the charismatic movement in recent years, probably because he was more interested in the 'work of the Holy Spirit in the heart'. 'You may as well try to bore a hole through a wall with a candle, as attempt to live the Christian life without the Holy Spirit', he once said in a characteristic comment that reflected a sound theology.

Any preacher as widely travelled as Gipsy would have known about 'counterfeits' in spiritual experience, and in any case his special emphasis was upon creation and the way that it spoke of a benevolent Father in heaven. But that, of course, related to his own childhood and youth in the forest, and on the lanes and byways of England, in the Gypsy wagon. His many references to the natural world, and the way in which it reflected the God of the Bible, seem tailored to our anxious age, in which we have claimed mastery of creation, and well nigh ruined it.

Gipsy Smith's influence on the course of evangelism and preaching was considerable, yet today many people seem to think of him as a Victorian figure, one who lived long ago, and whose inspirations are locked away with souvenirs and scrapbooks. They are surprised to learn that Gipsy lived into the age of nuclear fission and television. But he died not long after the end of the Second World War, during a period of austerity, and four-page daily newspapers. Whilst evangelical periodicals published tributes, Gipsy's passing was unnoticed by most. Merely surviving was a main concern in 1947.

Although Gipsy was a pioneer in so many respects, in his use of radio for example, he serves as a model for us in his genial humility. He was not afraid to acknowledge his limitations and he was always ready to smile. In his way, he was one of the great Christian humorists, and he echoed the advice of his Lord and Master: 'Be of good cheer' . . . 'cheer up!' The best thing you can do for your church, he would say to congregations, is to leave the meeting with a smile on your face, and with encouragement in your heart.

No single writer could hope to capture all that Gipsy did in a single book. Besides, there is today a booming interest in Romany/Gypsy life and traditions today, as I have discovered from the mail when I have written on this subject in magazines. Born in Epping Forest, Gipsy never lost his affinity with the Romany of his childhood world.

Apart from necessary secretarial assistance and organizational backup for missions, e.g. from the Free Churches or Methodist Home Missions Department in the inter-war period, Gipsy did not have an 'evangelical association' on the lines that might be considered necessary today. Indeed, some in the USA especially were surprised at the lightness of his administrative 'load'. He would offer such smiling comment, as 'Well, my Master orders the universe, so I believe He can order this mission.' Anticipating and perhaps pre-modelling the Billy Graham Crusades that came after his death, Gipsy insisted that local churches 'get together' in some kind of mission committee, and then extend an invitation to him. He was never in the business of 'hitting town and cleaning up' as, alas, some 'evangelists' were. By ensuring that local missions were sponsored by many churches (though probably held in a local hall or, in the USA, the Armory). Gipsy was able to concentrate on 'soul winning'. But in some respects his enduring influence was as great upon those already in the churches as upon those who had drifted away from them after the First World War.

Perhaps, most of all, Gipsy reminds us that we cannot find answers to our contemporary bewilderments in 'better organisation' (not even within the Christian fold). As he remarked to a lady as he travelled to a mission meeting in the USA, there would be no point in organizing any event of the kind unless 'we knew that the Holy Spirit would be present'. For those coping with the great political issues of our time, he might well advise that the only 'top down' revolution that works is the coming of the Holy Spirit.

There are many questions for all of us in the story of Gipsy Smith's remarkable life. Indeed, if you read this book without believing yourself to have been asked a question or two, you might need to read it through again! But it is designed to cheer and encourage, so, to quote Gipsy, 'Pass It On'.

1
A Romany childhood

When I was a boy, and my father pitched his tent
in the summertime, I would not be there for many
minutes before I had a garden.
(Gipsy Smith)

As Gipsy often told his audiences (and so graphically described in his 1901 autobiography) he was born in a tent, to a poor Gypsy family, in Epping Forest, on 31 March 1860. Britain then still had a large Gypsy (i.e. romany-speaking) population, and churches often undertook work in teaching its children to read and to write. But children raised in poverty were a widespread problem, and certainly not limited to Gypsy families, but young Rodney (the future Gipsy Smith) at least had the benefit of a close-knit family. There is some query about his date of birth, for in later years, an aunt who studied the parish records at Wanstead Parish Church in Essex, where his birth was registered, reported that Gipsy was a year younger than he had hitherto thought—a pleasant surprise for anyone in middle age!

The clergy of the Church of England took differing approaches to the baptizing of 'Gypsy children', not least because the marriages of parents might never have been registered, or might even have agreed upon under the old Romany practices. In the face of all the prejudice against these representatives of a truly ancient people, Gipsy emphasized the genuine commitment found among members of the extended family or clan, contrasting these with the breakdown of 'real' family life that he found, for example, in the USA between the wars. Where a parish church agreed to baptize a Gypsy child, there would sometimes be a kind of 'gift shower' by the parishioners, which, though well meant, did provide some excuse for visiting the Gypsy encampment. So, if the local clergyman visited the camp to make a prior arrangement with the proud parents, 'some of the ladies of the congregation are sure to accompany the parson in order to see the Gypsy baby, and they cannot very well do this, without bringing presents for the Gypsy mother and more often for the baby'. Gipsy Smith, noting these arrangements in his turn of the century memoir, thought that in those days (i.e. the early 1900s) Gypsies 'believed in christenings for the profit that they can make out of them', but he was careful to add that the Gypsy families had 'some kind of notion that it is the right thing to do'.

The giving of names to a Gypsy child was a serious matter, undertaken with more thought than many parents might take today. Perhaps here there was some lingering influence of the belief found in the east, that the name reflects the child's character—even purpose in life—whilst also relating him or her to a family lineage. Biblical and especially Old Testament names were given. Gipsy's father was named Cornelius, and his two brothers were named Woodlock and Bartholomew (they were later to form an evangelical trio known as the 'Three Gipsy Brothers'). Bartholomew ('Barty') gave a biblical name to every one of his twelve children, including both a Samson and Delilah. The fact that few Gypsies owned copies of the Bible, or possessed sufficient skill to read the Scriptures, prompted Gipsy to wonder as to the origins of the naming tradition. Tracing some similarities between ancient Gypsy practices and certain customs of the Jewish people (for example, designating pots and pans as 'clean' or 'unclean') prompted Gipsy to wonder if the true Romany people were in some ways related to the 'lost tribes of Israel'. Whether or not the 'tribes' were ever truly 'lost' is open to doubt, but Gipsy's autobiography appeared at a time when many Christian magazines were discussing the possible return of the Jews to their own land, Palestine. Like the Jews, the Gypsies were scattered in many lands. Gipsy reminded his readers that, in common with the Jews, the Gypsies had retained their ethnic identity and character, despite decades of persecution, wanderings and more subtle pressures to 'conform' and adopt the more settled, materialistic lifestyle of the native/settled population. More than ninety years ago Gipsy wrote, 'We gipsies can be traced back until we are lost on the plains of India, but even in those far off days, we were a distinct race.' Geneaology, so popular an interest today, was always of great importance to the Jews, and necessarily so. But the great and ancient Gypsy families and clans in Britain prior to the First World War, had almost as great an interest in forebears and kinship.

Father

Some details of Gipsy's father Cornelius Smith's origins can be found in a small, and rarely seen volume, published in the 1890s, *The Life Story of Cornelius Smith*, when Gipsy's father was the sole surviving member of the 'Three Gipsy Brothers'. Happily, much of the material was reprinted by Gipsy in his 1901 title, produced with the assistance of a Religious Tract Society editor, Grinton Berry.

We learn from this source that Cornelius was born in a Gypsy tent on 8 May 1831, in the parish of Burwell, Cambridgeshire. Cornelius' parents, James and Elizabeth Smith, had been married at Longstanton, in the same county, their occupation being shown as basket makers and chair caners, two of the traditional crafts by which Cornelius later earned an income. Elizabeth obviously exerted some moral influence, and Cornelius recalled that although she was 'only a gipsy', and in that sense would probably be thought ignorant of spiritual matters by most 'gorgios' (non Gypsies), she would never permit her sons to go to bed without saying the Lord's Prayer.

But even well-meaning men could turn to drink at times of economic hardship; it was a constant temptation for many in working-class life. Cornelius' father was a heavy drinker and Gipsy Smith may have been thinking of the traumas faced by his paternal grandparents when he warned that 'drink is the devil in solution'. Gipsy knew of course that going to public houses was often necessary to find work, and that engagements could be sealed with a drink. And since Gypsies often found employment at fairs and other places of celebration where liquor was drunk, the temptation to indulge in hearty drinking was persistent.

Indeed, Gipsy's own father Cornelius might have gone the same way, for he was a fine fiddler, and was much in demand for entertainment in public houses. Young Rodney used to 'take the hat around' and if his father was 'too far gone in drink', helped to guide him back to the wagon. Fiddlers (i.e. those able to play a violin well, for dancing and accompaniment) were much in demand, and became celebrities on their own account. Thus if any fiddler of note was converted, he could secure a hearing for some time afterwards—though his hearers might hope that good intentions would soon be abandoned.

Cornelius Smith secured an uncertain income, necessary to sustain his family, through exercising the crafts 'inherited from his parents', as well as making tin-ware items, clothes pegs and other small but useful objects that could be sold from door to door.

Cornelius also excelled in judging horses for stamina, performance and character, but a converted Gypsy could not be 'economical with the truth'. Gypsy during a meeting might refer to a Gypsy trader—now converted to the gospel—being asked to give his 'honest opinion' of a horse for sale, and struggling to be fair to both parties.

Mother

Like any basically earnest and well-meaning man, in any generation, Cornelius at times yearned to make a better life for himself and for his family. He married a young Gypsy, Polly Welch, but one has a passing insight into the problems of the couple in Cornelius' comment, in his 1890s memoir that, 'not being able to read . . . never having been to school, it was no wonder that I was so ignorant of the Christian way of life'.

We know little of Polly Welch, and, as she died when Gipsy was only five years old, he remembered little of her, much to his considerable regret. Polly was expecting a sixth child, when her eldest, Emily, fell ill, whilst the wagon was nearing the village of

Baldock in Hertfordshire. Called to examine the child, the local physician refused to enter the wagon, and made his diagnosis from the doorway. Seeing that the child had the dreaded disease of smallpox, he insisted that the wagon be placed in a remote spot, in a lane well away from any habitation, and ordered that the rest of the children keep clear of the wagon, and stay in a tent. Polly had not at that point contracted the disease, and only did so because she insisted on caring for the sick child. Cornelius believed that but for their being Gypsies, the sick child would have been allowed to enter the isolation hospital nearby, but we cannot know the kind of problems facing the doctor, because treatment for most diseases was very limited in the 1890s.

Polly contracted smallpox through caring for Emily. The baby was born, but died soon afterwards, as did Polly. Both Polly and child were buried at Baldock Churchyard, the authorities insisting that the interment be made at night, to minimize the risk of contact with local people. Gipsy's extensive recollection of the event, included in his autobiography, demonstrates how deeply he had been affected. He wrote, more than thirty years later, 'when I try to call back the appearance of my dear mother, I am baffled . . . her face has faded clean from my memory.'

Further disaster followed mere hours later, when the tent caught fire and many of the family's modest possessions were lost. The significance of the event was hardly lost on Cornelius, for traditional Romany beliefs required that on the death of any member of the family, all his or her possessions were to be destroyed by fire, this act being necessary in order that the spirit of the dead person could be released to travel to a better world.

Rev. George Hall, who knew many Gypsy folk and was something of an authority on Romany tradition, wrote that Gypsies possessed so deep a sense of grief that when any member of the family died, they would not eat any meal that would remind them of the one who had gone. He recalled the example of a Gypsy named Nookes Herne, who once had a child named 'Chasey'. But the child had died, and the mourning father would not use the name under any circumstances. When the ordinary business of life required him to refer to a man owning the same name, Nookes Herne would speak of 'that shovel mouthed man'.

Gipsy said that it was his mother's death 'which awoke me to full consciousness'. The family consisted of Cornelius and five children, of whom Rodney (Gipsy) was the fourth. He seems to have possessed a special affinity with Matilda (Tilly), born in 1862, who was to become no mean preacher herself in later life, and who (on marriage to George Evens, the Salvationist) was to become the mother of (Rev.) G. B. Evens, better known as 'Romany of the BBC'.

Travelling in their wagon towards Luton, that famous 'town of hat-makers', Cornelius and the children were delighted to meet Cornelius' two brothers, and their families coming *from* Luton, and making their leisurely way towards Cambridge. Cornelius decided to join the caravanserai, not least because his brothers' families could help his own children overcome their sadness. None of the brothers at that time had anything more than a 'natural religion' and, given the traditional Gypsy ideas, they had little of that consolation which comes to believers in the risen Christ. Yet Polly seems to have had some understanding of true religion; she had sung an old hymn shortly before she died, lines she must have learned at a meeting in the forgotten past.

The three brothers paused at a public house, just outside Cambridge, and, as they discussed their loss, the landlady overheard them. Interrupting their conversation, she said that she would send for a book 'that makes me cry whenever I read it'. She was not immediately aware that none of the trio was able to read, and on learning this was so, asked a young man if he would read aloud to the Gypsies as they took food and water to their horses. The book was not the Bible, but Bunyan's *Pilgrim's Progress*, one of the excerpts making a great impression. The reading had come to the passage in which Pilgrim's burden falls away as he gazes at the Cross. Gipsy records in his autobiography that his uncle Bartholomew responded to the words and that all three brothers 'felt the smart of sin, and wept like little children'.

2
A man of faith and fire

*I don't know anything about being
religious—what I want is Christ.*
(Cornelius Smith)

Cornelius has left on record an account of his spiritual awakening which he carefully distinguishes from his actual conversion to Christ.

On Sunday, we went to the Primitive Methodist Chapel in Fitzroy Street, Cambridge—morning, afternoon and night. At night, Mr Guns preached. His points were very cutting to my soul; he seemed to aim directly at me. I tried to hide myself behind a pillar in the chapel, but he, looking and pointing in that direction, said, 'He died for Thee.'

The anxious ones were asked to come forward, and in the prayer meeting the preacher came to where I was sitting, and asked me if I was saved. I cried out, 'No! that is what I want!' He tried to show me that Christ had paid my debt, but the enemy of souls had blinded my eyes, and made me believe that I must first feel it, and then believe it, instead of receiving Christ by faith first. Thousands make a great mistake there. I went from that house still a convicted sinner but not a converted one.

Although Cornelius gives no precise date for the service, attended by the three brothers, we can be almost certain that it was in late 1868 or early 1869.

Conversion of three brothers

Soon after his visit, with Bartholomew and Woodlock, to the Primitive Methodist Chapel in Cambridge, Cornelius and his family journeyed 'home' to Epping Forest, where his parents were living in a tent. Cornelius recalls that he put his horses to graze overnight in a piece of enclosed ground, as was custom, but on fetching them in the morning, he was convicted that he should not repeat the act. 'The Spirit of God told me it was wrong. I told God that it should be the last time that I would ever do such a thing or sin against Him knowingly.'

Hardly able to conceal his feelings, Cornelius told his brothers and relations, that he was 'done with roaming and wrong-doing' and that he meant to turn to God, 'by His help'. His brothers' response seems to have been one of alarm, Bartholomew exclaiming, 'My brother is going to heaven, and I am going to hell.'

Happily, the brothers had heard of the kindly and effective work of Henry Varley, a man who welcomed Gypsies and anyone else eager to hear the gospel. Although the Gypsies had sold their horses, they were able to 'borrow them' to draw their wagons to a piece of 'building land' close to Henry Varley's chapel in Shepherd's Bush, London, in the early spring of 1869. A fine example to believers in his day, as in ours, Henry Varley was a business man who addressed his practical gifts to 'reaching traders'. Known and respected in the markets and warehouses, and where everyday commerce was in hand, Henry Varley built a chapel to which all were welcome to come. He lived in Notting Hill, but was known throughout the land. As we will soon see, he had a very practical influence on the three Gypsy brothers, following their conversion.

Cornelius and Bartholomew found their way to a 'little mission hall' in Latimer Road, Shepherd's Bush, where a prayer meeting was in progress. Cornelius noted that its congregation included 'several working men', which suggests that they had come from their labours direct to the meeting. Today, when the issue of being 'slain in the Spirit' is often debated, it is worth noting that Cornelius had a similar experience in that mission hall, in the Spring of 1869.

As they were singing ('There is a fountain filled with blood') the power of God took hold of me. I was standing up, and my mind seemed to be taken away from everybody and fixed heavenward. I was unconscious until I fell to the floor and the people told me afterwards that I lay there for half an hour.

Rising to his feet, Cornelius

told the people that Christ had saved me. My dear brother Bartholomew was saved the same night. No human instrument pointed the way; God began it and God finished it.

The impact on Cornelius was awesome. He told the people at the mission that he felt so light that had the room been full of fresh eggs, he could have walked through and not broken one.

Woodlock resisted the brothers' testimony for a few days. Bartholomew and Cornelius began a prayer meeting in the tent of one of the Gypsy folk, and saw many conversions, some among their family. But, like all new Christians in any generation, Cornelius was faced with the issue of 'giving up' likely distractions to his new life:

My attention was drawn to my fiddle that I had played and loved in the dancing saloons. So that it should form no temptation to me, I made up my mind to part with it, although it had brought me in great gain (i.e. money collected at pubs etc.). I took the fiddle to a pawnshop in Shepherd's Bush, and asked the pawnbroker what he would give me for it. He said, 'What? sell your best friend!' I told him I had found Jesus, and He had taken away all my desire for earthly things. He wept, and taking my hand, said, 'May God bless you', and we parted. This was April 6th 1869. Mr Henry Varley heard of our conversion, and came to invite us to his tabernacle. He put a mission tent on the ground where we were staying, and called it 'The Gipsy Tabernacle'. A lady volunteered to teach the gipsy children in the daytime, and several young men came in the evening to give us an hour's reading, and to hold services on different nights in the week.

This practical help was almost certainly organized by a church in the area, quite possibly by Henry Varley himself. But Cornelius and his brothers were required to leave the location and, like the early Salvationists, found their gospel meetings attacked by rowdy and drunken people.

The Gypsy preachers

Cornelius and his two brothers—Woodlock finding Christ as Saviour on 11 April 1869—next travelled to Kent, for the hop harvest season. They had worked for a Mr Hodge at Orphan Green for some years, but now he was a little nonplussed at finding three fairly 'ordinary workers' suddenly turned into preachers. Mrs Hodge, the farmer's wife, urged her husband to give the trio employment; in the end, the Gypsy men were able to give personal testimony to the farmer and his family, and a tent was put up in the cherry orchard so that meetings could be held when the day's work was done. Henry Varley, who continued to take a practical interest in the work of the Gypsy brothers, came down to visit them; services were held throughout the picking season, and petty crime rates fell to such a low point that the local policeman reported that he could take his Bible rather than his staff to the meetings, there was so good a spirit. But perhaps the most remarkable of the events narrated by Cornelius Smith, in the memoir written in late life comes from this time, in late 1869 or early 1870:

> Soon after we wrote to my father and mother, telling them we were converted, and then we went to see them at Lowton Forest. They soon prepared something for us to eat. We told them that before we partook of food, now we prayed. All knelt down, and my father cried for mercy, and said he ought to have set the example. Instead of that, we had come to teach him, and both my father and mother rested on the promise of God. They were then seventy years of age. They lived five years after that, trusting in the finished work of Christ.

At the close of the hop harvesting season, the Gypsy brothers travelled to Cambridge, planning to spend the winter encamped on some ground near the Gas House at Barnwell, on the edge of the city. Meanwhile, with characteristic zeal, the Primitive Methodists recruited the three Gypsy brothers for their 'circuit plan', and as they preached in both Methodist and Baptist chapels, among others, we can see that there was no strict denominational bias on the brothers' part. Although William Booth, the founder of the Salvation Army, was to help the trio especially, and recruit the young Gipsy Smith as a preacher, it was the Primitive Methodists who had a special stake in all their labours.

Following their conversion, and their determination to follow a new way of life in Christ, the brothers decided that they would journey to Baldock, in Hertfordshire, where they would witness to old friends and members of the Gypsy clans. Magistrates in the area, showing it seems little sympathy towards travellers, had instructed the police to watch out for anyone likely to be a 'trouble maker'. The definition was possibly left open to interpretation, for the trio of erstwhile evangelists were suddenly apprehended and clapped into police cells. One wonders as to the response of the desk sergeant at the cheerful demeanour of the three men, who like Paul and Silas in the story in Acts, seem to have rejoiced rather than complained. Quite soon, news came that as any fine had been guaranteed by a benefactor, the men were to be released. If anything, this arrest helped their cause, for it acted as a kind of advance publicity, so that a large crowd awaited them, as they came to Baldock.

Given that the nineteenth century was rich in self-taught, home-spun preachers, there might seem little reason for devoting more space to 'the three converted gipsies'. Perhaps, though, better-trained and well-equipped speakers or writers of our time might learn from their directness. J. W. C. Fegan, founder of Fegan's Homes, had heard and met many preachers over the course of his busy and fruitful life, and was surely a fine judge of character. In the monthly magazine, published by the Fegan's Homes, 'Loving and Sharing', dated March 1906, Fegan wrote:

I heard with great joy and thankfulness of much precious fruit from a mission just held in Norwich. These recent meetings were conducted by Mr Cornelius Smith—father of the well-known Gipsy Smith—and his (i.e. Cornelius') second wife, formerly Captain Sayers of the Salvation Army.

With his brothers, Bartholomew and Woodlock, Cornelius constituted the trio of gipsy brothers who had no pretensions to learning. They were simple men; their books had been the hedgerows and the commons, and the stream and sky. They lived in gipsy caravans, and wore the usual type of gipsy clothing.

In 1881, they came to the village of Downe in Kent, where my aged mother (now in her 97th year) was living, in order to hold a mission. After breakfast and dinner, they used to get her to read the Bible aloud to them, while they gathered round and repeated after her, any special texts until they had committed them to memory. Woodlock could read best of them all, and was gifted with the clearest, purest Saxon speech I have ever heard. Poor Bartholomew's memory seemed to be, as a fellow countryman said of his own memory, 'what he forgot things with'. The other two brothers grew a little impatient one day over Bartholomew's futile attempts to remember a rather long text, and blurted out, 'Read on, ma'm, our Barty has a shocking memory.'

Then Bartholomew made what I thought was a wonderful answer: 'Ah, ma'm, what with drink and policemen and prison, my poor head's been that knocked about, I don't seem to remember anything. They do say that trying to teach me the Scriptures is like carrying water in a sieve. But I do say, ma'm, I thank God that it cleans the sieve anyhow.'

These three great-hearts served the cause of God for some twelve years together, until Woodlock, the second eldest, died following an accident during a mission at Chingford, Essex, in the Spring of 1882. Some measure of the reputation of this 'untaught gipsy' may be seen in the report of his funeral at Leytonstone, when over fifty Gypsies, and four hundred other friends came to the church. Indeed, the service was almost a mission meeting on its own account, as visitors spoke of how their own service to Christ had resulted from their response to Woodlock's preaching. Woodlock had been, as we would consider it today, quite young at the time of his death. He was just forty-eight years of age. When, two years later, Bartholomew died, Cornelius thought that his own evangelistic work might be over. But two years after that, Cornelius (who was of course a widower) found a second wife in a lady who had worked with William Booth. Together, they were able to press on in evangelism, Cornelius achieved a fine old age, living until he was ninety-one. As a preacher Cornelius had a winsome turn of phrase. His dramatic conversion experience did not, as sometimes is the case, give him any sense of spiritual self-importance. His influence upon his son was immense, an influence which Gipsy Smith gladly acknowledged in the dedication of his autobiography: to 'My father, to whom, under God, I owe all that I am.'

3
Early days

*Every crisis in our own lives can be, in
God's good purposes, a window opened in heaven.*
(Rev. Dinsdale T. Young)

G ipsy was to bring a breath of country air—as well as the breeze of revival—into the churches. Rare indeed was the sermon without some memory of his childhood, and life in the forest. Today, when we are so keenly aware of threats to the natural environment and loss of species through man's thoughtless behaviour, the issues raised by Gipsy seem especially significant. As a gospel preacher, Gipsy contrasted the sophistication that he saw in a modern world with the basic realities of life. True, he might put his sentiment into a half humorous comment, as when he claimed that he learned to sing 'from the birds'. But he was at times almost a modern Francis of Assisi, reminding his hearers that it was better to love creation and respect it, than merely to argue about its theological significance. Often enough, people would go to hear Gipsy, expecting to hear some reminiscence to stir the heart, and would discover later that, within all the stories, there was a sharp word to a careless generation. Reading through Gipsy's sermons and memoirs in the 1990s, one can find the challenge still, and in one sense only a Gypsy, born in the forest and raised among the trees, could have made it in such a way.

At the time of Gipsy Smith's birth in March 1860, Romany clans or families, who might differ in wealth and status, were associated with different parts of the country. Cornelius reminds us in his 1890s retrospect that certain towns and camp sites represented a sort of 'circuit'. Epping Forest, visited by thousands of Londoners, in search of a few bargains and souvenirs, was a popular haunt of the Gypsies. Popular magazines of the second half of the nineteenth century suggested that the entertainments (and encampments) in the Forest represented a useful distraction from the pressures of industrialized and urbanized existence, though this generous judgment was not entirely unanimous. Rev. Charles Bullock, the sturdy founder of *Home Words* and the Pure Literature League, suggested in another of his papers, *The Fireside*, in 1883, that 'if any of our London readers desire to see how gipsies live, they cannot do better than go to Epping Forest, especially on a popular holiday, when they succeed in draining a good deal of money from dupes who pay liberally to have their fortunes told.' Gipsy Smith, though a sturdy defender of his people, was no less severe in his view of fortune telling. Such superstition on the part of the Romanies did little to help them develop their real talents and value to the human race, and as for churchgoers, 'they say that they believe in the Bible and in God, and yet they go off to the seaside—Blackpool or Southend—and they look into a crystal, or trust to a pack of greasy cards, and believe a gipsy can tell them what is going to happen.'

If the young Rodney* (Gipsy) had any 'model' for a future 'career', he seems to have gained it from the fairground or sideshows. During the summer months, Gypsies could find employment in the fairs, and perhaps still do, but opportunities were much more plentiful before the First World War then ever they were afterwards. Rodney was especially attracted by the 'fairground barker'—that exponent of beguiling oratory who stood outside a sideshow or entertainment, urging those within earshot, to spend a few coins in entering within. A lad of rather earnest expression, the future evangelist must also have learned at least some communication skills in the door-to-door selling of hand-made clothes-pegs, made by his father and later by himself. According to tradition (and recollections from visitors to his missions) he sometimes sang on the doorstep, though usually on request. But perhaps some indication of his approach is given in one of his own memories from childhood.

---

* The first Baron Rodney (1718–2) was a British admiral whose surname became a forename in the nineteenth century.

There was, for example, the matter of securing a vendor's licence, as required by local authorities, and which the Gypsy folk rarely seemed to possess (which was hardly surprising, since many of them were unable to read or write). One day, young Rodney called at a house to display his basket of wares, only to find that the tenant was a policeman. Confirming that the young fellow on the doorstep had no licence, the policeman took him before the local magistrate for appropriate chastisement and punishment. But it says something for the enlightened magistrate (by no means all such people were) that he allowed the young Gypsy to speak up for himself.

Making good use of the opportunity, and possibly displaying early signs of that eloquence so characteristic of his later work, young Rodney explained that he was only trying to make an honest living, not stealing, as so many people accused Gypsies of doing. Further, the clothes-pegs made by his father were good ones—they did not break (he spoke the truth here, examples of Cornelius' pegs were brought to meetings held by Gipsy years later). Furthermore, his father would certainly pay for a vendor's licence if he knew how to secure one. A nominal fine was imposed. As he sometimes sold as many as five or six gross of clothes-pegs in a single day, the young Gypsy's approach must have been effective. Years later, when someone suggested that he might be elevated to the House of Lords, Gipsy joked that he would take the title of 'Lord Clothes-Pegs'.

It is sometimes thought that Gipsy wanted to become a preacher simply because his father and brothers were preachers. But it was the death of his mother Polly that brought him first to a sense of his own 'person', and that tragic sense of life that so often precedes a sense of mission. When Gipsy's father Cornelius was converted, his children at first did not know what to make of the event. Cornelius recalled that after his conversion at the Latimer Road Mission Hall, he 'went home a new creature in Him. When I arrived home, my children were called, and for the first time in my gipsy home, I knelt with them in prayer. I began at the right place, with my dear children.'

The change in Cornelius' life was dramatic, and given the

course of his subsequent life, one can hardly doubt its reality. Gipsy wrote in his 1901 autobiography,

> He [Cornelius] has often spoken of that great change since. He walked around the mission hall looking at his flesh. It did not seem to be all quite the same colour to him . . . When my father got home to the wagon that night, he gathered us all around him. I saw at once that the old haggard look that his face had worn for years had gone, and, indeed, it was gone for ever.

Gipsy's conversion

Gipsy states that he was converted on 17 November 1876, and at the time, he was hardly literate. This confirmation of his new life in Christ came during a mission at the Fitzroy Street Primitive Methodist Church in Cambridge, where the three Gypsy brothers were in membership. These are described (by J. Stephenson, in his biography of Rev. George Warner) as 'mighty men in processions and prayer meetings', the mention of processions indicating an emphasis on open-air missions which was characteristic of Primitive Methodism at the time.

Well known at the Fitzroy Street Church, Rev. George Warner conducted a campaign in the mid-1870s, at which Cornelius 'thanked God for saving his children, and prayed God that he might have a loving heart at home, and be kept away from everything that might grieve them.'

Gipsy was pointed to Christ by George Bell, who was a Primitive Methodist minister. In a jubilee sketch of George Bell's ministry, published in a 1904 booklet shortly before his retirement, the Rev. S. Seaman stated:

> Everyone knows Gipsy Smith, and the great work he is still doing for the Master. But everybody does not know that it was in a prayer meeting in the old Fitzroy Street Chapel in Cambridge that 'he first saw the light and the burden of his heart rolled away', and that Mr Bell was kneeling at his side, when it was done.

Gipsy confirmed the narrative, for at a meeting at The Dome Mission, Brighton, at about the same time as the 1904 booklet was issued, he clasped the shoulder of George Bell who was seated on the platform. Gipsy joyfully told the congregation, 'He was there when it was done.'

In 1874, D. L. Moody and Ira Sankey, the American preacher and gospel singer, paid a visit to Epping Forest. Cornelius' witness to the gospel must have been made known to the visitors, for they at once hastened to meet him. In the encounter, recalled by Gipsy in his missions in later years, Ira Sankey placed his hand on young Rodney's head and prayed that 'the Lord would make him a preacher'. Sankey, a thoughtful man, would not have made that benediction lightly, and it is interesting to note that the gospel singer was to help Gipsy when the latter at last arrived in the USA in 1889 (see p.48), a young preacher unsure of the reception he would receive on the other side of the Atlantic.

George Smith of Coalville observed, following his researches into the lives of Gypsy children, that there was nothing romantic about the hard life facing these travelling people. Yet Gipsy was to affirm, often enough, the close family life he knew in the gypsy tent, contrasting it with the affluent but emotionally empty lifestyle he found in the escapist years (in the USA especially) after the First World War. Gipsy did not dwell upon his conversion, though he never doubted its reality. The reason he did not do so is clear—he was far more concerned that people calling themselves Christians should be 'living the life *now*'. His conversion awoke in him a strong desire to become really literate, for at the time he was only able to spell and understand words of a single syllable.

Encouragement

Perhaps even more often than relating the moment of his conversion, Gipsy referred to the old man, walking with the aid of sticks, who crossed the street to greet the young Gypsy, on the morning following the meeting at which he professed conversion. A senior member of the Fitzroy Street Church, the old fellow did not avoid or ignore the young Gypsy lad carrying his wares, but rather made the effort to offer a benediction. Then, the old man, with a smile, hobbled on, and disappeared around the corner of the street. Gipsy did not recall ever seeing him again, but wondered if he would have remained a Christian if the old saint had failed to act so encouragingly. The after-care of converts was thereafter always close to Gipsy's heart. He sometimes warned churches somewhat careless in this regard that they allowed 'the wolf to run off with the lambs'.

Rev. George Warner was probably the main preacher for the service at which Gipsy was converted. He had been set aside by the Primitive Methodist Conference in 1874 for 'evangelistic work and especially for the promotion of Scriptural holiness'. Warner believed that the doctrine of 'entire' sanctification, properly preached, was the precursor of the revival. He insisted that

> the most elaborate sermons on holiness have failed to produce any practical results, for want of a connecting link between the rich theory and the heart of the speaker. The people go away feeling that a mountain crowned with snow is a grand object to look upon, but a poor thing to warm by. Let the same preacher—provided he enjoys the blessing—throw in gems of his own experience occasionally, and it will arrest attention and melt hearts that will otherwise remain unmoved . . .

George Warner died in April 1899 knowing that 'the young gipsy lad' had become a fine preacher, gifted as he was with an ability to tell stories, a good sense of timing and a responsiveness to the mood of the moment. The torch had been passed on, the fire still burned.

4
In the General's Army

The gospel was not to be preached in whispers
behind closed doors, but with bands and
banners, and loud hallelujahs.

In his 1901 autobiography, Gipsy Smith explained how he came to be called 'Gipsy': 'In order to be quite distinct from my father and two brothers, and who were always spoken of as "The Three Converted Gipsies", I resolved to call myself, "Gipsy Smith".' It hardly needs saying that the name 'stuck', so that Harold Murray, the evangelist's accompanist, was able to produce an early 1930s booklet called, simply, 'Gipsy'.

But it was probably William Booth, founder of the East End Mission that in turn became the Salvation Army, who first proposed the name. When young Rodney was enrolled into William Booth's mission work, he was introduced as 'the young gipsy lad'. William Booth, like John Wesley, was eager to see worshippers become active workers, and in both the Wesleyan and Salvationist Movements, men and women, with little education or none, were 'brought on' to be evangelists and witnesses. Although his mission work had started in the East End of London, William Booth's approach stirred churches up and down the land; some asked him to arrange local missions, or to send speakers.

At Cambridge, Cornelius and his two brothers found their talents as preachers much in demand. 'Again, we commenced work for God (in Cambridge) and gipsies, college gentlemen and others were seen marching through the streets, singing, "There is a fountain filled with blood", etc., the outcome of which was a general revival.' In fact, the work became so pressing that the brothers decided that they would 'leave our chair caning and basket mending and give ourselves wholly and solely to the work of saving souls'. Confirmation of their decision quickly followed, for a week's engagement at Biggleswade in Bedfordshire, had to be extended to a month, during which time some one hundred people professed to have 'given themselves to Christ'. From Biggleswade, they went on to Potton and Gamblingay, two villages in Bedfordshire, and 'everywhere signs and wonders were wrought in the name of the Holy Child Jesus'. Cornelius' narrative of those days includes a visit to Bedford itself, and a sort of pilgrimage to the memorial to John Bunyan. Here the three Gypsies, as they stood before the statue of John Bunyan, prayed that they might be blessed in God's work, even as Bunyan—despite all kinds of trials—had brought God's word afresh to the people.

From there we went to Bunyan's Chapel, and as we stood looking, the chapel keeper asked us if we would like to see inside. We accepted his offer, and sat down in the very chair that this man of God had sat in, and asked God to give us power to do something for Him in Bedford. A brother in Christ who was standing there, said, "You appear to be strangers to this part." We told him we were, but that we were not strangers to the Lord Jesus Christ. I told him we were known as the three converted gipsies. He shed tears of joy, and said the Primitive Methodist minister wanted to see us, but he did not know in what part of the country we were in.

We went to his [the minister's] house, and after talking the matter over, he asked us if we would commence a week's mission at once. We told him that was why we had arrived, and we began in the open air, and sang to the chapel, which was soon crowded to the door, and the power of God fell upon us, and very many souls were brought to the Lord.

But even in those less crowded times, prejudice against Gypsies was not uncommon, and Cornelius related a call at his wagon at four o'clock in the morning, by a policeman who explained that any Gypsies found stopping by the roadside for 'twelve miles around' were to be arrested without a warrant. The three brothers were handcuffed and marched the mile and a half to the 'lockup', preaching the gospel to their equally captive audience every step of the way.

During their missions in the villages of Potton and Gamblingay, the brothers received a message from William Booth, who invited them to join his mission. The brothers were favourably inclined, although—as events turned out—the demands for their services eventually became so great that, by mutual agreement, they returned to an independent (and seemingly sometimes unscheduled) ministry. Meeting the brothers at Baldock, in Hertfordshire, William Booth suggested that they go to Portsmouth, under the auspicies of the mission, and proposed that Cornelius take up the fiddle (violin) again as an aid in the work of evangelism. Thus the trio spent some time with William Booth's remarkable work, a chapter in the history of revival which would be well worth relating to a generation which, at times, seems to have forgotten such great days of abundant grace.

Young Rodney—yet to be identified as 'Gipsy'—Smith must have received many encouragements from his father (and customers!) in regard to his earnest intention to become a preacher, but he was barely literate. We know that this teenage lad possessed a Bible, and an English Dictionary and Dr Eadie's *Bible Dictionary*, the latter presented to him by a lady who had heard from Cornelius about the lad's intent. One advantage that Gipsy possessed was a retentive memory, and like his father and uncles (the three gipsy brothers) he committed long portions of Scripture to memory.

Struggling to read

How did Gipsy overcome the problems of so poor a formal education? He seems to have used a 'copy book' of the kind obtained by others in the same plight. A very basic educational aid, this required 'copying' simple words printed as if in conventional handwriting, at the top of the page. Word meanings were identified by drawings, although of course anyone able to read could help anyone engaged in this form of self education. It seems likely that even as he carried his clothes-pegs and other wares from door-to-door, he could call upon the help of at least a few sympathetic people.

'I was always asking questions,' he wrote. 'If I heard a new word, I used to flee to my dictionary. I always kept it beside me when I read, or *tried to read*.' Some indication of the 'learning curve' experienced by the young man can be glimpsed can be glimpsed in a conversation he had with a housewife in Cambridge. He had paused in his day's vending, to stare at a large poster-hoarding put up by a brewery business to push its alcoholic wares.

Noticing the look of puzzlement on young Rodney's face, and perhaps a slight movement of his lips, as he tried to read the message, the lady asked if she could help. At his request, she read the words on the hoarding to him, and then asked how well he knew his alphabet.

No doubt, Gipsy explained something of his own dilemma and ambition to serve God. At the close of this interesting exchange, the lady resumed her own 'mission' (probably some domestic expedition) but assured him that he would 'get on one day'. Remembering Gipsy's life-long opposition to alcohol, and the many problems that it caused, it is gently ironic that one of his lessons should have arisen from a brewery company's publicity.

Well wishers and Christian friends took an interest in Gipsy's potential, and at least one, a Mr Goodman of Norfolk, suggested that he apply for training at the college opened by C. H. Spurgeon at the Metropolitan Tabernacle. Gipsy was too free a spirit to take up a place at the Pastors' College, though Spurgeon would certainly have done all he could for the young Gypsy. Rather, William Booth, already in heart-felt sympathy with the labours of the Gypsy brothers, heard about Rodney from William Corbridge, who had been involved in arranging a mission in Leicester. William Corbridge had informed William Booth that Cornelius Smith 'has a son, Rodney, whom he thinks of sending to the Pastors' College. He has a great desire to preach. Get hold of him. He might be very useful in the mission.'

Soon afterwards, the Gypsy brothers came to London. Bartholomew accompanied his nephew young Rodney and his (Rodney's) sister, Emily, to a meeting being held by William Booth on Whit Monday, 1877. There seems to have been little if any prearrangement about William Booth's invitation to the 'young gipsy lad' to speak from the platform. Perhaps it was a testing of the young Gypsy's call to be a preacher. Whatever the truth of the matter, that Whitsun meeting was the true beginning of Rodney's new identity as 'Gipsy' Smith, though in a strange way, it was Gipsy's emphasis on his Romany origins that contributed to his eventual departure from the Salvation Army.

In the 'Army'

Invited to join the mission launched by the Booths, Gipsy was at first 'billeted' onto a couple whose home was close to the Salvation Army's headquarters in Whitechapel Road, London. Understandably, after his years in the countryside, he found his small bedroom claustrophobic, whilst some indication of financial stringency is indicated by the fact that for the first six months, Gipsy had no income at all, and his clothes were supplied by his father. But if William Booth could offer little more, he did ensure that the young Gypsy had some good training from workers at the mission, including Mr Thomas, Mr Bennett and Mrs Reynolds (he described the last named as a 'second mother' to him). He seems to have spent many hours with the dictionary as some of his hearers at meetings must have realized:

> I went on reading [aloud] slowly and carefully, until I saw a long word coming into sight. Then I stopped and made some comments—after the comments, I began to read again, but took care to begin on the other side of the long word. I used to struggle night after night in my lodgings, over the hard words and names in the Bible.

Late in 1877, William Booth decided to assign Gipsy to the work in Whitby, the busy Yorkshire seaport, where 'Hallelujah' Elijah

Cadman was in charge. Pugilist and chimney sweep in his earlier days, Elijah Cadman was largely responsible for the description of William Booth's uniformed mission as the Salvation Army. Cadman had devised a handbill for a mission at Whitby, advertising meetings by the 'Hallelujah Army'. Involved in a fund raising campaign, William Booth and his son, Bramwell, seemed to have adapted the idea, describing the workers in the East End Mission as the 'Volunteer Army'. On second thoughts, William Booth deleted the word 'Volunteer' and added the prefix 'Salvation'. Having been given the nickname of 'the bishop' in the early days, William Booth became, quite naturally, 'the General'.

Elijah Cadman and Gipsy did not see entirely 'eye to eye'. For one thing, Gipsy became 'interested' in a young lady who came to one of the meetings, Annie Pennock, daughter of a ship's captain. Elijah thought that 'sweet-hearting and soul-winning did not mix', and before long Gipsy was transferred to Chatham in Kent, returning to Whitby briefly to marry his beloved Annie in December 1879.

At Chatham Gipsy found a congregation of little more than a dozen, and these rather hard-pressed workers did not conceal their wish to have a more experienced leader. But Gipsy embarked on much open-air work, and overcame the disdain of some of the local troops. By the time that he left Chatham, some nine months later, the work had grown to a congregation of around two hundred and fifty.

Gipsy had also spent some short periods at Sheffield and Bolton, and although we know relatively little of these aspects of his early career, Gipsy paid tribute to Mr and Mrs Corbridge, with whom he resided during his six months in Bolton. To these kindly people, he attributed the securing of 'the true foundations of all the educational equipment that I ever possessed'.

Gipsy's pay was some eighteen shillings (90p) a week, out of which he paid for board and lodging, and also had to find cash to buy 'necessary items' in pastoral visitation since so many of those needing help were poor. Eventually promoted from Lieutenant to Captain, Gipsy began his married life on an enhanced pay of thirty-three shillings a week, with the provision of a furnished home.

There is no doubt that Gipsy enjoyed the work, and learned a great deal from it. His labours in Hull, in the early 1880s, read like an ongoing revival:

> It was quite a common thing for us to have gathered together a thousand people who had been converted at the services, and what is perhaps even more marvellous an attendance of about fifteen hundred at the prayer meeting at seven o'clock on Sunday morning . . . many a time, I have had to get to the platform over the coats, as the aisles were so crowded that nobody could walk up them.

His sister, Tilly (Matilda) also a Salvation Army officer, helped him. She married another Salvationist officer, George Evens, in 1883. (Their son, George Bramwell Evens, would half a century later become a famous radio broadcaster, as 'Romany of the BBC', combining this great work with that of a circuit Methodist minister.)

Gipsy's stay at Derby, the Midlands industrial centre, in 1881, was not as successful as he would have hoped. There are hints of discord, or at least a lack of unity among the workers. There were the inevitable tensions between local initiative and central control and policy. We know for example that, for the sake of evangelism (that is of attracting local interest) Gipsy sometimes dressed more like a Romany than a Salvation Army officer.

Gipsy asked the General to send him to 'the nearest place to the bottomless pit'.

Hanley

So it was, on the last day of December 1881, Gipsy, his wife Annie, and their one-year-old son, arrived on the local train at Hanley in the Potteries; there was no welcoming committee, nor even any prospect of accommodation. Gipsy, seeing the glow of the furnaces reflected on the clouds, could see why the General had thought Hanley fitted his request. Yet it was the beginning of one of the most fruitful periods of Gipsy's long service for God. Taking over a dilapidated building, formerly used by a circus, and working hard to make it physically habitable, Gipsy here developed the musical side of his ministry. Asking the General for a special 'attraction', Gipsy was gratified to welcome the Fry family, a father and three sons, all fine musicians and who almost certainly laid the basis for the Army's world famous band traditions.

It was sometimes a matter of good music turning away opposition, for the presence of the Frys at least diverted some of the ridicule and abuse to which Gipsy and his co-workers had been subjected. Eventually, the work at Hanley became second in importance only to that in London. Gipsy gained the friendship of the Mayor of Burslem and other civic dignitaries, and was in some respects a friend of all the churches, an anticipation of his service to the united free churches a decade or two later.

The problem as the work grew was simply that of *policy*. On Sundays, Gipsy Smith preached to crowds of seven or eight thousand people, but even though his photograph in Salvation Army uniform shows him as entirely orderly, he did not conform too closely to Army methods. True, the General must have faced similar problems elsewhere, given the individuals who found their way into the Army's service. But the work at Hanley was now so important to the Army's prestige. A wise policy from the General's point of view was to give Gipsy all he needed to launch the work in a given place and then, when it was established, to move Gipsy on to another spiritual battlefield, replacing him with a more experienced officer, with pastoral talents.

One can imagine the response of the Booths on hearing that Gipsy did not want to move on and also that the local congregation, or corps, proposed that Gipsy remain in Hanley. As if this was not bad enough, news came that, in reflection of their love for Gipsy and his wife, a presentation had been made to them by the local people. An inscribed gold watch was presented to Gipsy, and gifts of five pounds were given to Annie (Gipsy's wife) and to his sister, Matilda (Tilly). Silver watches were presented to the two lieutenants.

Strictly speaking, the presentations were in direct contravention of Army rules, but as Gipsy explained in his 1901 memoir, he had sincerely believed that the headquarters would be pleased that the work was being given such public appreciation; the gifts were small enough.

Bramwell Booth may have been more adamant on the matter than his father, but given the circumstances of the time, the Army leaders may have decided that Gipsy was too prominent an individual to let the matter pass. Gipsy was dismissed, and his two lieutenants disciplined.

Parting of ways

Local response to the news was predictable. Sympathy was probably deepened by the fact that Gipsy's second son, whom he named 'Hanley', was born to Annie on the same day that the letter of dismissal came from Salvation Army headquarters. But, the event is an interesting example of the ways in which the Almighty overrules the earnest disagreements of his people. Gipsy stayed in Hanley for another four years, now a freelance evangelist, backed by a committee representing the mainstream churches in the town, and with congregations that were probably the nation's largest outside of the capital. A new building, the Imperial Circus, had become available for Sunday meetings, its former owners having gone into backruptcy. In many ways, Hanley was a pioneering model of inter-church co-operation in the cause of evangelism, and presented the kind of model necessary if the churches were to face up to the problems of an increasingly secularized nation.

Gipsy often said that 'Hanley was written on his heart'. He refused at the time of his separation from the Army, or later, to criticize the General 'who gave me my first opportunity as an evangelist, and who put me in the way of experience which has been invaluable to me'. In recent years, one or two local church folk have proposed same kind of plaque or simple memorial noting Gipsy's links with the town, and the area generally. It would not be too much to say that Hanley, probably more than any other place in Britain, represented the first heart-beat of the ecumenical cause in its evangelical aspect. And even apart from that it demonstrated the influence of a young man whole-heartedly committed to evangelism.

5
First journey to the new world

*I tell you there is something
indescribable in the touch of a human hand.*
(Gipsy Smith: *As Jesus Passed By*)

Gipsy Smith could have stayed in Hanley—the town that had so clearly taken him to heart—for many years. But it was the spreading abroad of the news of revival at Hanley that finally prompted him to seek a wider ministry. That so many churches and congregations wrote to him, seeking his help, says something about the paucity of evangelistic effort in the land. Undoubtedly, Gipsy's response had much to do with the burden that he felt for the destiny of millions for whom the good news of the gospel meant little, if anything. Even apart from that his work at Hanley—reflecting a spirit of evangelical unity across formal denominational structures—was a great innovation. Gipsy's growing mission field in the last two decades of the nineteenth century embraced churches of many denominational traditions. He was in effect shaping the parameters of the missions he was to conduct within the new Free Church movement of the 1890s. In this, as in so much else, Gipsy was a true pioneer.

Gipsy, though of course a keen Bible student, read widely, not merely collections of sermons (a much under-rated aid for any preacher), but also for necessary light relief, e.g., favourite adventure classics like *The Three Musketeers*. The first collection of Gipsy's own sermons, published at the turn of the century, with the title *As Jesus Passed By*, suggest a consistent preaching of conversion and sanctification, linked to personal experience. Many of his

53

messages had to do with the church being less than it might be if it were more wholeheartedly committed to its message. Among the characteristics of Gipsy's preaching was a poetic use of language, and a dramatic emphasis that was more than mere emotionalism. True, Gipsy could be 'carried away' sometimes, but his view of the human condition was always heavenward, so that in our somewhat cynical times, we might learn from his approach. For example, in his sermon, 'Gleaning For God', Gipsy suggested that, compared with the apostolic church, modern Christians were 'too sober':

> Jesus always gives us more than we ask. You and I, who have tried to love Him for years, find every day a glad surprise. We thought we could not stand but we walked. We thought we could not walk, but we ran. We thought we could not endure, but we are living. We thought we should never hold on, but here we are, blessed be God. Live out your Gospel, and the people all round you will touch your hand, and through it they will catch the pulse of the love that went to the Cross, which is strong enough to save the world.

Samuel Collier

After he resigned in 1886, Gipsy retained links with the work in Hanley, and sometimes conducted missions there. In the same year, Rev. Samuel Francis Collier took on the superintendency of the Manchester Methodist Mission at Oldham Street in that centre of cotton business, and for a time Gipsy Smith became a member of 'Sam' Collier's staff. What lessons must have awaited the young evangelist, and what genial inspiration too. Born in Runcorn, Cheshire, 'Sam' Collier was encouraged to 'feed the flock' by his father, a grocer by trade and a preacher by calling. Modest, almost scholarly in appearance, 'Sam' Collier followed the philosophy of life advocated by Gipsy: surprise them! Whilst a student at Didsbury College, Manchester— 'the old ship', as it was known—in the mid 1870s, he arranged an impromptu mission among the railway navvies who were laying the track between Stockport and Manchester.

He used every device that his inventive wit could suggest to attract the people and make them come into the meeting, recalled his biographer, George Jackson, in 1922. 'He visited the ale houses, he made friends with the navvies, he patrolled the village streets ringing the hand bell borrowed from the College, he held open-air meetings in all weathers, and finally by a bold and clever stroke of policy, he secured the goodwill of a rather reluctant and doubtful vicar.'

No man could have been a better mentor for Gipsy Smith, who now had the opportunity to see how effective pastoral ministry, preaching and social care blended together. Exacting indeed was the schedule: four meetings every day, including a mid-day meeting for local businessmen; afternoon Bible readings; evening services at eight o'clock, and an evangelistic effort at midnight, as befuddled and sometimes homeless men were ejected from the bars and pubs of the vicinity. Among those who helped Gipsy and 'Sam' Collier, at varying times, were the young Rev. Campbell Morgan, later to become minister of Westminster Chapel, London, and Rev. F. B. Meyer (who seems to have brought some of the social care innovations to his work at Melbourne Hall, Leicester, where he was the first pastor).

Gipsy recalled the 10 p.m. march from the Methodist Central Hall, around the city's streets, to pick up the homeless, the drunk and the incapable, as well as the poor with no bed for the night. Fifty campaign workers and two brass bands were involved. Sometimes, a 'magic lantern' talk was arranged, though, as Gipsy said, one could not be sure how much of the gospel message 'sank in'.

But this was not mere 'bread and jam' religion. 'Sam' Collier developed practical ministries of many kinds, for children, young mothers, men down on their luck, and he sometimes worked so hard in these areas that he found he had little time left for sermon preparation. For those who today think that hours in the study combined with aloofness makes for an effective pastoring, 'Sam' Collier remains an object lesson. People loved him, and came to hear what he said because they recognized his sincerity. Gipsy particularly remembered one Sunday afternoon when 'Sam' Collier, having been too hard pressed to prepare an address for the evening service, sat at his desk and began to write. But he fell asleep. Even so, he was able to preach that night. As Gipsy told him, 'God would sooner stop the universe than let you go into a pulpit without a message.'

Visit to America

The tension between the church as a living organism and the tendency to lose sight of its original purpose in 'organizationalism' faced Gipsy when he went to the United States of America for the first time in 1889. Given the way that the States became Gipsy's second home (and would have been his permanent home had the Americans been able to persuade Gipsy to remain there) this first trip happened on a rather casual basis. Mr B. F. Byrom, who knew of Gipsy's work, was on holiday in the Holy Land, and fell into conversation with two ministers from America. Mr Byrom was engaged in the cotton spinning industry at Oldham, just a shuttle's throw from Manchester, so he probably mentioned, among other matters, Gipsy's good work with 'Sam' Collier. As Mr Byrom was to underwrite the cost of Gipsy's venture to the States, he may well have 'sold' the two Americans on the idea. They said that they would make necessary arrangements for Gipsy's preaching if he was able to come to America. But one of the two died, and the other withdrew from the undertaking. So when Gipsy boarded the SS 'Umbria' at Liverpool on 19 January 1889, he was armed with little more than a handful of letters of introduction, and his usual buoyant faith.

> A gipsy uncle—a brother of my mother—who having no children of his own, was very fond of me, travelled a hundred miles that morning from his wagon to see me off. I took him, attired in his gipsy costume, on board the vessel, and at once all eyes were upon him. When the simple man felt the movement of the vessel, and saw the water, his eyes filled with tears, and turning to my wife, he said, 'Annie, my dear, I shall never see him again.' Presently, I took farewell of him (the tears rolling down his cheeks), my wife, my sister and her husband, Mr

56

Byrom, and several other friends. I felt as we slowly sailed away from Liverpool docks that I was venturing out on a great unknown, but though my confidence in myself was poor and weak enough, I was very sure of God.

Journeying to the United States must have seemed an obvious matter for Gipsy, though he said that he was a poor sailor who during the voyage across the Atlantic was 'deeply moved'. Many Britons, including some Gypsies, had emigrated to America over the years. Gipsy not infrequently met Romany folk encamped not far from American towns and cities who sometimes had distant relatives or old friends of his from 'the old country' among their number. Churches in the United States often recruited ministers from Britain, and among Gipsy's letters of reference, one, especially helpful, was from the Congregationalist minister, Dr Charles A. Berry, who had recently been invited to succeed Henry Ward Beecher as pastor of his church in Brooklyn (in the event, Dr Berry turned the offer down).

Although set in a nation with a young history, churches in the States faced problems known to congregations in Britain. In both countries the impact of industrialization resulting in a loss of contact between the churches and 'blue collar workers' was evident, whilst churches were often more 'respectable' than 'apostolic' in their nature. W. T. Stead, who was to write a series of booklets about the 1904–05 revival, including one on Gipsy Smith, travelled to Chicago, to conduct a conference and write a subsequent book on the failure of the churches to shape a Christian conscience in civic affairs. *If Christ Came to Chicago* sounds more like an evangelistic book than it really is, but as a book on the need for Christians to 'live what they preached' it sold widely. Probably the best known example of this type of literature was Rev. Charles Sheldon's, *In His Steps: What Would Jesus Do?'* which began life as a mid-week discussion theme at his Topeka, Kansas, church. No less important in terms of shaping attitudes within churches was the new *Gospel of Wealth*, the title of a best-selling book by Andrew Carnegie, the steel maker and philanthropist. Some people took this to mean that the righteous person would never be poor, so, in one sense, the roots of the 'prosperity Gospel' were beginning to shoot, just at the time that Gipsy first arrived in the United States. He was not greatly interested in political matters, but his view of the accumulation of wealth seems clear enough, for he spoke of the young woman, heiress to a considerable fortune, who thanked Gipsy for his influence in her life. Now working hard for her church, she told Gipsy, 'God saved me from an easy chair.'

No less an issue for Gipsy was the sensitive matter of relationships between the races. Although the Civil War had ended in victory for the North, and thus for the anti-slavery movement, little had changed in the post-bellum South, especially in terms of real civil rights. It is significant that Gipsy in the States, and when he visited South Africa in 1904, did not compromise on the issue. If the 'colour line' (as he described racial prejudice) was permitted to flourish, revolution would be inevitable.

Gipsy, after settling in at the Astor House Hotel (recommended by Mr Byrom, his benefactor) attended the Monday morning meeting of the New York Methodist Episcopal (ME) ministers. None of those present seemed to know very much about Gipsy's work, but as a result of his visit, he looked up the pastor of the Nostrand Avenue (ME) Church in Brooklyn, Dr Prince. Given that the church was engaged in evangelistic mission on its own account, Gipsy's arrival proved to be timely, though at first Dr Prince seems to have had some reservations about Gipsy's unexpected appearance. But Gipsy had also visited the offices of 'The Christian Advocate' newspaper, whose acting editor had added his own recommendation to the considerable weight of correspondence that Gipsy carried.

Dr Prince introduced Gipsy at the close of that Monday's service, unexpectedly for the visitor as it turned out. Gipsy spoke briefly, and returned to his hotel, only to receive a letter on the following morning, to the effect that the people at the church believed that God had sent Gipsy to help them in their evangelistic mission. In New York, too, Gipsy was given practical help, not least in dress style for American church pulpits, by Ira D. Sankey. Gipsy's mission at the Nostrand Avenue Church lasted for some three weeks. Seating some fifteen hundred people, it was crowded at every service.

My way was made in America. I next proceeded to the Central Methodist Episcopal Church, Seventh Avenue, New York, the church of which General Grant was a member, and which is now the centre of the New York Methodist Forward Movement, over which Rev. Dr Cadman presided for so many years. The same scenes were repeated here. Then, I went to Trenton, New Jersey, where I had the exquisite happiness of meeting a great many persons from the Potteries who had settled there, who knew me well, and some of whom had been among my personal friends.

More old friends were met when Gipsy visited a Gypsy encampment at Cumminsville, on the outskirts of Cincinnati. The informative 1901 autobiography reprints a local newspaper description of the event, Gipsy being described as 'a neatly dressed gentleman with dark complexion and raven black hair . . . attired in a three button cutaway black coat and black and grey striped pantaloons, and a white tie (Ira Sankey had recommended this!) peeped out from under a turned down collar.' A middle aged, stoutly built man, who appeared to be the leader of the clan, explained that he was a 'Lovell' (an ancient Romany line) and that his family had been in the States for some twenty-three years.

Even apart from its value as a cameo of Gypsy encounters in the USA over a century ago, the narrative is also useful for its confirmation of a continuing migration of Gypsies from Britain (and Europe) to the new world. The unknown reporter added some of the conversation between Gipsy and his companions, Dr Henderson and Rev. T. A. Snider. Gipsy explained to them that 'the British Government is very severe with our women in the matter of fortune telling, and fines and imprisons them. This has driven hundreds of them to this country and there are not so many families over there as of old.'

Gipsy may have been right in his judgment, but there were many other pressures on gipsies in Britain, not least urban development and the use of formerly unwanted land by local authorities and industry.

Gipsy's first visit to the USA was a fruitful one, including meeting Dr DeWitt Talmage, well known in Britain, not least for his preaching at the Crystal Palace in south east London. He also visited the former home of the radical thinker, Tom Paine, author of *The Rights of Man*, at Germanstown in Pennsylvania.

In August 1891, Gipsy paid his second visit to the USA, sailing on the SS 'Etruria', and to the end of his days, he was a man of two continents, or perhaps one might say of two worlds, the Old and the New.

Reflections

Always sensitive, and rejoicing in the hopefulness and encouragement he thought should be characteristic of Christians, Gipsy loved America and not infrequently said so. He believed the Americans to be often more earnest about their church life and witness (and more supportive of their ministers) than was often the case in his home country. Decades before churches in Britain began to take well planned adult education seriously, Gipsy explained how US churches worked to make their Sunday schools effective for all members of the family.

Perhaps even now there is something to be learned from Gipsy's reflection, made more than ninety years ago: 'In England, when the benediction is announced, we rush for the exit door; in America, they rush for each other. There is more friendliness, more brotherliness in the church life of America. You will see more handshaking after one service in America than after ten in this country.'

Modern expositors might consider Gipsy's preaching light on scholarship, rich on sentiment, whilst hard-pressed preachers of our time might sigh for the kind of popularity the evangelist seems so easily to have won in the States. One reason for Gipsy's acceptability was not of his own making, but related to the Jeffersonian tradition of making rural life and the moral farmer-father, the bedrock of the nation in contrast to the self-seeking, money-centred life of the city. Thomas Jefferson, one of the founding fathers, set a moral tone which, to this day, prevails in the USA, or at least in a good part of it. So Gipsy, whose father and uncles had worked in the hop fields and practiced rural crafts, who had been diligent if financially poor fathers, was something of an heir to this tradition. Gipsy did not denounce city life—indeed, he preached in major cities across the North American continent—but his reference to the life he had known, in the forests and fields, touched a chord in an idyllic America, the nation under God. Other homespun preachers from Britain also found attentive congregations in the USA, among them Henry Moorhouse, whose preaching on the 'love of God' served to change the course of D. L. Moody's ministry. Rev. Mark Guy Pearse, the Methodist preacher and writer of west country stories (from Cornwall, his home county, in the main) also found a hearty reception in the USA.

Churches in the United States were also enthusiastic about annual, or even more frequent 'revivals', though the word referred more to missions, than to the nation-shaking event that we consider the appropriate meaning of the word in Britain. 'Special attractions' were welcome, and publicity could be flamboyant. Gipsy was not impressed by a poster announcing that he was 'the greatest preacher in the world', and suggested it be removed (as indeed it was). Once Gipsy had been welcomed to a pulpit or platform, it was clear that he was an effective evangelist, not much interested in reputation or financial reward. Opportunities in the United States, to the end of his ministry, were more abundant than ever they were in Britain, perhaps because of the practice of annual 'revivals' which at least kept evangelism on churches' calendars.

A final factor was that Gipsy had some link with many of his hearers. Since some had emigrated from Britain, they were interested to hear 'how things were at home', and sometimes Gipsy was recruited to carry messages between family members on both sides of the Atlantic, and even to trace 'missing persons' (e.g. emigrating sons or other kin who had stopped writing home). After the First World War, Gipsy might find in his congregations, former doughboys (i.e. US servicemen) who had heard Gipsy during his service with the YMCA in France (see pp.000). But even in the States where churches often had advantages of income and manpower denied to so many ministers of the gospel in Britain, some did not welcome his kind of evangelism (or, one suspects, *any* kind of evangelism). His early missions were primarily within the Methodist Episcopal denomination, which whilst holding Wesleyan doctrines had an episcopal ecclesiastical structure.

There are hints that Gipsy's sermons were by no means lengthy, and when he was invited to speak at house meetings, or 'drawing-room meetings', as they were known, in New York, he ensured that these lasted no more than about seventy-five minutes from start to finish.

Having developed his memory as a youth—and committed appropriate sections of Scripture to memory—Gipsy could easily quote, or perhaps sing a verse of a Wesley or other classic hymn, in the course of a sermon, i.e., on the prompting of the moment. Evangelists years later were to report that among enquirers at the crusades of the 1950s and later, many had been moved not so much by the preaching, but by a hymn or chorus that had stirred memories of other days, other places.

Gipsy was a popular preacher. But modern communicators using him as a model need to realize how willingly he accepted the hard labours of travel, preparation, and prayer. His visits to the United States meant the sacrifice of much family life. Thus when he returned from his second visit to America in 1891/2 Gipsy had been away from home for seven months. 'It looked easy', but his preaching was a reflection of an earnest discipleship in which self-denial was central.

6
Learning to stand aside

Send us no more doctrines,
we are tired of them. Send us Christ.
(message to Henry Drummond
from churches in Japan)

Gipsy was still a young man, in his early thirties, when he accepted an invitation to conduct a mission at one of Scotland's most prestigious churches, Free St George's, Edinburgh, under the ministry of Dr Alexander Whyte. This 1892 mission started as a fortnight's event at the Fountain Bridge Free Church, but the vast crowds coming to hear Gipsy could not be accommodated. Dr Whyte was a fine scholar, something of a Puritan, and at times almost severe so that someone observed that 'he made me frightened to go to church'. However, this was outcome of the seriousness with which he regarded the issues of life, and he might not be an easy companion at some gatherings today. Dr Alexander Whyte might have seemed an unlikely supporter of Gipsy's informal, and often joyful approach. But they had much in common. Dr Whyte had experienced the upheavals of true revival, in the 1850s and afterwards, when people met in grassy places and market squares to make their repentance.

Ernest H. Jeffs, a Christian journalist who knew Dr Whyte well, wrote in his studies of *Princes of the Modern Pulpit*, published in 1930, some ten years after the preacher's death, that

he preached with all the intensity of a Puritan divine, or a medieval friar. There never was a preacher more infinitely remote from the optimistic humanism of modern religion. His venerable old world figure stands in the history of the kirk, as the last of the sternly gracious prophets and deeply learned expounders who, for three centuries mounted the Scottish pulpit as if it were a throne, as, from the point of view of national leadership, it is.

Gipsy had an easy rapport with the older man, and recalled in his autobiography how Dr Whyte had encouraged him at the end of his (Gipsy's) testimony, given to the St George's congregation: 'I have heard many great men in the pulpit, but I have never felt my heart so moved as it was tonight by your story. I do not envy the man who listened to it with dry eyes.' Gipsy thought Dr Whyte's comment, and smile, 'the effluence of a rich, noble, generous soul. It suggests a quarter of an acre of sunshine.'

Missions in Scotland

Gipsy's missions in Scotland in the 1890s were an important preparation for his new role as missioner for the united evangelical Free churches.

In Glasgow, for example, where a mission was held from September 1893 to the end of January 1894, the sponsoring committee consisted of twelve Free Church ministers, with about the same number of churches involved in the schedule of meetings. Dr George Reith, pastor of the Free College Church (whose son, John, would later become first director-general of the BBC) thought the mission the most remarkable since the visit of Moody and Sankey in 1874. Gipsy reported that some 'three thousand people went to the inquiry-room', i.e., for counselling and commitment to Christ, but in this 'Glasgow Pentecost', as a regional newspaper put it, there were some anticipations of the great revival that began in Wales in late 1904. Gipsy described one aspect of the Glasgow services that certainly has some similarity to the events in the Principality just over eleven years later:

At one service, and that the most fruitful, there was no sermon, because the people began to go into the enquiry room immediately after the hymn. I have no doubt that many of them had already made up their minds and really came to that meeting with the intention of taking their stand publicly. We spent that whole evening in simply saying to the people, 'Come, come!' I think God taught us a great lesson that night. We are so apt to think that this must be done, and that that must be done, and that a certain fixed course of procedure must be followed or else we must not look for results. Too often I fear our rules and regulations and orders of service simply intrude between men's souls and their God. We all need to be taught when to stand aside.

Gipsy's approach encountered one or two obstacles. He met for example an austere attitude to the use of 'musical accompaniments', because to 'staid, sober, decorous Presbyterians instrumental music was a desecration of the regular services in the sanctuary'. Gipsy was permitted musical instruments (piano, organ, etc.) at the evening service, which was primarily evangelistic in nature, but not in the morning or afternoon services.

Since 1894, however [he wrote in 1901], things have greatly changed even in Scotland, and most of the Presbyterian Churches I am told have now organs or harmoniums. I do not believe for a moment that the result has been a diminution in the solidity and gravity of the Scottish character.

Missions to Gypsies

Gypsy clans were common in Scotland, and an encampment on the south side of Edinburgh was well known in the nineteenth century, local churches doing what they could to educate children, and even willing-to-learn adults. During his 1892 campaign in Edinburgh, Gipsy was introduced to a lady who, in a former residence in 'a great Lancashire town' had been engaged in work among the poor, including Gypsies. One of the people mentioned by this lady in her conversation with the evangelist proved to be a relative—an aunt (his mother's brother's wife). The lady asked Gipsy how she might help the work among Gypsies in a practical manner, and offered to finance any work Gipsy might suggest. From this encounter, the Gypsy Gospel Wagon Mission was born, a sort of 'parsonage on wheels', not unlike some of the itinerant ministries being developed by the Church of England and others at this time. A Mr Wesley Baker, and an assistant, visited Gypsy camps, fairs and other places, to offer counselling, caring, educational and other assistance. Gipsy knew that the work was difficult, but thought it important even if it did no more than give young Gypsy children some basic literacy education. Among those helped by the Mission was a member of one of the best known Romany clans, Algar Boswell, who became a Christian whilst at camp in Blackpool.

At this time, more than twenty years after state education became a right for all children, guaranteed by the Education Acts under Gladstone's administration of the early 1870s, Gypsy children were neglected. George Smith, of Coalville in Leicestershire, a campaigner for the poor, mobile population (including 'canal boat children') estimated in the 1880s that the thirty thousand Gypsy children in the land had little or no educational opportunity. Some so-called 'Gypsies' were victims of unemployment, and had taken to an itinerant life because they could no longer afford a settled existence. Typical of George Smith's correspondence to the religious press is the following, in an issue of 'Hand and Heart' (17 December 1880):

A few days since, at a village feast in this locality, I took occasion to invite the poor women and children living in the show and cocoanut vans to tea. During tea and previously, I elicited the fact that not one of the twelve children, although ten were of school age, could read and write a sentence.

The father of six of the children had been for many years a member of the Independents, was well educated and had earned an honorable living, living till the last three years as a collier near Aberdare (in south Wales). His wife, previous to their marriage, had for many years been a lady's maid. At the present time, they are tramping around the country with a van and horse worth about £4, in which they exhibit a working model of a colliery, 'a prize baby', and boxing gloves. They and their children are fast settling down to a vagabond gipsy life. The father is undergoing a month's hard labour in goal for cruelty to his horse. The children have begun to wear brass rings upon their fingers. The mother is content to eat her food off a soap box.

George Smith urged that reforms be effected to bring education to this 'outcast portion of the population'. But the issue was equally that of poverty.

Home and family

Gipsy made his family home at Cambridge—the ancient university city—in the mid 1900s, for, much as he regarded Hanley, the pottery town, with great affection, Cambridge held attractions linked to 'family feeling'. It might seem paradoxical that Romany people, who seem always to be travelling on, might have a strong sense of place (more so, perhaps, than many householders in modern urban life). But so it was, and Gipsy's home, 'Romany Tan', at Cherry Hinton, Cambridge, became one of the most famous addresses in the land. One might have described the place as 'homely' rather than 'spacious' or 'dignified'; it was, as its name implied, a family home, a place to keep in mind and heart when the evangelist was hundreds or thousands of miles away, as was so often the case.

Both Gipsy's sons were to become preachers, Albany, as 'Gipsy Smith Junior' in the southern states of the USA, following employment at sea and later in business, and Hanley, as a Methodist minister (neighbours of the present writer had attended the Walcot Methodist Church, Bath, during his pastorate.) Zillah, Gipsy's daughter, like Hanley, clearly inherited Annie's gentle, reflective features, and no doubt much of her similar personality. Albany, the older of the two sons, had greater resemblance to Gipsy. Although the evangelist devoted a chapter of his 1901 book to his family, details are sparse, and focus in part on the defence of Gypsy people necessarily given by the boys, and the children's interest in their father's work. There is also an engaging reference to George Bramwell Evens, Gipsy's nephew who, like Hanley, was to become a Methodist minister in later years.

Gipsy sometimes described himself as a 'timber merchant', joking that he had sold clothes-pegs (or 'clothes-pins', as the Americans described them) in order to make a living. The truth was that even in his thirties, Gipsy, with his abundant moustache, thick black hair, affable and dark features, looked like a businessman. Indeed, the mantle of maturity fitted him at an early age, chronologically speaking, and clergymen who were in fact years older, seemed to regard Gipsy as a mentor, an equal, not as any kind of junior partner.

Australian Visit

Gipsy's mission in Australia in 1894 was intially almost a repeat of his first mission in the USA—he arrived, in Adelaide, with little more by way of schedule than letters of introduction, including one from his friend and fellow preacher, Dr Alexander MacLaren of Manchester. Gipsy had a good answer for those ministers who asked, reasonably enough, 'Why didn't you tell us you were coming?' He would respond along the lines that missions often did well through their very spontaneity, also that too much 'booming' (advance publicity) could hinder the work of the Holy Spirit.

Gipsy arrived in Adelaide—on 22 May 1894—close behind Rev. Thomas Cook, the well-known Wesleyan Methodist evangelist, who had been leading a month's mission at the Pirie Street Methodist Church. But Thomas Cook had to keep to his schedule, and had been unable to meet a suggestion that he conduct another mission locally at the Archer Street Church. This minister and a leading layman of this congregation rejected Gipsy's suggestion that he should conduct a mission in Thomas Cook's place, so Gipsy turned to the minister of the Franklin Street Bible Christian Church* in Adelaide. A prominent member of this church was

---

* The Bible Christians had their roots in the south west of the British Isles, and were in time to become part of the wider Methodist movement.

Chief Justice Way whom Gipsy had met in America. Here a door did open and Gipsy had ten days of fruitful ministry in a building which seated seven or eight hundred people, and which was crowded every night. Then Gipsy moved on to the Archer Street Church which was now willing to have him. In all Gipsy preached for six weeks in Adelaide to ever increasing congregations. He rather wryly observes in his autobiography: 'If my Wesleyan Methodist Brethren had received me with warmth and cordiality, I should perhaps have stayed only a fortnight in the town, but I stayed six weeks, because I was determined before I left to make myself thoroughly felt.'

Gipsy left Adelaide for Ballarat, a gold-mining town, but while he was there he received news from England that his wife was seriously ill. Unable to get passage on a ship for three weeks he joined Thomas Cook in his mission in Melbourne. At these meetings Gipsy sang and Thomas Cook preached. The 'crowning gathering', as he terms it, was the Thursday night meeting when he told the story of his life.

> The meeting was announced to commence at 7.30, but by four o'clock the place was crowded, and there were two or three times as many people outside. Wherever a window could be reached from the ground that window was broken, and whatever could be found to stand upon was seized and utilized.

The last week of Gipsy's visit to Australia was spent in Sydney. He preached in the Centenary Hall, the headquarters of the Forward Movement. Though the Hall seated 2,500 people, it proved far too small to hold the crowd that wanted to hear him. Another cablegram reached Gipsy: 'Wife very seriously ill. Come home at once.' He sailed on 20 June for home. 'Two thousand people came down to the boat to see me off, and sang, "God be with you till we meet again"', he recalled.

Gipsy's impressions of Australia make interesting reading today, especially in the light of the popular image of its people as being generally indifferent to the gospel.

'Many of the people are from England—from home as they

say—and the moment you begin to talk to them about the old country they are home-sick.'

Their hearts become tender and receptive. There are not a few people in Australia who have been shipped there by their friends in England, so that they may redeem their careers and stand erect on their feet again. Such people gain from their new life not only new opportunities, but fresh susceptibility to moral and religious influences. They make the material among which good evangelistic work can be done. They come to your meetings, and because you are from home, you make a particular appeal to them. You are a link between them and the people they have left behind, and they think you are speaking to them in the name of their friends in the old country. It seemed to me easy to get the Australians to attend evangelistic services. It fell that my visit immediately followed their great financial collapse, and it may be that their distress and difficulties made their hearts more hungry for the Gospel.

Gipsy's journey home took him across the Pacific via Fiji to Vancouver, then overland by way of Montreal to New York. There a cable awaited him informing him that his wife was much better 'and that there was no need to hurry to England if work demanded my stay in America.' Gipsy decided to pay a short visit to Ocean Grove which was then the largest 'camp meeting' site in the world, a town-ship of several thousand people formed into a Christian co-operative. He became an enthusiastic supporter of its work.

In the height of the summer season, the hotels, cottages and tents of Ocean Grove are crowded with a population of 70,000 to 80,000 people from all parts of America. I have sometimes seen as many as 250 ministers on the platform (of the Ocean Grove Temple, etc.). The enthusiasm and fire of Ocean Grove live all over the continent, maintaining alert the revival spirit. Ministers have told me that but for Ocean Grove, many a church in America would have been closed.

A month's mission in Indianapolis followed, during which Gipsy suffered from the recurrence of a throat problem. Dr Clyne, a throat specialist, who was related to the pastor of the church in which the mission was held, was present at one of the Sunday services. 'The doctor could see', wrote Gipsy, 'that I was having trouble with my throat, and he sent a message to me through the pastor saying that he wanted to see me at his office the next morning.' Dr Clyne sucessfully treated Gipsy and when the evangelist asked him for his bill he replied 'in deeply moved tones: "Sir, two of my boys have been converted during your mission. Will you give me your bill for that? Can I ever pay you for bringing those boys to Christ? How much is that going to be worth to me? I cannot preach, but if I can help you to preach with ease and comfort to yourself, I have a share in your business."'

After an absence of eight months, Gipsy Smith arrived home on 23 November 1894.

7

More missions on
both sides of the Atlantic

Shucks, that man is easy to listen to.
(small boy at the Indianapolis mission, 1921)

Before embarking on the round the world tour described in the previous chapter, Gipsy had promised the Rev. Andrew Mearns, Secretary of the London Congregational Union, that he would undertake three months evangelistic work in London. Gipsy travelled with his friend (and relative by marriage), Mr B. F. Byrom, to London a week before Christmas 1895, to arrange the final details. While there, news of his wife's collapse reached him. Gipsy returned home at once, and in consequence did not ask as many searching questions about the itinerary as he might have done. In any case, he was bound to leave the programme details to Andrew Mearns. When his wife had recovered in measure, Gipsy returned to London in early January 1895 to begin his mission. It proved to be something of a disaster:

I must say frankly that I do not look back on this work in London (i.e. in 1895) with any real satisfaction. I was sent to several churches which were practically deserted. Indeed, my work was mostly among weak causes, and in a few instances causes without a pastor or any organised band of workers. And most of the missions were only for a week. It took one quite a week to make oneself known in these localities, and just when one was beginning to get a good hold of the people, one had to leave and go elsewhere. Good was done, I am sure, and in every case before the week was out, we had crowded

73

congregations. But it was surely unwise to send me to chapels which were without pastors, because there was no-one there to look after any converts that God gave us. In this campaign, I worked at ten or eleven places. The right plan would have been the selection of six or seven of the strongest churches, and a fortnight's mission in each. In a live church, with a capable minister and a competent band of workers, something great might have been accomplished. To send a missioner to some deserted, disorganised chapel, situated perhaps in a godless wilderness, and then expect valuable results in a week, is like sending a man to gather apples in the Sahara desert.

Gipsy's forthright diagnosis shows that if spontaneity has its strengths for the evangelist, mere wishful thinking has no place in mission planning. His comment confirms that even in an era which seems rich in 'Victorian Values', from our rather biased perspective, the description of 'godless wilderness' could be applied to areas in the capital of the land. In the Christian press generally in the 1880s and 1890s, there was no little alarm at the ineffectiveness of the churches in reaching urban populations. This sense of failure prompted the inter-church initiatives in which Gipsy was soon to become engaged.

Gipsy's three-month-long London mission was interrupted by a short mission at Union Chapel, Manchester, of which Dr Alexander MacLaren, the notable biblical expositor, was the pastor. Gipsy wondered whether his unsophisticated approach to evangelism would suit the congregation. 'The tempter whispered: "Your methods will never do for Union Chapel. Do you know that this is the most brainy and cultured congregation in England?"'

The response to Gipsy's preaching proved his fears to be unfounded. There were many professions of conversion and later the co-pastor, Rev. J. E. Roberts, recorded that 'Some of our best workers to-day were converted under Gipsy Smith.' Gipsy himself viewed this mission as 'one of the most remarkable missions of my life.' He regarded it as helping to establish his credibility as an evangelist. 'I have needed no further recommendation to many ministers than I have had a mission at Union

Chapel. As a consequence I have reached hundreds of people who from ignorance have had no sympathy with evangelistic methods.'

Gipsy closed a busy year in which he conducted a number of short missions with a six-week evangelistic effort in a number of Free Church congregations in Edinburgh. His 'gift of song added greatly to the charm and fascination of his testimony', reported the press, whilst his 'bright, hearty, happy Christian spirit strikingly commended his Christian message.' The meetings generally 'conveyed the marked and unmistakeable impression of a true evangelist endued with spiritual power.'

To America again

After a brief visit to his family for the Christmas holiday, Gipsy was once more on the move, sailing to Boston on New Year's Day 1896, on his fifth journey to the new world. On this occasion, Gipsy had been invited to conduct a mission at the People's Temple, the largest church in Boston, pastored by Dr James Boyd Brady. So important did Gipsy regard this work, that he refused to fill in his diary with other bookings that year, until the Boston mission was over. He must have been given some special sensitivity on the outcome of the event, for more than any other mission of the decade, one senses a foreshadowing of the great time of revival in which he was to be involved in the early years of the new century. Of the Boston mission, he wrote:

When the month was finished, it was evident that we could not stop the work. The four weeks extended into seven. On the fifth Sunday, I preached to a crowded congregation on 'Be Filled with the Spirit', and at the close of the sermon, a memorable and indeed indescribable scene was witnessed.

Dr Brady rose, and in tones of deep emotion said, 'The sermon this morning has been for my own soul. I feel my need of the experience of which brother has been speaking, and I am going down to the Communion rail for myself. I am going there to seek my Pentecost. I shall never be able to rear the young souls that have been brought to God during this mission unless I am filled with the Spirit.' Presently, between two hundred and three hundred people from all parts of the Church were kneeling at the Communion rail on both sides of their pastor. When we dispersed, we all felt that we had seen strange things that day . . .

As a result of the mission, eight hundred persons were received into the Church on probation. I was asked three times to become pastor in succession to Dr Brady when his term of the pastorate was fulfilled. The people were willing to free me during three or four months every year for evangelistic work, to give me an assistant and a handsome salary. But I did not see my way clear to accept their offer.

It was during the tour that Gipsy met the chaplain to the US Senate, Dr Milburn, who was a member of the Metropolitan Episcopal Church in Washington DC, where Gipsy conducted a mission:

I chanced to mention in the course of an address that I was not ordained. At once the old man (Dr Milburn, who was blind) rose and placing his hands on my shoulders, said, 'I will ordain you, without a question.'

Dr Milburn presented Gipsy to the President, Grover Cleveland, yet for all his associations with the great and learned men of his day, Gipsy remained entirely without affectation. Aware of the many pressures upon their time, busy Christians often give the impression that even in casual conversation they have a stop watch in their hand, but Gipsy always seemed to have 'the time of day' for anyone.

Learning from others

One reason for this relaxed approach was his eagerness to learn from others. His great friend, Rev. Peter Mackenzie, as a young preacher borrowed books of sermons 'to get a few plums for his cakes' (as he described his own addresses). Gipsy was always out to find good plums, and gave the impression that he was enthusiastic about meeting people.

One of those who certainly influenced his ministry was the writer, Henry Drummond, whose *Natural Law in the Spiritual World* represented a thoughtful counter to those who argued that Darwinianism had 'disproved' Scripture. Henry Drummond had studied with Dr Marcus Dod, the Principal of New College, Edinburgh, and it was Dr Dod who most of all encouraged the younger man's writing activity. During D. L. Moody's campaigns in Scotland, Henry Drummond was sometimes described as Moody's 'right hand man' because he was so effective in reaching university students and other young people. Indeed, it may have been Drummond who especially encouraged Gipsy to develop this aspect of his work for by the end of the 1890s, Gipsy was lecturing to students on evangelism, and the methods by which people at large might be reached with the gospel.

Like Gipsy, Henry Drummond was to travel widely in the cause of the gospel, and for all his learning, he showed a modesty and sensitivity to young people that itself spoke of a deeply-held faith. There was for example that message given to him, at the end of a lecture tour in Japan, and which he was asked to take to the churches of the West: 'Send us no more doctrines, we are tired of them. Send us Christ.'

As already noted, Rev. Peter Mackenzie was another influence on the Gipsy's ministry, so much so that Gipsy devoted a chapter of his autobiography to this ebullient Wesleyan. Peter had died in harness in the mid 1890s, after an awesome work for God, as Bible lecturer, circuit minister and 'stoker up of flagging fires'.

Born in Peterhead, Scotland, and spending his early life as a coal miner in the north east of England—that part of the country which most shaped his personality—Peter was accepted for ministerial training, although he was married, an unusual arrangement for the time. Never a 'conventional' circuit minister, he was able to attract crowds comparable to those seen in John Wesley's day. Like his fellow labourer in the Wesleyan cause, Rev. Morley Punshon, Peter raised vast sums for local chapel causes through his lectures which were more like dramatic presentations based on Bible characters—'Samson, the Hebrew Hercules', 'Jonah, the Runaway Prophet', 'Gideon, the Mighty Man of Valour', to mention a few. Although at times he allowed his enthusiasm to run away with him, Peter was one of the most spiritual men of his time, beloved in the land to the point that he was referred to most often by his Christian name alone.

Rev. Dinsdale T. Young, the second advent writer and Methodist minister, whose pastorates included that at Central Hall, Westminster, so admired Peter's work that he gave public lectures about him, after Peter's death. Certainly an unusual labour—few busy ministers today could find the time to lecture (on many occasions) about a fellow servant of Christ, gone to his reward. In this case, Dinsdale T. Young's tribute was reflected in a book, published by Hodder and Stoughton in 1905: *Peter Mackenzie as I Knew Him*. Some of the original sermons and lectures, in the main transcribed from notes, were collected by Rev. Joseph Dawson, and published together with a best selling and poetic biography. One could hope for their reissue today, for Peter Mackenzie spoke to a time, as Gipsy did, when religious inspiration was in short supply, and the glory of God seemed all but forgotten by the majority of the people.

Gipsy could well have written a study of his fellow worker, given the sense of sympathy expressed in his autobiography:

I met Peter for the first time sixteen or seventeen years ago, on the platform of Hull railway station. We were leaving in the same train but not in the same compartment, as our destinations were different. I told him that a great work of grace had been accomplished in Hull. 'Glory to God!' shouted Peter. 'I will send you a goose for Christmas.' Three months passed away. I had forgotten all about the goose, and Peter's promise, but he had not forgotten. He sent me the following letter: 'Honoured and dear Sir, I have had no time to purchase a goose. But I send you ten shillings, and a photo of yours truly, which when you receive it, you will have goose enough. Peter Mackenzie'.

Peter came to Hanley while I was there, to preach in the

Wesleyan Chapel and to lecture in the Imperial Circus building on 'The Devil, his Personality, Character and Power'. The lecture was announced all over the town in black letters on a huge green poster.

As I was passing along the street, a half tipsy man accosted me and pointing to the placard said, 'What nonsense! There's no such person as the devil.'

I asked what he had been doing of late.

'Oh,' he said. 'I have been drinking. I had a six-weeks' spree. I've had a fearful time—the blues terribly.'

'Oh, indeed,' I said, 'what do you mean by the blues?'

'Don't you know? Little 'uns.'

'Little 'uns?'

'Yes, little 'uns. Don't you know what I mean? Little 'uns. Little devils, scores of them.'

'Well,' I said. 'Don't you think now, that if there are scores of little 'uns, there must be an old 'un, too?'

When I seconded the vote of thanks to Peter for his lecture, I told this story. Rising from his seat, and waving his chair over his head, he shouted, 'Glory, glory. I'll tell that all over the country'.

When Peter was brought home ill to Dewsbury, the Wesleyan minister of the town, Mr Martin, called to see him.

'I'm very sorry, sir,' said the minister, 'to find you in bed, and so ill.'

'Yes, yes,' said Peter. 'I am in dry dock, undergoing repairs.'

A few days later, Mr Martin heard that Peter had become much worse, and again called on him.

'Ah,' said Peter. 'Father is going to send down the angel and let old Peter out of prison.'

A few days later, he died.

8

Co-operation in evangelism

'We march to holiness through fire.'
(Rev. J. H. Jowett, at the first
Free Church Congress, 1896)

Gipsy was a great believer in co-operative evangelism—in churches working together in joint evangelistic missions—as the following quotation makes clear: 'I consider my present sphere of operations the biggest and most important field I have ever touched . . . it will do more to break down local prejudices and to bring Christians and churches together than anything has done for ages.'

Gipsy was referring to his work as missioner, or staff evangelist, of the National Council of Evangelical Free Churches (hereafter identified as the NCEFC, or Council), a position he assumed on 1 September 1897. That Gipsy should take on the new position had been suggested by Rev. Samuel F. Collier, of the Manchester Central Mission, though much the same proposal came from others, including Rev. H. J. Pope, whose expertise had done much to erect and maintain church buildings in the Wesleyan Connexion.

On a larger stage

The story of this great endeavour is something of a romance in evangelical history. The visionary in the work was Rev. Thomas Law, a minister of the United Methodist cause, who had agreed to serve as General Secretary of the Council. A man who finally wore himself out in the work, Thomas Law pioneered new mission management and follow-up systems that were to serve evangelists well in the new century. For some time, he also served as Gipsy's missions secretary. Aware of the apparent inability of the churches to reach growing numbers of the population outside the reach of the gospel, Thomas Law proposed that churches should work together at local level, through Free Church councils, emphasizing co-operative evangelism. So the national Council—although its membership included some of the land's best known preachers—was a reinforcement for local evangelical strategy. It looked, as historians say, for a 'bottom up' revolution in church life, rather than a 'top down' attempt to revive the Christian cause.

Many were aware in the 1890s that the churches faced something of a crisis. When Rev. Hugh Price Hughes, the revivalist minister of the West London Mission, addressed the first Free Church Congress in Nottingham in March 1896, he outlined some reasons for the formation of the Council, of which he was then President. He argued that the new spirit of inter-church co-operation was possible was due not not to any lack of conviction, but rather

> like Wesley and Whitefield, we all 'agree to differ' on points of interpretation, while we realise our fundamental agreement on the essential facts of the Christian religion.
>
> This astonishing theological calm is something so totally new in ecclesiastical history, and has been brought about so gradually and so unintentionally, that not only do we deserve no credit for it, but it has scarcely yet received even from ourselves the consideration it deserves.

With the prospect now of the churches working together to 'confront every external foe', Hugh Price Hughes spoke optimistically, but he soon turned to an issue which was certainly a sensitive one at that time. It was, as he put it 'the portentous revival in our midst, of extreme medieval clericalism, which our fathers believed to have disappeared for ever from England'. Although, he added, it was entirely possible that one could exaggerate the extent to which 'medieval clericalism obtains among the clergy . . . the attack upon us (i.e. free churches) especially in the small towns and villages, has of late become so vigorous and so bitter that it has forced us together in self defence'.

Given that the NCEFC was to become deeply involved in political matters, notably the issue of church schools, there is a certain irony in Hugh Price Hughes' comment in 1896 that the Council was not to take a political line, though he lists contemporary campaigns that demonstrate the preoccupations of evangelical Christians in that last decade of the century—temperance, anti-gambling and holiness movements were hard at work, as was the peace movement, which embraced many ministers and free churchmen to the outbreak of war in 1914. Fundamentally, as Hugh Price Hughes put it, the work of the Council was the deepening of a spiritual life in the churches, to make more effective witness to 'the vast unreached majority of the people'. Most important of all, he thought, was the defence of the New Testament doctrine of the Church, though this was more than the mere assertion of theologically correct positions. At a time when poverty and social evils of every kind were all too apparent, Hugh Price Hughes looked not only for a 'holy people but a holy city too'.

There is no better definition of what became known as the Nonconformist Conscience, and its historic setting, than his address to the Council members and conference visitors of 1896. Given the revival that was to come within ten years of the Conference, there was a special significance in the closing words of the address, which referred to the actual numbers of people who could be accommodated in church buildings. Research undertaken by Mr R. W. Perks, MP, in relation to a Parliamentary Blue Book of the 1880s, indicated that together the Congregationalists, Baptists and Methodists provided places for seven millions of worshippers, more than the Anglicans. If revival came to the land, the issue was not merely: would there be enough ministers and pastors to care for the newcomers and converts, but also, would there be enough buildings to house them?

Although he did not seek the appointment, Gipsy's status as Council (NCEFC) missioner, or staff evangelist, brought new opportunities to work in interdenominational contexts and, for that matter, to become involved in writing. His first book of sermons, and his 1901 autobiography, covering the first forty years of his life (written with the help of W. Grinton Berry, editor of the *Sunday at Home* magazine) were published under Council auspicies.

An early assignment from Rev. Samuel Chadwick (the later principal of Cliff College of Evangelism) was to speak at the 1897 Wesleyan Conference at Leeds, preaching in the Colosseum twice on the Sunday of the Conference, to some six thousand people on each occasion. Over careful on matters of ministerial etiquette, the compilers of the printed programme, omitted Gipsy's name, because a former ruling had stated that names of ordained ministers only were to be included in its pages. It was because of this rather unexpected formality that the organizers almost lost Gipsy's services, as he assumed that he was no longer wanted! Fortunately, Samuel Chadwick with Hugh Price Hughes and W. P. Watkinson, another well known preacher of the time, made sure that Gipsy was welcomed officially. 'Their conclusive argument was that if a man was fit to preach, he was fit to be announced.' Gipsy's wry, and indeed humorous comment, suggests that whilst etiquette is appropriate in its place, you do not need so much of it that you miss a blessing available on a less formal basis!

The Council was a source of encouragement throughout the British Commonwealth of Nations as was indicated by its handbook's listing of branches in many lands, including Australia, New Zealand, South Africa, as well as New York, Rome and Berlin. George Cadbury, the businessman and philanthropist, helped finance the Council's work, and the first President of the NCEFC, Dr Charles Berry, was a Congregationalist, whose earlier home was the mill town of Bolton in Lancashire. Harry Jeffs recalled that Dr Berry had

a smiling delight in alarming the uncommonly good and the sticklers for ecclesiastical propriety. He would appear in the pulpit wearing a tweed suit with a bright buttonhole. Later visits to the Grindelwald Reunion Conference organised by Sir Henry Lunn had the effect of converting him into a high churchman in the free church sense. He dressed in sober ministerial style. When the movement for uniting the free churches into a National Free Church Council was launched, Charles Berry became its flaming apostle.

Dr Berry had faced a punishing schedule, and at times he confessed himself 'drained' or 'empty'. His church at Wolverhampton —attended by Gipsy's sons during their studies at nearby Tettenhall College—was a major cause in Congregationalism.

Dr Charles Berry died in the midst of his work, as it were, and his son, Rev. Sidney M. Berry carried on a family tradition, becoming minister of the Carrs Lane Congregational Church in Birmingham, possibly the best known Free church of England's second city. But it was Charles who was especially remembered by Harry Jeffs, as 'the soul of good fellowship', and who had been one of the initiators of the NCEFC vision, and Gipsy's part in it.

Working hard and cheerfully to meet as many of the requests for his services as he (and Rev. Thomas Law) could arrange, Gipsy was certainly a national celebrity long before he reached his fortieth birthday in 1900. Not that he was interested in celebrity status. His final mission of the old century was at Luton, in Bedfordshire, a town then famous for its hat making industry. The response was impressive, well over one thousand enquirers, around one in forty of the total population. George Evens, Gipsy's brother in law came to Luton at Gipsy's request, to help conduct the overflow meetings.

On the Saturday, I took him to the place of my mother's death and burial, at Baldock, about twenty miles away. I pointed out to him almost the exact spot in Nolton Lane where she lay sick unto death, and together we trod the path along which her coffin must have been carried to the grave, with my father (Cornelius) following as the sole mourner. When we stood by the grave, I said to my brother in law, 'I have been feeling for some time that I should erect a stone here.'

'I am rather surprised', he answered, 'that you have not done so before.'

'Yes, indeed, but I have made up my mind to do it now.'

Alderman Gittings, the Mayor of Luton, presided at my

lecture ('The Story of My Life') on the Monday evening. When I reached the part where I tell of the death and burial of my mother, he turned to Mr Evens, my brother in law, who was sitting beside him on the platform, and asked, 'Is there a stone over that grave?'

'No', said my brother in law.

'Well, I will put one up. That is my business.'

At the close of the meeting, he (the Mayor) told me of his decision. The incident seemed to be a remarkable comment on the text: Before ye call, I will answer. While ye are yet speaking, I will hear.

The stone is still to be seen, or was, on the present author's visit in the 1980s.

John Clifford

Especially supportive of Gipsy's work at this time was Dr John Clifford, whose work in the Baptist cause was well respected. Scholarly—some might even say 'Venerable'—John Clifford was born in 1836, and began his ministerial training in 1855, some five years before Gipsy was born. With a string of degrees, and a streak of radicalism inherited from his East Midlands origins— John Clifford was one of the great democrats of his time. For all his justifiable claim to theological distinction, he refused to use the prefix 'Rev./Reverend', and explained, 'Nothing is secular to the Christian man—every calling ought to be a religious calling, and if a man cannot look upon his vocation as religious, it is time for him to have done with it and to take up something else.' There is almost a prophetic anticipation of renewal movements of our own time in his refusal to recognize any difference between the layperson and the minister.

Elected President of the NCEFC for the 1898/99 session, John Clifford took his duties seriously, and, despite many demands for his services (and his age!) he spent on average two to three days in every fortnight on Council business, visiting various towns and encouraging local evangelical enterprise and inter-church co-operation. Nor was 'mere busyness' a concern; local Free Church Councils were urged to 'give as frequent opportunities as possible, for united waiting upon God and also by the appointment of Quiet Days.' Here we see an anticipation of the spiritual retreats and prayer movements which were to develop in the late twentieth century.

When he visited the United States towards the close of his presidential year, in 1899, John Clifford found a similar concern for closer relationships between churches, although the idea of Civic Christianity (much advocated by W. T. Stead) was probably more debated there than in Britain. This was a project, not sponsored by the NCEFC but having clear links to its mission, which looked to the churches to shape better city/civic government, by active participation of church members (in councils, etc.) and the development of local welfare/social services, run and financed by churches. But there was irony in the fact that in the same year that the South African, or Boer War started, the NCEFC was busy arranging events to honour Oliver Cromwell, the tercentenary of whose birth was also celebrated in 1899. Rev. Thomas Law, the over-worked Secretary of the NCEFC, recalled an open-air meeting led by John Clifford in Huntingdon market place:

> It was a gusty day, and the gathering was held in the market place under cloudy skies. Aware of the Doctor's (i.e. John Clifford's) rule to arm himself on special occasions with copious notes, Mr Law said to him: 'How are you going to manage today, doctor? Won't you be at some disadvantage?'
>
> 'Oh, no,' he replied, 'just wait a bit.'
>
> Sure enough, he managed his notes without serious difficulty. As usual, he divided them into three portions—the full note, the outline and the quotations, and though the wind was high, kept them in order as easily as a deft card-player manipulates his cards.

The two evangelists—John Clifford and Gipsy Smith—were to work together in some remarkable meetings at Birmingham in the 'Simultaneous Missions' (or 'New Century Campaign') in

1900. But another foreshadowing of work to come was of a more solemn nature—the outbreak of war with the Boers (the Dutch settlers in the Transvaal and the Orange Free State) on 11 October 1899. In its aftermath, and to aid the divided Christian Community in South Africa, Gipsy was to conduct his 'mission of peace' in 1904.

The Boer war divided Christian opinion in Britain, and not a few Liberals, many of whom were found in Free Church Councils, opposed the war. President Kruger, leader of the Boers, was undoubtedly a 'difficult character' to deal with, but the tensions between British and Dutch settlers ought to have been settled without resort to arms. Given that there was a not inconsiderable 'peace movement' in Britain, it seemed to some that the government was embarking on a foolish war which would ultimately solve little.

It might be argued that there was an element of prophetic judgment, too. Many young men, volunteering for military service, were found to be physically underweight and in relatively poor health, the outcome of the poverty and inadequate diet facing so many of the nation's population. Pigeons coming home to roost in Westminster and the War Office, one might think. The colour and pageantry of patriotism had concealed the fact that Britain was becoming isolated in Europe, and that it enjoyed little support in its fight with the Boer settlers. Germany's support—in print and pronouncement at least—for the Boers might have had some virtue, but it served to alarm those who were already arguing that Germany's industrial power, technical competence (and care of its citizens) might soon mean its dominance of the Continent.

By early 1901, more than 100,000 troops from Britain and the colonies were involved in the war, which was costing the UK exchequer an alarming amount, £2.5 million per month. The burning of farms and setting up of concentration camps by the British appalled many, who did not appreciate perhaps the new forms of guerilla fighting being developed by the Boers. Even those who had initially supported the war tended to become 'war weary', as the conflict dragged on. Finally concluded in mid 1902, and after

Queen Victoria's death in the preceding year, the war had its impact on the churches. The old certainties about Britain being a nation especially blessed by God were decaying, and were all but destroyed in the 'great war' that began in 1914.

Increasingly, too, evangelists were coming to see afresh that 'individual salvation' had to be accompanied by concern for the nation as a whole. Rev. A. T. Guttery, writing in the early years of this century, would have been in sympathy with the high purposes of the NCEFC, and looked for individuals turning to Christ. But at the same time, he said that the young men of his time, some of whom would have been caught up in the South African/Boer War had a 'perfect right to ask their seniors what they had been doing with England during the last ten years. They had allowed the nation to drift, and to become worse in many respects. They had had ten years of decadent ideals.' Strong words indeed, in the still prestigious days of the British Empire!

Because Christians today spend too little time considering the recent history of our land, say the last century or two, they sometimes assume that the spiritual questions of our time are new to our generation, or that church leaders of previous times ignored them. Closer to the truth was the NCEFCs sense that the country was going 'downhill' in its moral life, and that the older churches were more concerned with 'internal arrangements' and ecclesiastical priorities than with saving people who had been for generations untouched by the gospel.

The Simultaneous Missions—or 'The New Century Campaign' as it was sometimes known—was an ambitious enterprise, calling for leading preachers to travel throughout the land, conducting services and meetings as a challenge to local believers and for that matter non-believers also. Thus, 'simultaneously', missions would be held in a great number of churches, capturing local and national attention, and showing that the churches were now united in labour and spirit. In a somewhat unlikely pairing John Clifford and Gipsy Smith were teamed for a mission in Birmingham.

'Surely that is a remarkable combination', remarked someone at the local meeting announcing these arrangements. Remarkable indeed! *The Baptist Times* was to report that it was a remarkable combination, and as felicitous as remarkable, and it probably fell to the lot of no other city or town in the provinces to enjoy the services, day after day, for an entire week of two men so differently endowed, and yet by the superb exercise of their different gifts, contributing to such magnificent results.

Dr Clifford's first appearance was made in the [Birmingham] Town Hall at noon on Monday, the special duties allotted to him being to conduct a series of services during the lunch hour of the business people in the city. Although it was Monday, and the Doctor had travelled up from London after a hard day's work, there was no trace of fatigue in his face. Dr Clifford's audience (about twelve hundred people) filled the body of the great hall and overflowed into the gallery.

The general theme of Dr Clifford's addresses was 'Reconciliation with God' and the same text was announced by him each day, except Friday, 2 Cor. v 19, 'God was in Christ reconciling the world to Himself, not imputing their trespasses unto them'. The final exhortation on Friday was appropriately based on Phil. ii, 12, 'Work out your own salvation'. These remarkable deliverances were magnificent, cogent in argument, luminous in illustration, impassioned in appeal, and deeply impressive in their spiritual earnestness. They must have been a revelation to those good people who cannot be persuaded that a man can keep abreast with the critical and intellectual thought of the age, and yet maintain the simplicity and fervour of an evangelical faith.

Gipsy expressed his own appreciation of the older man's messages, and for his prayerful support when he spoke at meetings in the city. Perhaps in our own age of techniques and management know-how, we give too little attention to wisdom, which was so often to be found in John Clifford's discourses (though some might have mistaken it for mere radicalism). His biographer, Charles Bateman, writing during Dr Clifford's lifetime, spoke of the ready welcome that he always found at NCEFC meetings :

The thousands present will listen to him for an hour without counting the minutes. They love the little round-shouldered Baptist, with the massive head and shaggy hair. He is their hero of many fights. His glowing periods, filled with the Puritan spirit, stirs their souls and consciences. They cannot hesitate to resist a bad law after such deliverances . . . To doubt would be disloyalty, to falter would be sin.

The Education Battle

The 'bad law' which did so much to divert the NCEFC from its original evangelistic aims was the Education Act of 1902, and the further legislation of 1903. John Clifford described the Bill, introduced by the Conservative leader, Rt Hon. A. J. Balfour, MP, as 'the worst of the five bills that the government has introduced'. That distant battle might seem a storm in a teacup now, but the Bill appeared in 1902 to be a threat to independent schools, managed by local boards and reflective of Free Church attitudes. The government probably meant only to bring independent schools into the state (or local authority) sector, but it did seem to nonconformists that the end result would be Anglican domination of education policy, certainly in respect of religious education. There was also, as we have seen, no little alarm in the Free Churches at the resurgence of 'clericalism' in the established church. A great crusade against the Education Act was launched by the NCEFC at St James's Hall, London, on 15 April 1902, and in the November of that year, a well attended meeting (estimated at 15,000 in the main building, and up to 5,000 outside) was arranged at the Alexandra Palace. Even more impressive was a demonstration in Hyde Park in May 1903, which must have attracted more than 20,000, whilst King Edward VII watched, 'Free Churchmen marching by battalions into Hyde Park to protest against an iniquitous Bill' (Charles Bateman).

For most onlookers, announcements that this or that church leader was refusing to pay his rates, until the Bill was abandoned, seemed incidental to the real problems facing working people. Of course, John Clifford believed, not without reason, that he was defending the traditional Protestant position, and, throughout the campaign, he insisted 'upon the prejudical effects of clericalism and Romanism upon the state'.

Given the need to modernize the nation—a lesson arising from the long drawn out battle with the Boers—it was hardly surprising that the government wanted a better system of elementary and secondary education. A. J. Balfour, something of a scholar and philosopher himself, would have taken a high minded view, though in the wake of the war, and popular disenchantment with politicians, it was hardly surprising that the administration was looking for a victory over someone, even if it was only over 'Liberal Free Churchmen'.

Free Church Missions

All this served as a distraction from the evangelistic thrust of the NCEFC, although much evangelism was still planned from its spacious offices at Memorial Hall in Farringdon Street, close to the traditional publishing centre of London. Gipsy's co-worker in missions was Rev. J. Tolfree Parr, and W. R. Lane served as Lay Missioner. All but forgotten now, W. R. Lane was a fine speaker, and his testimony/lecture, 'From Gambling Table to Mercy Seat' told of his rough-and-tumble life prior to becoming a Christian and a witness for God's grace in the 1880s. The format of a testimony-cum-lecture was popular in mission meetings, and Gipsy adapted it better than most. His *Story of My life* was always a special attraction. They were often given on the last evening of a campaign or mission, with tickets sold in aid of church funds. Gipsy did not himself make any money out of these marvellous discourses.

Converted gamblers and former drunks could be very effective preachers, as were one-time pugilists and street fighters, like 'Bendigo' and Albert Shakesby. To capture the attention of men leaving saloons in the early afternoon, W. R. Lane and his NCEFC friends would hold afternoon meetings for men, and counselling was linked to this evangelistic work. As an experienced tent evangelist and, as we might term it today, Christian social worker, he had no illusions about the ease with which a pledge to abstain could be signed and then forgotten even as the 'convert' left the tent or hall. So among other labours, he tried to encourage anti-drink and also care ministries within local churches. Indeed, like many in our time, he believed that nurturing and caring for families (especially those facing tough times) was a priority. One of his lectures was a presentation of *The Pilgrim's Progress*, but his recollections of his own life in the gutter, *Eight Years in Darkest London*, was more truly 'shocking', showing the perils awaiting so many in the land.

Rev. J. Tolfree Parr was an excellent expositor, and during NCEFC missions, he delivered Bible expositions in afternoon meetings. He recruited men from the local churches to join in 'orderly processions of 300 or 400 men preceding the service for men' and which, he told the NCEFC, had been 'impressive witness for God, and has swept many out of the public houses and from the street corners and into the meetings.' But, he warned, the point of any mission was not that of arranging meetings alone, but joining in with church workers to reach the ungodly and indifferent.

In the few years between the Simultaneous Missions of 1900 and the coming of the Welsh revival in late 1904, much earnestness was being expressed in evangelical circles, along with some hard thinking and much praying. And outside the churches, as within them, people seeing the nation's apparent isolation and weakness during the 1899–1902 conflict in South Africa, were asking, 'What next? Where is the nation going?'

The debate on national purpose—and power in an increasingly hazardous world—acted as a sort of sub-text to preaching in the decade preceding the outbreak of the Great War in August 1914. Gipsy was to return to this theme, both in Britain and the USA, in the 1920s .

9
The mission of peace, 1904

*The first call of every church is to go into
all the world and preach the gospel to every creature.*
(Rev. F. B. Meyer, NCEFC Conference, 1904)

The sense of national uncertainty, following the end of the
Boer War, was nowhere more reflected than in the arguments about Empire (Free) Trade and Tariff Reform. Joseph
Chamberlain, the businessman turned parliamentarian, believed
that Britain's future prosperity depended on a system of free trade
within the British Empire, i.e. the English-speaking nations of the
Commonwealth. He also believed that the nation's political insti-
tutions needed reform into a federal system. In the end the arguments helped bring down the Conservative government in 1905,
for at most only about a third of the government supporters
believed that imperial preference would work. It has to be said that
the politicians, in discussing the issues, tended to treat the elec-
torate rather as children arguing that 'a little loaf' would be bought
if Chamberlain's ideas were accepted, and a 'big loaf' for the same
money if they were not. A tax on corn—and thus bread—was
involved in the debate, but the heart of the argument was strangely
close to issues of recent years. Were City (financial) interests to be
paramount in the economic priorities of the nation?

The answer, at the beginning of the century, was a resound-
ing 'yes'. With war breaking out between Tsarist Russia and Japan
in 1904, and evidence of other turmoil in the world, there was no
easy self-assurance in the land. The Entente between Britain and
France, though couched in glowing terms of friendship and shared
cultural perspectives, turned out to be an unwritten naval agreement, and a factor in Britain's involvement in war in 1914—as

was the arms race between Britain and Germany developing in the first decade of this century.

Social issues

Thus, in the early years of the century, evangelically minded Free churchmen were taking a long, hard look at the social life of the nation. A flow of books and reports showed that poverty and unemployment existed on a wide scale. Rev. R. F. Horton, President of the NCEFC in 1905, took up an issue which continues to perplex Christian leaders today—how could the churches reach working people? In his presidential address at Manchester in March 1905, Robert Horton noted that working-class movements had often drawn their leaders from the Free Churches, yet by the turn of the century, this sympathy seemed no longer evident. Robert Blatchford, the champion of working men's rights, through his paper, 'The Clarion', and his best selling critique of society, *Merrie England*, had attacked the churches (though he became a worshipper toward the end of his life). But at least Robert Blatchford spoke in words that working men understood.

We shall win men like Robert Blatchford to our faith (declared Robert Horton) when we carry out in the England of today the Gospel of the Kingdom of God, as our Lord carried it out in the world of his day. It is the omission of so large a part of the Gospel of the Kingdom which causes these bitter assaults on the Christianity of our time.

The Free Churches should repair the omission. And is it not possible that one reason why the working men are so difficult to bring into Christ's Church is that the preaching is not strong enough or concrete enough to win and to hold them?

Men who work with their hands acquire much mental ability of the practical but not of the speculative order. Abstract reasoning is to them intangible, Hegel is unintelligible, even the poets are unsubstantial. A preacher who would win them must be concrete, must touch them at the practical point of life as they know and live it; he must be full of information; he must give definite and verifiable facts. He must grapple with things as they are.

Robert Horton—a former President of the Union at Oxford University—was more than a scholar, and was once described as 'just what would have happened if Matthew Arnold had become a Salvation Army captain'. Although involved in many causes, including social work and foreign missions, he only ever had one church, and that 'from scratch'. He took on the pastorate of a new Congregationalist Church in Hampstead, on a year's engagement, and remained there for the rest of his life. Something of his influence was suggested by Alexander Gammie, when he wrote in *The Glasgow Citizen* in November 1938, after Robert Horton's death: 'At the close of a sermon, his hearers, instead of wishing to rise and cheer or express admiration of such an effort, felt that they should fall to their knees in prayer.'

His challenge to the churches, shown in his presidential address, was that they had to imitate Jesus Christ in deed as well as in word, and for that matter, in words that made sense to working people. Gipsy had been pressing a similar argument for years, though he was never especially interested in working class *movements*, as such, and probably knew little about them. Indeed, one of the few occasions that he made no impact on his listeners, according to Harold Murray, was when he attempted to speak to a group of unemployed men in an industrial town, and who were reportedly 'Communists'. But there is no doubt that, had Gipsy had time to prepare his arguments, he could have made one or two telling points which they would have recognized.

He was wise—and experienced—enough to see that enquirers or converts at evangelistic meetings needed effective nurturing and friendship. It was not enough to welcome them at Sunday services, and ignore them for the rest of the week (a lesson one might think for some churches today). When Gipsy conducted a campaign at Woolwich, in south London, during 1904, he encouraged the establishment of a local branch of the Young Free Churchmen's Auxiliary, a fellowship which had much in common with the Christian Endeavour movement.

Gipsy's approach can be seen in the mission he conducted at Leeds in the early months of 1904, and as a result of which 'a rescue home' (or 'shelter') for homeless teenage girls and women was opened:

The town was paraded by a large procession and thousands of people were gathered inside the Coliseum. At about one o'clock in the morning, when the enquirers were being dealt with, it was found that the number included three girls who had been brought in, off the streets. Evidently, they were under deep conviction and wanted to leave the life of prostitution they had been leading. The problem of what to do with them at once presented itself. Arrangements of a temporary nature were made, but on the Saturday night, a meeting was held at which Gipsy asked, why not start a home under the auspicies of the local free church council? A fund was at once started, a suitable house found, and the services of a matron secured. Even before the furnishing of the house was completed, three women were brought to the home, and ever since, the capacity of the house has been fully engaged. (Free Church Year Book, 1905, pages 191-192)

Gipsy thought such initiatives 'normal' if the churches were to be taken seriously, though, of course, the impetus was the care of 'the least of these', not any kind of public relations campaign.

One whose ministry was seemingly revolutionized by Gipsy's influence was Rev. W. J. Dawson, whose *Autobiography of a Mind* recalls his early life as a preacher, and is something of a neglected spiritual classic. Writing some decades ago, F. R. Webber (in *A History of Preaching in Britain and the USA*, published by Northwestern Publishing House, Milwaukee, Wisconsin, USA) recalled the impact of Gipsy Smith on his hearers, most of them ordained ministers, at the NCEFC conference held at Brighton, Sussex, in the spring of 1903. Proceedings seemed to have little life until Gipsy rose to speak:

Here we are in this large city of Brighton, with the drunkards and the wastrels all about us. We pass them by, we come to this convention hall, and bewail the fact that the religious forces of Britain are not reaching the neglected. I propose that every man present at this conference go out into the back streets of Brighton tonight, right now, and bring into this hall whatever (sic) we might find, and bring them under the influence of the Law and the Gospel.

Impressed by the call, the thousand or so members of his audience went into the streets of the seaside town, and within an hour or so, the hall was filled with 'perhaps the largest assembly of outcasts that had been gathered in many a year'. Gipsy delivered his call to 'start a new life', in his characteristic heart-to-heart fashion, but with clear biblical direction. At the close of this midnight sermon, 'scores of drunks and outcasts poured into the enquiry room, confessing their sins, and seeking to know the requirement for Christian living.'

That night must have been quite a learning experience for many who had come to the conference expecting just another conference of sermons and reports. Gipsy had learned the 'basics' from Rev. Samuel F. Collier at the Manchester Methodist Mission, and in any case, had much in common with that clergyman hero of a P. B. Power story, a man who had many long words in his head but made sure he left them at home when he wanted to speak to ordinary folk.

Returning from the conference to his church—Highbury Quadrant Congregational Church—in north London, Rev. W. J. Dawson saw his ministry take a new direction. Gipsy was asked to take a mission at the church as soon as he was able to make a space in his diary.

The climax of the mission came one night when almost a thousand people, headed by a brass band, went through the streets. They returned, three thousand strong.

Gipsy Smith addressed one of the most unusual congregations that north London had ever seen. During the weeks that followed, interest did not die out. So many of the unchurched, the poor and the neglected came to Highbury Quadrant Church that it was actually necessary to ask the older members of the congregation to stay away, in order to give the newcomers room. A great Thursday evening service was started for such people as these. Within a period of ten days, 20,000 people attended services at Mr Dawson's church. Not only did they reach the poor of the community, but many cultured people, of the well-to-do classes, who had not been in the habit of attending church. (F. R. Webber)

Soon to become an evangelist in the USA (and pastor of a church in Newark, New Jersey, from 1912 to 1925) Rev. W. J. Dawson conducted a mission at Plymouth Church, in Brooklyn, New York, in the same year that Gipsy went to South Africa, 1904.

He (W. J. Dawson) told the story of his experience at Highbury Quadrant, declaring that one reason for indifference and decay in a large congregation, is due to a lack of interest in the outcasts and the poor of the community—this, and a pastor who neglects to plead with men for their redemption through Jesus Christ, the Saviour of mankind.

Well known in the USA for his writings, as well as his preaching, he spoke of his personal 'revival' often and at a meeting at Des Moines, Iowa in October 1904, gripped his audience with his discourse. In reporting the event, *The Christian Advocate* thought it a 'promise and a beginning' of an evangelistic movement which would permeate the denominations and bring many into the churches, and also bless the nation at large.

Revival in South Africa

There is a link between this urging of revival through prayerful service, and Gipsy's agreement to visit South Africa in 1904, despite receiving some four or five times the number of invitations to conduct missions in Britain, than could conceivably be accepted. In one sense, the story of the 'mission of peace' of 1904 began long years earlier, for in the same year (1860) that the evangelist was born, a tide of revival swept over South Africa. It began at the recently opened Dutch Reformed Theological Seminary at Stellenbosch in the Cape Province, where Gipsy was to address students during his 1904 visit.

In 1860, its academic staff were summoned to a special conference to review the progress of the churches. Held at a small village with the English name of Worcester, this included a session on the subject of 'revival', a subject which was probably related to reports of the evangelical awakening in Britain and America during the late 1850s. However, it was the witness of an old saint that moved the people present, more than any reports from afar. Rev. Andrew Murray, senior, father of the later well-known writer and preacher of the same name, had devoted every Friday evening to prayer for revival in South Africa, since the days of his first pastorate at Graaff Reinet, the family home. By the time of the conference he had been seeking the outpouring of the Holy Spirit for some thirty-eight years, and had thus started his entreaties years before some of the seminary staff were born.

Soon to take up an appointment at Worcester, the old prayer warrior was invited to address the conference, following two earlier speakers from the Seminary, Dr Robertson, who had taken 'Revival' as his topic, and Dr Adamson, who had pointed to the conditions under which the Holy Spirit could be given to the Church.

> When Mr Murray Senior attempted to speak on the subject, his heart was too full and he broke down. Those addresses made a deep impression on those present, and sent them home with a renewed sense of responsibility, and an earnest expectation that God was about to visit His People. (*Andrew Murray and his Message*, by Rev. W. M. Douglas, 1920)

Anticipating by more than forty years, the invitation sent to Gipsy Smith, the 1860 Conference decided to ask churches in Europe (especially Britain and Holland) to send out teachers and preachers, to help meet the needs of congregations in South Africa.

Rev. Andrew Murray, son of the speaker at the 1860 conference, was born in 1828, and by the time of Gipsy's work for the NCEFC was well known in Britain and the USA. The two men had different emphases in their ministries, for Andrew Murray was more a teacher of intercessory prayer who also emphasized divine healing, but this was, we should note, merely a difference of emphasis. It seems likely that Andrew Murray, who knew Gipsy's work, had a hand in the decision of the South African churches to ask for Gipsy's help in restoring unity and power in the churches, divided as a result of the 1899–1902 war.

A plea for help

This plea for help from South Africa arrived in Thomas Law's always weighty postbag some time in 1903, and the hard-pressed secretary of the NCEFC suggested the name of another evangelist. Perhaps Rev. J. Tolfree Parr was proposed (he had taken missions overseas, and was a most competent preacher and evangelist) but the South African churches were adamant that Gipsy had to come! They had prayed long and earnestly, they explained, and were now convinced that Gipsy was the man for the moment. Looking back, one can hardly disagree with their insistence. Gipsy was always something of an 'outsider', that is, a man outside the élites and structures that men (even good men) so often make for themselves. He was of course a patriot, but he was not essentially an English stereotype, and thus could not be identified with any 'side' in the recent bitter conflict. In short, he was ideally placed, in God's grace, to be a peacemaker.

Gipsy must have realized, too, the extent to which Rev. Andrew Murray was caught up in the tensions that followed the end of the war. As Murray's biographer, Rev. W. M. Douglas wrote, some seventy years ago, 'many of his old friends turned away from him, on the side of the English-speaking people because he was too pro Boer, and on the side of the Boers, because he was too pro British. Oh, it was a sad, sad time, but it came on both sides, because of the failure of the church leaders—both Boer and British—to come together in humiliation and prayer, before the storm broke. Each side was ready to pray for its own success,

'but', said a Quaker editor of a Midlands paper, "I feel I can never forgive the ministers and churches, that not one voice gave a call *for both sides to come together to pray.*" Andrew Murray did sound the call, but it was unheeded.'

During the war (alas, between two professedly Christian peoples) Andrew Murray worked to help the prisoners of war of both sides to maintain their faith. Christian Endeavour societies were organized, and it is noteworthy that after the war was over there was a crop of candidates for theological training. It was hardly surprising that Andrew Murray suffered a breakdown in health, nor was it really so surprising that Gipsy—who had a host of invitations for work in Britain—decided to go to the aid of his comrades at the Cape and elsewhere in that suffering land.

The NCEFCs official send-off was given at the annual conference at Newcastle upon Tyne, at which Rev. F. B. Meyer, NCEFC President in 1904/1905, was a main speaker. Thomas Law was to have accompanied Gipsy on his visit, but the pressures of work at Memorial Hall were too great to permit him to leave. When Gipsy sailed on 19 March 1904, he was accompanied by his wife, Annie, and daughter, Zillah, who proved a most acceptable singer at the meetings (sometimes in duets with Gipsy himself).

In South Africa there had been more requests for Gipsy's services than could ever have been met. As it was, he visited Cape Town, Kimberley, Johannesburg, Durban, Bloemfontein, East London, Pretoria and Port Elizabeth, with engagements including 'drawing room' (i.e. house) meetings for women, temperance rallies, talks to ministers and other chores, in addition to the great public meetings.

Blessing

Looking at the reports, coming from ministers of churches in South Africa, and published in 'The Free Church Year Book, 1905', one can hardly escape the impression of great blessing and spiritual revival. From East London, for example, the secretary of the local mission, Mr W. G. Cooper wrote:

It is difficult to speak of Gipsy Smith's mission without seem-

ing guilty of exaggeration. Yet it can be truly said that exaggeration is impossible, for words cannot be found to describe the things we have heard and seen during the wonderful ten days that the mission has lasted . . . about 750 persons have passed through the enquiry rooms, and others are still daily coming to the resident ministers to ask what they must do to be saved. The ministers realise that they have got to carry the great revival on . . . not the least effect of the mission will be the encouraging and stimulating effect upon the ministers.

At Pretoria, where the Dutch Reformed Church enjoyed most benefit from Gipsy's visit, it was suggested that the 'best effects' had been upon those already in some contact with the churches: 'the Mission had only just begun to grip the people whom we specially wanted to reach; if the mission had been allowed another fortnight, we should have witnessed a great movement among those who rarely entered a place of worship.'

At Johannesburg, the large marquee was crowded night after night, so that overflow meetings had to be held at the Dutch Reformed Church. The planning of the mission had been effected with noteworthy detail, the Witwatersrand Free Church Council reporting: 'Arrangements were made for extensive visitation work. The whole of Johannesburg and the suburbs, being mapped out, and notices, with invitations, distributed from house to house.' The 1904 'mission of peace' deserves attention, for the way in which Gipsy related to a society devoted, as it seemed, to material gain, and in which social divisions were evident, not least as a result of the recent conflict. Gipsy was impressed with the spectacular and beautiful terrain that met him at Cape Town, as indeed elsewhere, but he did not close his eyes to the preoccupations of the people in general.

They are made up of thousands of white people, British and Dutch, and thousands of coloured of all shades. These, for years, have had one overwhelming passion—the making of money. Money and pleasure, drink, gambling and lust stand out large in the lives of thousands of men in Cape Town and, I think it is safe to say, all over the country. The churches were

largely divided (i.e. at the commencement of the mission); on the one side, stood the British, on the other side, the Dutch. I early saw the racial difficulty was a big one. Patience, wisdom and a deep spiritual revival in all the churches would be needed in order to bring these people together into one Christian whole.

Gipsy did not always receive a warm welcome. When it became apparent that no secular building in Cape Town was large enough to accommodate his campaign the use of the Dutch Reformed Church was sought. The request was rejected, promptly and curtly. At the time the town hall had not been completed, so in the end, the organizing committee had to rent an old and somewhat derelict corrugated iron building. Someone said that it was 'consecrated' iron! 'Well,' the Gipsy smiled, 'we shall certainly consecrate it!'

The committee spent almost eight hundred pounds (a not inconsiderable sum) putting the building in order. From the very first night of the mission it was packed to capacity with a multi-racial audience of three thousand people. 'It was a sight to witness,' Gipsy wrote , 'white and black, rich and poor, British and Dutch, Episcopal and Nonconformist, sitting side by side, and here and there one could see a Malay, with his fez in his hand, listening like the rest. There was no difference—all had sinned and Christ is the Saviour of all.'

Undeniably, Gipsy used 'good old fashioned sentiment' in his preaching at Cape Town, but then, that was hardly novel. In a report of one of the midnight meetings, a Cape newspaper thought one of the evangelist's secrets was his tender approach, an ability to touch chords that stirred old memories. 'Gipsy Smith believes that the memory of a good mother lives always, in spite of the most deadening influences. He can tell a hundred stories in which a man's recollection of his mother has saved him from ruin. He appealed specially to those who lived evil and degraded lives, emphasizing the belief that no human being is quite destitute of manhood, and that a chance word or incident may cause the faint spark to glow, and eventually burst into flame.' However, Gipsy was brief, succinct in his appeal, perhaps three minutes or so were spent making it, before he invited his hearers (no few of whom were drunk) to join him in prayer.

The point, as we might see it, was his promise that any man, or woman, drunk or sober, religious or irreligious, could make a new beginning. This aspect of the mission was quite noticeable, reflected in the comment of a minister that, prior to Gipsy's visit, he had been impelled to dismiss the members of his church choir, because they were so worldly. But, he added, 'in this mission, they have all got new hearts, and have come back to me.' Another reported several ministers were rejoicing that their own children had now fully decided to follow Christ.

When Gipsy, with his wife and daughter, left Cape Town on the afternoon of 10 May 1904, en route for Wellington and the home of Rev. Andrew Murray, they were given a splendid farewell by a large number of new converts. They were for the most part wearing a badge they had made, of white and red ribbon, symbolizing the old text, 'Though your sins be red like crimson, they shall be white as snow.' The stop-over in Wellington was to permit Gipsy to preach at Dr Murray's church, a building that seated some 1500 people. Some 150 people rose to commit themselves to Christ on Gipsy's invitation, and though he had to proceed to Kimberley on the following day, he later heard that 'for ten nights in succession, meetings were held in which enquirers were dealt with, as a result of that one night (in which Gipsy had preached), showing how ready and ripe the harvest is in South Africa, only waiting to be gathered.'

A feature relevant to present-day evangelists and their co-workers, was the absence of any sense of competitiveness. As Gipsy put it, 'From the first day of the first meeting in Cape Town to the last in Port Elizabeth, there was not a hitch, not a cross word, no unpleasantness, in any committee, nor with any particular worker. Every man, from first to last, seemed to forget self, and to lay his all at the feet of Christ, and the service of his brother.' Gipsy undoubtedly ascribed much of this refreshing atmosphere to Andrew Murray, who had once counselled a young lady in words that certainly ring true today. 'Your greatest difficulty is Self Occupation', he had told her. 'Your only cure will be

Self Oblivion, forgetting Self. Let it be a settled thing that you are not going to trouble about what you find, or do not find, in yourself. Believe that the Holy Spirit of God is deep hidden within you, and enabling you to believe and to love. Do not look for Him in sudden thoughts, and impulses and suggestions. He lives deeper down, where you cannot at first find Him.'

'Experimental Christianity'—that was certainly the Gipsy's theme, and it was Dr Murray's too. It was not enough to have the right theology, important as it was, but to live as if it mattered more than anything else. Gipsy surely anticipated the events of the revival that burst upon Wales, and then Britain in the later months of 1904, for we find in his South African sermons very many urgings to seek the Holy Spirit: 'Oh, to preach the old Gospel story more and more in all its fullness, grandeur, and eternity, in all the power of the Holy Spirit. What a difference it makes when we preach in the demonstration of the Spirit and with power.'

Although Gipsy referred often to his 'mission of peace', no meeting meant more to him than the invitation from Professor Hofmeyer, to address the students at Stellenbosch Theological Seminary. This was no small door to become open, as the Dutch Reformed Church student body had little if anything to do with the English churches, since the outbreak of the conflict in 1899. Among searching questions, one student asked Gipsy for his views on reconciliation. Perhaps the student had in mind the need for a political reconciliation as well as between the churches. But Gipsy applied the lesson more deeply.

> Our nations have fallen out. And it's the duty of Christians in both lands to give a lead. We have to forgive and forget, and give opportunities for meeting together in fellowship. If we Christians give a lead, the politicians will have to follow . . .
>
> Suppose, we got to Heaven, leaving behind a sore spot we could have healed, but didn't. We would not like to hear Jesus say, 'You were in that place, and you failed to heal that sore spot.' We are all responsible for reconciliation, and it is an everyday task.

The final mission was held at Port Elizabeth in stormy weather.

However, this did not prevent the crowds coming to hear Gipsy at The Feather Market Hall. Two of the ministers helping in the campaign proved to have been converted through hearing Cornelius, Gipsy's father, preaching in Britain, years earlier. About a thousand people went to the enquiry rooms, a final 'praise meeting' being held on Tuesday 13 September 1904. At this cheering close of Gipsy's visit, ministers spoke of the blessings they had themselves received. One said that 120 people had applied for church membership, another beamed, 'My church has a new pastor, and it's me!'

Return home

There was a brief and well deserved holiday in Cape Town, before the return to his home country. Accompanied by his friend, Mr W. Cuthbert, President of the YMCA in South Africa, Gipsy, with his wife and daughter, was taken to the heights of Table Mountain, overlooking the Cape peninsula. Gipsy said that it was impossible to describe the beauty and grandeur of the scene.

A great welcome-home meeting was held in Exeter Hall, London, on 12th October, and at his home church in Cambridge (Hills Road Wesleyan Church) a week later. Gipsy had spent some six months in South Africa, and was soon prompted by his friends, and no doubt the ever faithful Rev. Thomas Law, to produce a book about his experiences. *A Mission of Peace: Evangelistic Triumphs in South Africa* is a rare enough book now, but on its publication at the close of 1904, was widely read and discussed. In his 'retrospect' at the end of the book, Gipsy explains that he determined to avoid 'taking sides' on political issues, but, on the other hand, he did not treat any ethnic or racial group better than any other. He practiced an earnest, genuine equality.

Only in our own time have the issues that Gipsy encountered really been attended to by statesmen. But the vigorous Christian presence in South Africa, and its bounty of faithful preachers, must be regarded as a fine aftermath of the work that the Murrays began, and which, in an all too short mission, Gipsy Smith attempted to extend.

10
A chapter of revival

We are on the eve of a great
revival—do not think the writer a madman
(Evan Roberts to the editor of
Sunday Companion)

So much has been said, and written of the spiritual revival that occurred between 1904 and 1905 that the following account is written only because Gipsy Smith was so deeply committed to that period of fruitfulness in the churches, and had in part prepared the way for it. A further reason is to remind present-day Christian preachers and writers, of the need to inform congregations of past revivals, not in terms of nostalgia, but in readiness for a new outpouring of the Holy Spirit, 'upon all flesh', as we are promised.

The author of this book formerly lived in an area greatly blessed by the revival, and worked in a mining community, in the early 1950s (Pontycymmer, in the Garw valley) which saw some of the earliest revival meetings conducted by Evan Roberts, the so-called 'boy preacher'. In 1985, the former *Observer* columnist, Tom Davies, published a novel, *One Winter of the Holy Spirit*, set against the revival period, a serious and well-written book, which captures the sensual as well as the spiritual in the Wales of 1904 and later. Evan Roberts is a central character of the novel, and wonderfully descriptive as the book often is, the young preacher is not presented sympathetically. There is, dare one add, an element of hysteria in the meetings described in the book, an issue which had a wider airing in the Welsh press. Indeed, it was to answer some critical articles in a Cardiff newspaper, published in the 1970s, that Dr Edwin Orr—resident in the USA, and respected as a scholar on revivals—came to Wales to defend Evan Roberts' good name. But probably the best recent source of material is the 1986 reprint of Brynmor Pierce Jones' *The King's Champions — Revival and Reaction 1905–1935*. It shows how some of the arguments about the revival's 'staying power' and the emotional stability of Evan Roberts arose. In this brief chapter, an attempt will be made to show how the National Council of Evangelical Free Churches (NCEFC) sought to encourage revival, and to further its influence.

Debate

A major debate within the NCEFC and strangely anticipating our time, was whether 'spirituality' ought to be the main focus for the churches at a time when most people in the land had no interest in churchgoing. To say the least, attendance at NCEFC gatherings was a testing, learning experience for many pastors and church leaders, whose faithful ministry seemed now a sustaining of the faithful few rather than reaching the nation at large. Much the same problem faced all the mainstream denominations though it was a Methodist evangelist, Rev. J. Ernest Rattenbury, who added fire to the debate on 'the institutional church' at the NCEFC Conference in Manchester in the spring of 1905.

> It is sometimes said that nothing is needed today for the salvation of the world but the naked spiritualities. It was just because naked spiritualities would never save the world, that the Word was made flesh, the spiritualities were clothed, the spiritualities became incarnate in Jesus Christ, and they remain incorporate in the Church of Jesus Christ. The Church that most truly represents him is the Church which most deeply spiritualises the common life . . . Mr Law asked me to suggest methods in this paper which I had found useful in filling empty chapels. When I began to think, I found I had only one, and that can be told in a single sentence: *to find a point of attachment with the people*. I have found it in a common democratic ideal.
>
> I never believe what I have so often heard, that the people of this country are longing to return to Jesus Christ. No more than

anyone else are they anxious to take up the Cross and follow Jesus. But they do believe in Jesus the Democrat. So do I! Here is a common platform. But in the churches as a whole, the democratic ideal is absent. The ideal of the majority of the Free Churches is not democratic but middle class . . . In many churches, the working man is simply not wanted, and in others he is wanted only when he will come and conduct himself in a proper manner, and take his proper(?) place.

Ernest Rattenbury was too well respected a worker and preacher for his words to be dismissed, but some of his hearers, and those who read the transcribed sermon in the 'Free Church Year Book', must have 'wriggled a little'. For he was saying in effect that after ten years of apparently earnest endeavour by the evangelical free churches, and indeed the churches generally, there was still a lack of sympathy and communication with most of the nation's citizens. Strangers, he observed, were too often made to feel like strangers: 'They are treated in the Sunday house of the proprietors of the Church, as they would be in their week-day house, to a straight-backed chair in the passage among the draughts . . . God's houses are preserves for the middle class.'

This trenchant speaker held out hope for the 'institutional church', of course, but only in the sense that it ceased to be so much an institution and became more an instrument of God's purposes in the world. Churchgoers needed to have the needs of ordinary people laid on their heart, and to repent of their self satisfaction.

We can see that the religious revival came at a time of questioning of so many matters—the effectiveness of government, the purpose of the Empire or Commonwealth, the real motives for economic policies, and so on. International events, 'wars and the rumours of wars' were being shadowed by a new sense of competition with industrializing powers in continental Europe. Mass media, and the new novelty of the cinema, were diverting attention from more serious issues, whilst the churches, far from being secure in their domain, were beginning to see their failure to bring working people into their life. The glamour of the Edwardian Era concealed miserable living standards for too many people, and the

111

sinking of the Titanic in 1912 was for many people a sort of cosmic comment on the way that the nation was going. W. T. Stead had compared the luxury liner to 'a floating Babylon'.

This backdrop to the revival needs noting, for it is sometimes assumed that, like some spiritual rainstorm, the revival came 'out of the sky', without much prior warning. Prayer for revival had been characteristic of many churches in Wales for years, and in the land as a whole, prayerful consideration of church life had accompanied the 'Spontaneous Missions' of 1900, and subsequent work. Almost forgotten now, the Torrey and Alexander missions of the early years of this century, also served to create a spirit of anticipation.

Rev. Thomas Law seems to have spent a considerable amount of time in Wales, as indeed did Gipsy Smith. Writing in early 1905, only a few months after the beginnings of the revival, he (Law) observed:

> A movement without genesis, without any machinery (i.e. formal organisation) has suddenly swept through the whole of South Wales and many other parts of the Principality. A revival of some sort had been anxiously anticipated, but it has come in a way that was least expected. No organisation can take the credit of the Welsh Revival simply because there has been no organisation in connection with it. It has come about by the prayerful entreaties of the body of the Church in Wales, and by the will of the Holy Spirit.

Evan Roberts

This 'Free Church Yearbook' of 1905 does not refer to Evan Roberts, but rather to local evangelical free church councils who had been 'preparing the way for the revival'. Evan Roberts, though described as a 'boy preacher' was in his twenties, and some six feet tall, and a mature student rather than ordained minister. It says much for the open-heartedness of his contemporaries that he was welcomed into so many pulpits (which would normally be reserved for ordained ministers and other seniors in the denominations). He had assumed a sort of leadership of the revival initially through work with young people. Evan, a winsome and intelligent bilingual young man, had studied hard on his own account, geometry, shorthand, theology, etc. He had decided to train for the ministry, and was beginning his advanced studies when the opportunity came. Perhaps it was because of the churches' sense of their own weakness that they sought his aid. At Pontycymmer in November 1904, those attending a temperance conference were so appalled at the drunkenness and associated crime and family stress in the Garw valley, that Evan was sent for. He was taking services in the Rhondda valley at the time, this being the early period of the revival, and thus was able to come to Pontycymmer promptly. Rev. D. M. Phillips, in his 1906 study of Evan Roberts and the revival, thought that the 'sweeping power of the meetings' at Pontycymmer in mid November 1904, 'determined definitely the success of the movement'. Certainly, when the present writer worked at Pontycymmer in the early 1950s, some spoke of Evan Roberts as if he had passed that way only a few weeks earlier.

According to D. M. Phillips, Evan opened his first meeting at Pontycymmer with the words: Let us have the quietness that we can make, and then we shall have the quietness that God can make. Although on that occasion, Evan spoke to the crowded chapel for over an hour, some later meetings had almost no preaching but were characterized by singing, praise and prayer. The 'pentecostal' nature of even that first meeting at Pontycymmer was well described by D. M. Phillips:

Sceptical critics were disarmed by the simple and unostentatious manner of Evan Roberts. He did not indulge in high flowing language, rhetorical efforts, nor any other means which would appeal to people's emotions . . . The enthusiasm of the meeting developed from stage to stage until at last men and women poured out their hearts in prayers and appeals, and in some of the richest hymns and tunes. Strong men were choked with weeping in their attempt to speak, and others overwhelmed in agony; some piteously cried for forgiveness and to be right with God. The majority of the people were anxious to express themselves somehow, and in the effort, a good number

113

took part simultaneously. Evan Roberts now sat under the pulpit in the big pew*. He clapped his hands, and occasionally laughing joyfully, urged the people to go on. Not until four o'clock (on the following morning) were they able to close the meeting.

This was indeed 'the people acting in democratic praise', that is, expressing their spiritual needs and praise without benefit of liturgy, order or service, or even formal leadership. It is sometimes said that 'revival is untidy', in the sense that it does not conform to our agendas and arrangements. Some idea of the criticism coming from more staid if sincere church members is seen in the prayer of Rev. John McNeill, a well known preacher of the time (and whose ministry like that of Gipsy Smith, was enjoyed on both sides of the Atlantic). On the last day of the mission led by Evan Roberts in mid Rhondda (Penygraig and Williamstown) on 22 December, John McNeill closed his prayer: 'We have heard of this revival being called the debauch of emotionalism. If it is, O Lord, may we never be sober any more. If this is debauch, then there is no sobriety in heaven, where we are going to.'

Careful to avoid any financial reward for his work, and, where possible, publicity that seemed likely to bring him personal prestige, Evan Roberts showed a wisdom beyond his years, but in the end the burden proved too heavy. Following a collapse—probably severe nervous exhaustion—he left Wales and for some time stayed with Mrs Jessie Penn-Lewis and her husband in Leicester. A well-known speaker and writer her *Overcomer* ministry took her to many places in Britain and overseas. Evan eventually returned to Wales, where he was supported by kindly Christian friends in Cardiff, from the early 1930s onwards. He died in the Festival of Britain year, 1951.

It has been suggested that Evan never recovered from his breakdown, and suffered some kind of mental impairment. In fact, he sometimes spoke publicly, albeit rarely, and one can find

---

* The big seat under the pulpit faced into the congregation, and was occupied by elders and deacons or officers during the service, usefully checking if any older or sick members had not been able to attend.

references to his doing in the Christian press; for example, when visiting his father at Bargoed, Glamorgan, he was also invited to speak at the local chapel, which he did. Intercessory prayer became the centrepiece of his life, but one is bound to regret that he wrote so little (if anything) about his personal involvement with the revival, from a later, more mature perspective. Perhaps his ministry is summed up in one of his 'sayings' collected by D. M. Phillips for his 1906 study: The path of life is obedience.

Dr J. Edwin Orr told the present writer, in a personal letter of March 1985 that 'it is true that Evan Roberts suffered physical breakdown in 1906. He was still an invalid when I had cordial fellowship with him from 1934 onwards, but his mind was clear. In 1934, I toured every county in Wales, and found converts of the revival very active.' Dr Martyn Lloyd-Jones, as shown in Iain Murray's biography, was also clear that many of the most active church leaders in Wales had been fruit of the revival.

Gipsy in Wales

Less recognized, perhaps, is the contribution that NCEFC arranged missions made to the revival, in terms of preparation, and reinforcement. Gipsy knew Wales well, especially South Wales—where there had been an influx of labour from other parts of Britain to work in the coal mines. The Principality has had its own Gypsy clans and traditions, of course, so it was understandable that Gipsy, preaching in Swansea in 1895, had been thought of Welsh lineage:

At the beginning of a career as an evangelist, a Welshman taught me a verse of a Welsh hymn. At one of my Swansea meetings, making the most of my knowledge of Welsh, I sang this verse. It was the only verse I knew.

But, when I had started the people at hymn-singing, I could not stop them. My Welsh accent must have been good, because I was asked by some if I would preach in Welsh. 'No,' I said reflectively. 'I think I prefer English'.

Closer in time to the revival, Gipsy was well known and ever welcome in Wales, and there is no doubt that he did much to lift the hopes and spirits of the people. A former editor of *The Western Mail*, Mr E. James, wrote of a mission, early this century, held in the spacious market hall in the centre of Bridgend, a splendid, light place which, in the present writer's childhood, held stalls of many kinds, with cockle-sellers in their immaculate white aprons, to fruit, clothing and pet sellers, plus a colporteur whose cloaked bookstall looked rather like a large tent. When Gipsy came, the hall was entirely cleared of business activity:

I don't know how many thousands got into the hall, but the enthusiasm was overwhelming and it is true to say that this and other tours helped to create the atmosphere and the spirit that led to the revival led by Evan Roberts, a revival that filled the churches, emptied the public houses and put crime into suspension. Gipsy afterwards told me that the Bridgend meeting was one of the most tremendous occasions of his life. His power was overwhelming. I recall part of his address:

'There are many things we do not and cannot understand. I cannot explain and you cannot explain how the power of God is manifested in the mighty cataract, how the tremendous power of God is reflected in the face of a child as it smiles in the summer sun, how the love of God is found in the cold water which brings relief to the fevered brow of a suffering soul, how He bestows joy to those who have all lost all but their faith—I cannot explain these things. And I cannot tell you the precise process by which the loving Father lifts a saint from the mirest gutter and makes a saint of him. I don't know *how* He does it, but I *know* He does it, because He did it to me, Gipsy Smith.'

His poetic touch was shown that night in wonderful phrases. Here is an example: 'When I campaigned in Portsmouth, I had wonderful help from a dear old lady. I wish I could describe her to you. I know . . . she was like an old country church, lit up for divine service.'

A resident of Porth in the Rhondda valley (Mr T. Powell) remembered a mission, during the period immediately preceding the revival, in a huge marquee on the old fairground, a plot which later became the site of the Rhondda Transport depot.

I can remember Gipsy well, a man with dark, swarthy complexion, black curly hair and eyes that seemed to bore into you. His meetings were packed to the door, and there was great enthusiasm at each meeting. One of the men converted at the meetings was a very rough character named 'Billy Bach' (little Billy). This man joined the Salvation Army, and I often saw him banging the bass drum at the open air meetings. When he died, such was his reputation as a Christian worker, that his funeral was the largest seen in the Rhondda up till then, although the weather was atrocious. Many people were converted at the Gipsy's meetings. One man became a member of our little chapel at Ynyshir, and was a faithful member for forty years.

Mr Powell recalls that Gipsy

played the violin and accompanied the hymns. I remember him well as a very big, swarthy man, and I particularly remember that after one of the services, he came amongst the congregation and put his huge hand, as it seemed to me, on my small head and said, 'God bless that lad!'

I think that incident had more to do with the course of my life than perhaps I have hitherto realised. (The writer of this letter had some fifty years service, or more, as a local preacher).

With his ever lengthening itinerary, Gipsy preached in many places during that period of revival which overflowed from Wales into England, Scotland and beyond, touching the lives of many preachers. Women preachers too were greatly blessed, among them Rosina Davies, known as 'the little Welsh girl' in the early days of her work, which continued into the 1940s. It is significant, to say the least, that in her 1942 autobiography (published by Gomerian Press, Llandysul) Rosina Davies refers both to the neglect of preaching (doctrine) during the Revival and of sound teaching of converts in its aftermath. This point about the lack of essential nurture is made by other writers, and is a pointer to some areas needing attention today. Rosina refers to the period of rest she had to take during the 'high water mark of the revival' (i.e.

the early months of 1905) 'when the people were demonstrative, and the sermons were put aside'. In that year, she recalled in 1942,

> it was perceptible that a sort of exhaustion was setting in . . . had there been more Bible reading, and scriptural knowledge, the Holy Spirit would have had something to lay hold of, and the joy of the Revival would have turned into actions, and those that were filled with the Spirit would have gone, Bible in hand, to teach others. Without Scriptural knowledge, every professing Christian is weak and uncultured . . . The Revival we need now is in Bible reading, without prejudice or criticism and selfish opinions.

The Revival in Wales may have been a lost opportunity in some respects, though Brynmor Pierce Jones' *The King's Champions* has shown how diligent pastors and students became 'spiritual instructors and guardians' of many who were brought in during those great days.

11
Songs of glory

Drink is the devil in solution.
(Gipsy Smith)

Charles Alexander, the gospel singer and preacher, worked in a similar cause to that of Gipsy in that dramatic winter of 1904–05. Brought up in mountain country in Tennessee, he became a committed Christian in his early twenties, and like Gipsy travelled widely as a missioner. Some of his most successful work was done in tandem with Dr R. A Torrey—the Torrey and Alexander Crusade Song Books becoming almost as popular in local church meetings, as the older Moody and Sankey collections. Some seven years younger than Gipsy, Charles M. Alexander developed his interest in gospel singing whilst studying at the Moody Bible Institute in Chicago, and his comment (in an article that he penned soon after the revival of 1904–05) reflects a great deal of Gipsy's own thought on the matter.

I do not recall any religious awakening without Gospel singing. Music was a vital part of the Revival under the Wesleys. The revival of 1859 was a time of hymn singing. Gospel songs were fully half the power of the Moody and Sankey meetings, and we all know what a prominent part music played in the Welsh Revival. I have yet to see the first church that remained empty for long, where each person entered heartily into the singing of hymns. When singing is delegated to the few, with no responsibility on the rest of the audience, the interest dies, the numbers dwindle, and all kinds of expedients must be resorted to, in order to draw the people. This method crowds out music from its proper place which should be co-ordinate with preaching. In order to maintain this equality, every individual must be made to feel his responsibility in the singing part of the worship. This is as true in a church service, as in an evangelical meeting.

The Torrey and Alexander mission at Bingley Hall, Birmingham, beginning in January 1904, opened an eventful year. A link with the National Council of Evangelical Free Churches is seen in the fact that a major supporter of the Council's work, Mr George Cadbury, participated in the opening event, a public welcome to the two Americans. Dr J. H. Jowett also spoke, and Rev. Luke F. Wiseman (later Secretary of Methodist Home Missions) took prayers at the closing meeting.

As the ministry of Evan Roberts in the Glamorgan mining valleys was beginning in the closing months of that year, a Torrey and Alexander mission was held in Cardiff, throughout October, before the two evangelists went on to Liverpool for a mission that lasted from 4 November 1904 until 23 January 1905. The highlight of their work in 1905 was the great mission to London, lasting some five months, from early February to the beginning of July. The theme tune of the mission, 'The Glory Song' ('That will be glory for me') was whistled and sung in the streets, as well as in the meetings. It was as popular as Gipsy's 'Count Your Blessings' had been during the Metropolitan Tabernacle campaign some years earlier (and as 'Blessed Assurance' was to become during the Billy Graham Harringay Crusade of 1954). Charles Alexander might have observed that every time 'The Glory Song' was heard, it was further publicity, not only for the mission at London's Albert Hall, but for the gospel message that Dr Torrey preached. A graceful man, with a consistent and lively enthusiasm, Charles M. Alexander influenced many people across the world, and probably more than any other individual in his time, encouraged well-ordered singing in churches. He died at Birmingham (England) in October 1920, a relatively young man, and the pace of life must have contributed to his final illness. He had been looking forward to further work, and to a 'Bible revival'; thus, for all the sadness that existed everywhere after the close of the First World War, he died in the spirit of hopefulness in which he had lived. Perhaps even more than Gipsy Smith, he seems a somewhat neglected figure in the history of revival.

Gipsy was a more popular preacher than Dr R. A. Torrey seems to have been, in Britain at least, but Dr Torrey's style was shaped in the USA, where churchgoing was still a habit for most families, so that he could easily have overlooked the long years of drift away from the churches in Britain. It was not enough to preach the truth, but to understand why so many of the nation thought it 'beside the point', as far as their own daily preoccupations were concerned. Gipsy was more 'a working man's preacher', clearly one who had toiled manually, and his lack of a seminary education may well have been an advantage to him, in showing that he had no special advantages over those who had left school at twelve years of age, or fourteen, to face humdrum and unpromising job prospects..

Drink is the Devil

There was, however, a special facet to Gipsy's work in the first decade of this century, as indeed at other times, and that was his opposition to alcohol. This was no mere cause to attract support from like-minded people, for one suspects that in his childhood Gipsy had seen many examples of husbands and fathers falling into crime and family discord through drink. Remembering that Evan Roberts had been summoned to Pontycymmer in late 1904, because local churches seemed powerless in the face of drink-related crime and family breakup, there is some special interest in W. T. Stead's comment in the Revival Pamphlet he published in February 1905 ('The Story of Gipsy Smith / The Missions of the National Free Church of England'):

No one can spend any time in these Welsh villages without being impressed by the fact that in south Wales at least, Drink is the Devil. Satan is short for alcohol. The real struggle that is going on is between the Revival and strong drink. It is a fight in which the odds are very heavily in favour of the Devil. He goeth about not as a raging lion seeking whom he may devour, but as a subtle and cunning tempter who has practically the monopoly of the field. Man is essentially a social animal and the public house and the drinking club are the only places where the young men can meet their friends, except in the open air.

W. T. Stead, an experienced journalist (and son of a Congregationalist minister) saw the relevance of the anti-alcohol message, for whilst missionary preaching could be dismissed by 'the liquor interests' as mere piety that might pass off, and which might have relatively little effect on sales, Gipsy's well-informed, effective attack on alcohol and its outcome was far more dangerous to their business. One might have thought Stead would be primarily interested in the revival meetings themselves—certainly he and Gipsy spent a day at Maerdy (a mining community in the Rhondda) with Evan Roberts just before Christmas 1904; further, Stead thought the revival a great psychic event, i.e. with national implications. He was also interested in the NCEFC's form of inter-church co-operation, and mistakenly thought that it was the forerunner of a new united free church of Britain in which denominationalism would be buried once and for all. So it is significant that Stead devoted so much space in his 'Revival Pamphlet' to the issue of alcohol, as being the great foe of reform in the community, as well as the enemy of true regeneration in the individual. He certainly chronicled the extent of the temptation facing miners in the valleys, from free drinks to saving clubs, sponsored by the public-house owners and the brewers, to ensure frequent visits by members. Stead wrote, for example:

Drink, which has its fortresses in the public houses, its outposts in the drinking clubs, has its flying column in the travelling wagon. This is the resource of the brewers who have not tied houses. To avoid being frozen out, they have organised a very effective system of travelling wagons, which scour the country, halt at any wayside house, and book orders for a couple of gallons of beer, which are consumed at leisure in the bosom of the family, with or without the assistance of neighbours . . . the absence of opposition at the beginning of the Revival is being succeeded by a stubborn, ruthless determined attack, all along the line.

Given the influence of the commercial brewing interests in the nation's political life, it was hardly surprising that the government averted its gaze from the damage done by heavy drinking, until war came in 1914. Unable to evade the issue any longer, the government considered possible nationalization of public houses, and initiated controls in areas where drunkenness might be seen to interfere with production in armaments factories. Gipsy would no doubt have appreciated the limitations of political action, and in later years would see the way that prohibition in the USA added to lawlessness. But he certainly believed that the life of Christian discipleship called for a clear mind and sober judgment, even if joyfulness was to be encouraged in one's spiritual life. The effect of the Gipsy's preaching in South African communities paralleled the impact of the revival in Wales during 1904–06:

In this city (Pietermaritzburg, the seat of government of Natal) we encouraged the most bitter opposition from the people in the liquor, theatrical and gambling circles. Everywhere in this country, where the mission was held, these people were hit hard. Theatres and beer-shops if not emptied, were left by thousands to attend the meetings.

I was slandered and abused by the papers representing these interests as 'King of Bunkum', 'A Fraud', 'The biggest humbug that ever came to South Africa'. Some of my words were twisted into all sorts of meanings, the foulest lies that could be told, were circulated . . . The abuse was really so bad that I began to fear for the mission, for it was the talk of the city before I began, or had even arrived; and as I did not reply, or refer to it in any way, the man in the street began to believe it, and said he would not listen to one who could not contradict what was being said.

Gipsy faced a situation which many were to encounter as mass media became major shapers of opinion. Biased reporting could damage a man or woman in the public eye, with the vast number of readers being unaware of the true motives behind the news story. 'The wildness of the storm', as Gipsy called the thundering press attacks, seemed likely to discourage the mission workers: 'Still, my hope was in God. I knew He would not forsake me, and I was prepared to look a fool and to be a fool if He could be honoured and glorified.'

Such was the impact of the mission that the press had to report it, and to back pedal on its attacks. The episode, by no means unique, may serve to encourage those who today stand for scriptural standards, in an age of easy virtue and mercurial publishing.

W. T. Stead, who had fought for diverse causes himself (including the raising of the age of consent, landing him in prison on a trumped up charge) sympathized with Gipsy's stance, and when he attended Gipsy's mission at Pontypridd, in mid Glamorgan, in January 1905, he gave the temperance mission prominence in his report:

Against these devices of the Devil (i.e. the various strategies of the publicans and brewers) Gipsy warned his converts. The moderate drinker who is a church member is much prayed for in South Wales today. 'Touch not . . . taste not . . . handle not' the accursed thing.

Hence the constantly reiterated appeal to the converts to sign the following pledge—

PONTYPRIDD FREE CHURCH COUNCIL
GIPSY SMITH MISSION PLEDGE CARD
'I promise by Divine Assistance to abstain from all intoxicating liquors or beverages for Christ's sake and my weaker brother's.'
Name   ....
Address   ....

Gipsy Smith was tired out when the meeting (at Pontypridd Town Hall) closed. He went home. But the enthusiasm of his converts and fellow-workers knew no abatement. They made a drive of the streets and public house and gathered in a motley crowd of men who were not exactly teetotallers. A midnight meeting it was of the approved Mission style.

It was true that Gipsy pressed for a decision. Stead noted, for example, the Gipsy's call for committed Christians to stand and profess their faith (which, of course, meant that uncertain or unpersuaded people remained in their seats). And because Gipsy could sing so well, he could—like the old Welsh preachers— suddenly burst into a hymn, even in the midst of a sentence or theological argument. 'Almost persuaded', for example, was a hymn used by Gipsy at this time. But Stead, no stranger to religious occasions (and well able to sort out the phoney gospel-mongers) could report that Gipsy's influence was of hopefulness, and encouragement to those who had a 'faith of the heart' rather than 'of the head' alone. It was true, as he said, that many would be quite unmoved by Gipsy, the choir and all the manifestations of spiritual revival. But there was more to the occasion, as to Evan Roberts' labours, than mere 'well intentioned enthusiasm'. Stead's closing words on the January 1905 mission at Pontypridd seem to characterize the entire revival period:

Something—they called it the Spirit—keener than a two-edged sword, pierced the heart, and roused the conscience, bringing to light neglected duties, forgotten ideals, spurring one on to fresh resolves and nobler aspirations. What I felt others felt.

There is something profoundly affecting in the sacred contagion of a strong emotion, especially when at the back of it stands a deep conviction, logical, unanswerable, as hard as adamant—the knowledge of one's own exceeding sinfulness, one's own miserable failure to be the Christ to others which He has been to us.

But Stead was careful to show the cheering aspect of the spiritual tension. As he waited at Pontypridd Railway Station for his train, he saw (and heard) a large crowd of people waiting for the local train to Merthyr. This great crowd was singing, he wrote, 'like a trained choir, with all their hearts and voices', the chorus,

'Oh, happy day that fixed my choice'. 'Even the surliest sceptic', Stead suggested, 'must have admitted that the singers were for the time, as happy as the larks who sing their matin song in mid-heaven.'

Gipsy had a great regard for Wales which had of course been home to long established Gypsy clans for generations. Emotion was as evident at the meetings of Evan Roberts as ever it was at the Gipsy Smith missions, though, as a veteran of evangelism, Gipsy was always careful to preach a sound if necessarily basic message. Mere emotionalism was not, in the present writer's view, to be found in either man's approach. Mrs Elizabeth Baxter—who had a special ministry in looking after young women in the metropolis—journeyed to Swansea to see and hear the young Welsh revivalist. The meeting, she said later, was reminiscent of 'the more deeply spiritual meetings of the Society of Friends'. On that occasion, Evan Roberts preached in Welsh.

Newspapers were not slow to see the potential of 'sending up' the preacher, and those 'feeble minded people' who attended. A journalist on a satirical paper in Liverpool came to one of the meetings, planning to write a lampooning article, but changed his mind. He thought that here was something in the meeting that awakened 'the deep springs of the soul'. Evan Roberts 'acted like a silent dynamo, giving off the energy that moves the mighty machinery of the mission'. This seems a little akin to poetic licence. If anything, Evan was the fountain effect not the source of the spring, and in the end, he suffered a break-down in his own health. Gipsy had a well-managed and staffed organization behind his work, and though he was to part from the National Council of Evangelical Free Churches in 1912, for many years he was able to focus on his special ministry. There was a network of support which Evan Roberts did not have, at least not in the same way. Also, Evan Roberts was criticized even within the churches for allowing women to take an active part in the meetings. Yet there is no doubt as to the beneficial outcome of the Revival, of which Evan was but part, and among changes in behaviour that one might welcome today, is the comment that 'after conversion, people went home and paid their bills'. Given that in our time small and vulnerable businesses have often closed because they could not get their bills paid, one can see how spiritual and economic life overlapped.

Many leaders of the Free Churches in England went to South Wales, to hear Evan Roberts for themselves, a subject 'most sympathetically and earnestly dealt with', when some of these ministers gave their report to a NCEFC conference in London, beginning on 31 December 1904 and lasting into the New Year. *The Free Church Year Book for 1905* thought that there had never been such a gathering of ministers in London: 'the leading note of the Conference was that those who were in the habit of preaching to others desired to carry the truths they had so often proclaimed to their own inner lives, and to promote the revival there first.'

The revival spreads

As the Revival spread beyond Wales into other parts of the United Kingdom, there was no shortage of local co-operation, so that as one church was filled, an overflow meeting would be held in another, or meetings for converts/enquirers could be held in one building, and youth or men's missions in another, all under the same local Free Church banner. It was, as a report from Torrington, North Devon puts it, a topic even discussed in public houses! The expression on the face of the landlords is not specified. At Torrington, as elsewhere, the churches had joined together in a Week of Prayer proposed by the NCEFC as a local church activity between 9 and 16 January 1905. 'Hundreds of decisions have already been made', reported the Secretary of the Nuneaton and District Free Churches Council in early 1905. 'The whole of the Free Churches are united as one church, drawing the nets full of fishes. We have meetings every night, and numbers of decisions at each meeting. We no longer expect a revival, we have got one.'

As Dr J. Edwin Orr, and other writers have shown, the description 'Welsh Revival' is something of a misnomer, as there was a sweep of renewal across the land. The fact that local clergy rather than 'evangelical personalities' were involved meant that this aspect has been overlooked in later decades. Dr Edwin Orr said

127

that God's gracious Spirit was given in the 1904–05 revival, bringing into the churches many young men who would later be drawn into the terrible conflict that began in 1914 (and which decimated British churches for at least a generation).

The Welsh Revival had been a sort of spiritual yardstick, as the 1905 'Year Book' affirmed—for many Councils were seeing a growth in prayerfulness and evangelistic work that had much to do with the news from the Principality:

Undoubtedly the Welsh Revival had acted as a great stimulant to all spiritual work. It is quite possible that we are on the eve of such an outpouring as has not visited these shores for many years. When this comes, it will be found, that Free Church Councils will energetically take their part.

The birth of the Pentecostal movement dates from about this time, although Dr Edwin Orr assured the present writer that he had been unable to find any record of 'speaking in tongues' during the revival, until a meeting, held in a home in 1907. Whether one would define 'speaking in tongues' as a necessary measure of pentecostal worship depends on one's theological stance (the present author has an open mind on the matter) and in any case, the congregational worship found in some Welsh chapels at that time—some singing, some praying aloud, in Welsh or in English, with the whole shaping a rhythm of its own—would make any measure of whether or not 'speaking in tongues' was occurring difficult to judge, all the more so if the hearer was not Welsh-speaking.

An aspect of the revival which seems to have had little attention was the upsurge in adult education that appears to have accompanied it. At Pontycymmer, one of the centres of revival, local educational work flourished in 1905, not least with the local co-operative society. For decades economic expression of the gospel was thought to lie in self-help, so that many free churchmen were volunteer members of local Co-op management committees. In South Wales, the valleys' tradition of adult education, or the virtue of study and learning, is probably related to spiritual revival. 'Revival' could not be merely considered as a sudden

Cornelius, Gipsy and Zillah Smith, with the two sons of Albany Smith, Jack and Wilbur (photograph provided by Romany Watt)

THE WELL-KNOWN EVANGELIST, says:-
"I cannot understand how any Methodist can live without
the 'Methodist Recorder.'" It is published every Thursday,
lavishly illustrated, price One Penny. May be ordered from
any Newsagent or Bookstall.

A promotional portrait of Gipsy Smith
(photograph provided by David Lazell)

Gipsy and Annie, his first wife

THEME SONG
THE GIPSY SMITH MISSION
NEW YORK CITY

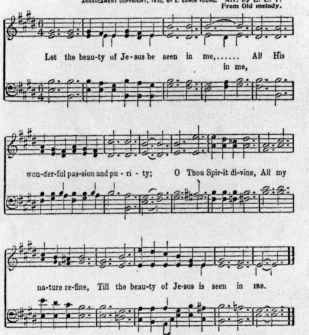

Sing it with Gipsy Smith,
in Grace Methodist Church
104th Street, between Amsterdam and Columbus Avenues

A chorus (song) popularized by Gipsy Smith.

An invitation card to a Gipsy Smith mission

JOHANNESBURG CYCLE BRIGADE ADVERTISING THE MISSION.

Johannesburg Cycle Brigade advertising Gipsy's mission in 1904 (from *Mission of Peace*, facing page 160)

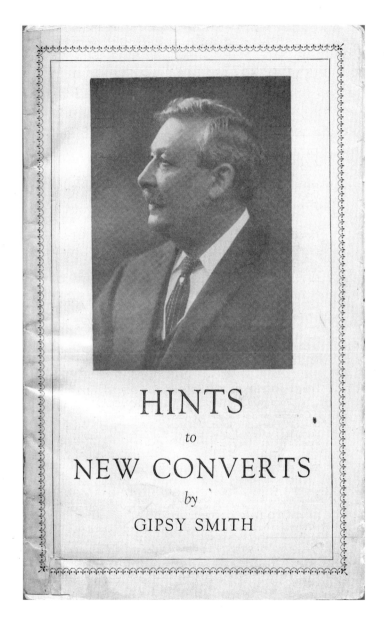

HINTS

to

NEW CONVERTS

by

GIPSY SMITH

Cover of the booklet *Hints to New Converts*.

Gipsy with his second wife, Mary Alice

rush of the Holy Spirit, permitting an absence of hard thinking. If anything, the revival period posed searching questions to pastors, preachers and church leaders. It also raised issues for those who were in the vanguard of new models of inter-church co-operation, new ideas on ministry, and new arguments for 'women's roles in political and religious life'. Gipsy, even in the height of all the excitement, insisted that the Bible had to hold its central position, a piece of advice hardly to be neglected today:

There are not a few hearers who are carried away for the moment. It is at times difficult to discriminate—to separate the chaff from the wheat, and to make sure that the faith is well grounded. We do indeed need the inspiration of the Holy Spirit in dealing with such cases. *I never allow any excitement during the reading of the Scriptures.*

I insist upon silence and order. The Bible holds the field till God recalls it. I remember having to wait ten minutes with the Bible open before me, before I could begin reading. But I put my foot down, and was determined to have silence—and I got it.

Gipsy not infrequently discussed the role of the evangelist in relation to the local church, and his thoughtful views, expressed in the early 1930s (in his memoir, *The Beauty of Jesus*, published by Epworth Press) deserve attention in any generation. He stated, for example, that the evangelist is essentially a reaper. 'How many ministers would there be in the ministry, or members in the churches for that matter, if there had been no such evangelical reapers?'

When the Religious Tract Society—a magazine and book publisher, later to become the Lutterworth Press—invited Gipsy to write a piece for a 1906 book on revivals, he pointed to the magnitude of the task:

It is impossible for the ordained minister of a church to attend successfully to all the demands of Christ's flock. In one sense, the evangelist comes first, and then the pastor. As far as human vision can extend, it seems to me that a vast extension of evangelistic work is absolutely vital for the in-gathering of the millions. I believe that this country, and other countries, are waiting. (*Stories of Great Revivals* by Henry Johnson, RTS, 1906)

The debate was not confined to the Free Churches, for in the established Church too, the impact of the revival, and the beginnings of the modern Pentecostal movement were being felt. One of the best evangelists in the Church of England, Canon Rev. W. Hay Aitken, thought that

> nothing is more to be depreciated in revival work than mere physical excitement and hysterial emotionalism . . . the noisy and frothy ebullience of feeling that one often witnessed in the past were not altogether fruitless for each 'revival' left some permanent ingathering, but the large proportion of 'backsliding' was deplorable, and the last state of those who were merely superficially affected was worse than the first (also from *Stories of Great Revivals*, above).

Undoubtedly, some churches eventually rejected what they regarded as 'noisy and frothy ebullience', or perhaps felt that they could not change their traditions to accommodate new forms of worship, in which congregations could be more expressive. Understandably, in those days as in our own, some ministers and church leaders thought that in an age of change and novelty, it was necessary that the church show a stability, and in that a resistance to change. Churches with a formal liturgy, and a traditional 'order' could not allow much in the way of the spontaneity which was inherent in Pentecostal, charismatic worship. Then there was the matter of hierarchy: if members of congregations, especially 'converts' and 'newcomers' were to be allowed expression of their spiritual gifts, what would happen to the idea of 'priesthood' and a trained ministry?

It was a matter of 'testing gifts' and 'doing things in order', but the end result, all too often, was that enthusiastic young Christians were left high and dry in the pews, except where local pastors and clergy really focused efforts on 'bringing them on' in Christian service. But this kind of nurturing in itself called for time and insights not always available to clergy, and for that matter, a subject not often included in their seminary education. Gipsy, who was largely self-taught, and who had followed the Spirit's guiding rather than traditional ways of shaping ministry, could offer encouragement. Mrs M. Entwistle, who remembered Gipsy's visit to Blackburn early this century, recalled Gipsy's influence on neighbours who were often drunk:

> We lived next door to a very drunken family, all men. One of these was blind; his younger brother had thrown a pair of scissors at him years before, and blinded him. When this man, Edwin, came home drunk every night, he would pull his brother out of bed, and kick him around the floor. The rows were terrible, and we youngsters were terrified.
>
> On the first night of Gipsy's mission, this blind man was the first to go into the enquiry room, as we called it. My mother could just not believe it, and said that it would never last. He went (to the mission) every night, always the first, and even went (as he always did) to the public houses to hold a meeting.
>
> He never broke his vow of dedication, nor did he touch a drop of alcohol afterwards. He joined the Church of England, and was successful in gradually getting his brothers to give up the drink. He held cottage meetings in his own home, and started a mission for the blind. If there was anything in the town of a religious nature, Edwin was there, collecting for this and that, from door to door. He was a power of good.
>
> He lived to a ripe old age, a good life owing to the ministry of Gipsy Smith. I shall never forget the Gipsy saying, 'A blind man shall lead them.'
>
> I often saw Edwin miles away from home—no buses in those days—with bundles of leaflets under his arm, such as British and Foreign Bible Society. I remember, just after his conversion, at one of his cottage meetings, his old mother standing at the kitchen door, with a jug under her apron, to fetch her supper beer, listening to what Jesus had done for him. I was not as ready with my pen as I am today, or I would have written and told Gipsy about it. (personal letter to the author, 1970)

The impetus to local evangelism, conducted by free churches working in tandem, flagged after the first decade of this century, and Gipsy eventually left the NCEFC (in 1912) though with mutually expressed good wishes. Perhaps the movement had become too concerned with political reform and social change—issues outside Gipsy's immediate interests. Yet he regarded as brothers, and with affection, many who might be said to have preached a 'social gospel'.

12
Visits to Gypsy camps and Paris

Aimez-vous Jesus?
(Gipsy Smith, Paris, 1908)

Gipsy may well have kept a notebook summarizing his impressions of missions held in so many places, over so many years, for he was in many ways a meticulous evangelist. Watching him relax after some great meeting, in the home of a somewhat awed host, as he stood by the fire enjoying small talk with the children of the house, one might think Gipsy able to make himself at home in any situation. But he had learned a lesson which so many today ignore: there is a time for work, and a time for rest, and the latter is essential if one is to perform one's God-given task. Harold Murray, his friend and accompanist, reported that Gipsy could 'bend down and touch his toes' when he (Gipsy) was seventy years of age, and that does not seem at all unlikely. One of the secrets of his enduring impact, was his 'naturalness'. Watching him 'talk' to the birds in the garden, or as he inspected some wild flowers on a stroll between meetings, was to observe a man for whom creation was not so much a subject of philosophical debate but rather a source of prayerfulness and praise. That he so often went out of his way to thank those who cared for a church, or arranged its flower displays, was characteristic. For Gipsy, each day was a 'day of great things', but it was a 'day of small, precious things' as well.

In his observations in the first decade of this century, Gipsy must have realized that the old Romanichel (true Gypsy) families and clans were in decline, or at least were departing the 'old country'. It is true that one may find examples of Gypsy people attending his meetings, as at Southend in 1904, when the large hall of the Kursaal entertainment centre which held some six thousand people was filled each night for some nine days. A co-operative Free Church input was seen in the choir, of some one hundred and fifty people, recruited from the town's churches. Miss Edith Benson, a member of that choir, recalled that those present were

very, very conscious of the Spirit of God brooding over the meetings. As a result of that mission, six hundred and eight souls gave themselves to God so, for many years afterwards, the impact of that week was felt and known.

Every night, the first two rows of seats were reserved for gipsies only, there being a gipsy camp at Eastwood, then just outside the town. They came night after night, and sang with great fervour, 'Jesus is mighty to save'. Many came out for God. One, known as 'the gipsy queen', with her black curls on either side of her face, came to our house one day, selling clothes-pegs. She recognized me and my mother, and said, 'Oh, my dear, do you have a piano or organ? Do play and sing with me, 'Jesus is mighty to save'. And we did.

As a further result of that week, eight gipsy couples went to the Avenue Baptist Church, and asked the minister (the Rev. James McCleery) to marry them, which he did. They had been living together but now wanted to do the right thing. He married them, together in a row. Every night of the campaign, Gipsy sang to us, and his voice still rings in my ears, just like a bird, so clear, every word distinct, and a message. One night, he sang, 'Never lose sight of Jesus'; on another, 'I will sing the wond'rous story' to the Welsh tune, 'Hyfrydol' and in the last line of the last verse, everybody was moved to tears, some weeping heavily. Every night, he insisted on all doors being closed to any late-comers, and everybody quite still while the Scripture was read. He said, 'Before I speak to you, let God speak and listen to Him.' Doors could be kept open at all other times during the meeting. His ministry was a great help to me, a young, dedicated Christian. (personal letter to the present writer)

Gipsy held some of his greatest missions in Essex, the county of his birth, and which, of course, had been home to Gypsy clans for generations. When Gipsy visited the Methodist Central Hall, Barking Road, East Ham during the period of revival, he was only a stone's throw from his birthplace. That he was a preacher active on the platform is confirmed by Mr C. Thompson, who was a member of the Ilford Gospel Choir, which helped Gipsy's mission:

> Our choirmaster and conductor was a Mr D. J. Simons, and we sang hymns chiefly from Alexander's Hymnal (i.e. the song book for the Torrey and Alexander Missions being held coincidentally with Gipsy's). I well remember Gipsy Smith preaching to a full audience at this fine Central Hall, and he did get worked up to his sermon. He did a fair amount of gesticulating, then took off his coat and carried on, and knelt down on one knee with hand clasped. Truly, a wonderful inspiration to us all . . . I well remember two of the hymns we sang at Gipsy Smith's service—'The Glory Song' ('When all my labours and trials are o'er') and 'Oh, it is wonderful' ('I stand all amazed at the love Jesus offers us'). (personal letter to the present writer)

Declining numbers

Among researchers attempting to trace the movement of the old Gypsy clans, Rev. George Hall was probably best known to readers of religious papers. He wrote of his experiences 'on the road', for George Hall was no mere armchair theorist, but visited Gypsy wagons as they travelled on, and shared meals at camps. Reasons for the decline in the numbers of true Romany people were not hard to discern. Unused land, used by Gypsies for generations— and to which they assumed some kind of unwritten 'right by tradition'—was now wanted for local authority development schemes, for factories, or for roads to accommodate that mixed blessing increasingly known for its hazardous progress, the motor car. The old crafts which had provided part of a Gypsy family's income were also in decline. Official policy in Britain seems to have been the encouragement of emigration to the relatively underpopulated countries of the Empire, or Commonwealth, so it is hardly surprising that some Gypsy clans followed this route in search of 'breathing space'. Gipsy John Hawkins—an evangelist who worked with the Railway Mission and the Fegan's Children's Homes—recalled in a slim biography of the mid 1940s, saw that every year, 'parties of destitute boys, after training in farm work, were sent to Canada and placed in selected situations with farmers all over Ontario'. In 1909, for example, the 'unusually high number', some one hundred and twelve, necessitated Gipsy Hawkins' accompanying the party. An outcome of that unexpected journey was that the evangelist spent a number of years in Canada, from 1909 to 1927.

Other children's charities were responsible for sending children—with little by way of natural family ties—to English-speaking countries, including Australia, and in the 1980s, there has been understandable investigation into the true status of some of these young emigrants. Were they orphans at all, or merely members of 'problem families'? Changes of attitude in child care and social case work have helped raise the profile of these issues, but one can hardly blame those well-motivated charity workers of long past decades for their concern to give young lads a promising life in a new country.

This brief explanation serves to show how easily emigration was accepted in the years prior to the First World War, and indeed after it, as a way to solving long term problems of employment and survival in Britain. Few seem to notice, or care, that so many of the old Romany folk were leaving, and when Rev. George Hall's informative article appeared in the Christian magazine (*Leisure Hour*) in 1909, he was hardly campaigning for any new government policy.

He wrote that Birmingham had all but lost its once large Gypsy population, and that the community of Gypsies who had lived near Blackpool had also 'dispersed'. Yet Lancashire was still accustomed to the sight of convoys of Gypsy wagons making their way along roads, now seemingly the preserve of the automobile. By this time the University of Liverpool was initiating research, whilst

The Gypsy Lore Society had also been formed in 1888. In the summer of 1908, George Hall stated he had seen 'a host of splendid Continental gipsies, who might have stepped straight from the pages of an oriental romance, camped at Birkenhead'. But it seems likely that they were on their way to a new beginning in the USA. He estimated that Britain's Gypsy population, five years before the outbreak of war in 1914, was probably no more than twenty thousand in England—including those now involved in a sedentary way of life—with around ten thousand more in Scotland and Wales. But Rev. George Hall was careful to point out that 'totals' were largely meaningless, given the varying backgrounds and character of the clans.

As Gypsy men gave up the old ways, and married into 'gorgio' (non romany) families, old Gypsy family names entered into the population at large. Over recent years, the present writer has had a large number of letters from people wanting to know if their surname indicated Gypsy origins. One would need to be a geneaologist to answer these enquiries, but the answer often seems to be in the affirmative. After a generation or two a family descended from a true Romany might have lost all of its sense of tradition. Some indication of the transition to a settled life was provided by Gipsy, when he recalled how his father Cornelius was advised that if he married again (as he did to Captain Sayer, a Salvation Army Officer) he would have to buy some land, and settle down. Eventually persuaded, Cornelius and his two brothers bought some land at Leytonstone, east London, and built three wooden cottages. But in their design, the cottages were apparently 'stood on wheels', to give the illusion of being wagons, and that therefore the families could move on in any new spring or summer.

Growing reputation

Gipsy's reputation as a preacher grew, even as the National Council of Evangelical Free Churches seemed to become preoccupied with social issues, despite assertions that its original purpose was undiminished. During the 1906 General Election, for example, there was a well orchestrated campaign against the government's proposals that denominational schools should be brought under local authority control and funded from the rates. Some idea of the fervour of this campaign is suggested by the Christian journalist, Harry Jeffs, who accompanied Rev. F. B. Meyer and Rev. Thomas Yates in a tour of the west country, during the campaign. Mr Jeffs explained that he was going as 'war correspondent'. Perhaps after the great events of the revival, which, beginning in late 1904, continued for almost two years, it was time to consolidate. Certainly, there was a trend towards presenting the gospel in terms of its social outcome, not solely in relation to individual conversion. But this social emphasis could not be avoided, given the problems of poverty and unemployment being increasingly brought to the attention of churchgoers. What has become known as 'the comfortable pew' in recent years was certainly known ninety or more years ago. Here, as in the matter of pentecostal gifts and ministries, the churches were being stirred up.

'Passion in preaching' seemed to be a disappearing quality in the years immediately preceding the First World War. Perhaps this was because a new generation of more questioning preachers was replacing the old Victorian 'giants', though new forces were abroad in society. Rev. Vallance Cook, brother of the fine evangelist, Rev. Thomas Cook, observed (in 1914) that there were 'more millions outside the call of the gospel today than when John Wesley moved up and down with such majesty and power', adding that 'the present condition of the church, with the utter inability to cope with the difficulties that confront us, are eating the heart out of numbers of the brethren'. In his widely selling sixpenny booklet, *Our Church Membership and How to Increase It*, Vallance Cook clearly thought that a spirit of pleasure had captured the nation, and that in general the churches had failed to counter antichurch propaganda. No less an influence was the way in which a spirit of reform, based on religious values, now sought expression in working-class movements, as indeed Keir Hardie chose to do. Vallance Cook, good man that he was, might have been reinforcing the sense that the churches were oriented to the comparatively affluent and well-educated when he wrote that 'a large section of the population has made socialism a religion, and social betterment a crusade . . . once they filled the galleries of the churches'. Perhaps they did, but were those in charge of the nation's economic and social destinies listening to their entreaties?

Other divisions, strangely resonant of our own time, included controversy about women's role in political and church life. Campaigns for universal suffrage, for women's right to the vote, divided families, as it divided churches. In this, earnest men—and some women—opposed to the suffragists gave the impression that the church was against that democratic spirit of which Rev. J. E. Rattenbury had spoken at the Free Church conference of 1905.

Missions in Paris

Gipsy did not get caught up on these issues, and in any case he must have taken a wider view of inter-church co-operation, as societies on overseas mission-fields began to model new patterns of working together, creating a ripple effect that washed back to Britain. His decision to go to Paris in 1908, and again in 1909, may have been encouraged by W. T. Stead, who had foreseen a United States of Europe emerging eventually, and had written of this prospect in the magazine that he produced, *The Review of Reviews* Methodists and other free churches had been active in France for some years, as indeed had the Salvation Army, in whose work Gipsy continued to take keen interest. France and Paris in particular, had long welcomed Gypsy communities, and if anything, Paris represented a better prospect for progress in the city's art and musical community. That Gipsy spoke from the stage of a theatre rather than from a church pulpit was due in part to the NCEFC's concern to reach the maximum number of people. Anticlericalism was not uncommon, but whilst Gipsy was quite at home on a stage, as long as he could preach, there must have been some who regarded Gipsy as some kind of entertainer, fitting in with the expectations that many had of the Romany musicians and singers.

Many of Gipsy's initial audience spoke English, and publicity had been aimed especially at the English community in Paris. Opera glasses, available at every seat as for usual 'performances', were much in use, and Gipsy's act of kneeling and praying at a small table on the stage was undoubtedly a fervent one. How was one to speak to so cosmopolitan, so sophisticated an audience? After singing a gospel hymn, Gipsy talked 'heart to heart' with his hearers, explaining that he was no more than a man who believed that the power of God was available to all, and that it would change any person's life if sought.

His simple and heart-felt testimony to God's grace was brief and to the point. At the end of it, he invited those in the audience, in need of prayer, to stand and join him in a simple prayer of dedication. Some two-thirds of those present stood. There was no enquiry or counselling room, because the organizers had recognized the problems of it being regarded as some kind of confessional. Remember, this was little short of a century ago; crusade style evangelism is better recognized today, and has crossed some at least of the social and cultural barriers that faced Gipsy Smith and his contemporaries. Rev. Thomas Law had ensured that 'decision cards' were provided, and the wording was simple enough: 'Believing Jesus Christ to be the only Saviour for sinners, I do here and now accept Him as my Lord and Saviour, and promise by His Grace to love and follow him.' There was room for signature and address and/or church connection if any follow-up was requested. On the first evening, about one hundred and fifty cards were issued and used.

After the initial meetings, the English-speaking majority of the audience gave way to those whose only language was their native one, French. This says something for the 'word of mouth' publicity that Gipsy's mission must have achieved. A stand-by interpreter was brought in, but this usually efficient individual found it quite impossible to translate Gipsy's fine flow of language. Gipsy did not speak 'commercial English'. Finally, when the interpreter gave up, Gipsy facing, as he said later, a 'time of utter agony', asked his hearers, 'Aimez-vous Jesus?' At once, the people roared approval, and many came to their feet. That question, 'Do you love Jesus?' was the shortest sermon he ever preached.

Gipsy's return in 1909 was characterized by house meetings, one especially being at the home of a wealthy lady, who had been converted at Gipsy's mission in Paris the year before. Twenty-five Protestant pastors in the area had been invited to lunch, which would give the evangelist good opportunity to encourage their own evangelistic enterprise. Gipsy was a little hesitant, not least because he had found on his earlier visit the pastors to be inclined to Unitarian views, some expressing ideas that he would have considered 'rationalism'. Even today, evangelical witness in France often encounters philosophical objections or questions which are not so commonly found in Britain. It may be that Gipsy was under-rating the earnestness of the ministers he had met in 1908.

The lunch with the pastors was considered a great success, and for more than two hours, Gipsy answered questions usually through an interpreter (this one, at ease on the occasion). Indeed, another similar dinner was quickly arranged, and some seventy pastors came to hear Gipsy's views, and no doubt a few stories. Had Gipsy been able to speak French, he could have occupied a number of pulpits around Paris and its environs, after these encounters.

Gipsy finally severed his formal associations with the NCEFC in 1912, and in that same year his mercurial, much-talented friend, W. T. Stead, died in the 'Titanic' sinking. His years as NCEFC missioner had been of great benefit to Gipsy, but as the movement became more 'political' and the need of the churches more acute, in terms of spiritually-based ministries, Gipsy may have decided that the time had come to find a new trail.

13
In time of war

*Peace does not follow the munitions train
—it follows in the wake of the Prince of Peace.*
(Gipsy Smith)

Euphoria, panic, predictions of great disaster, bitter disappointment, wild optimism—all were to be encountered in Britain in the first days of the 1914–18 War. Many businessmen and managers were to see their male personnel all but disappear, as volunteers flocked to the colours. Tom Mercer, manager of a retail store in Reigate, Surrey, was by no means untypical when he said that by the third week of August, 1914, his shop staff was reduced to an old man, and a young lad too young to join up. Units were raised locally, so that the wives and mothers of a town or suburb could stand on some main street, and see their loved ones march away. Many, alas, never returned, and the war memorials in numerous communities today silently speak of a generation of potential community and church leaders who died in the first bloody campaigns. Gipsy's post-war missions were thus shaped in the crucible of conflict, for his theme during the 1920s was that the Christians who had survived should pay a debt of gratitude to those who had not.

Yet the coming of the war seemed to unite a Britain which had been divided on many issues, not least the settlement of the Irish question. Historians have suggested that the violence building up in British society before August 1914 found a sort of release valve, but there were many sad hearts not least among Christian leaders who had campaigned for the peaceful settlement of international disputes. One Methodist minister, who was also known as a successful novelist, withdrew from preaching when war began, feeling that his work for peace had been wasted. He had nothing more to say, by way of comfort and hope.

Some clergymen marched off with the battalions and companies raised locally, and often faced dangers no less real than the combatants. In battleships, or dreadnaughts, as they were known, small churches were situated in the very bowels of the ship, and in the event of a direct hit, there would be little hope for the priest or padre conducting a service or engaging in his private prayers therein. Although some clergymen who went to front-line service found themselves unable to cope with the day-by-day destruction of men and materials, it was true that many developed a ministry that lived up to the best aspirations of the National Council of Evangelical Free Churches. But it called for a new dimension of worship, far from the formality, even sense of 'habit', found at home 'in Blighty'.

A chaplain's experiences

Rev. Thomas Tiplady—later to do good work at the Lambeth Methodist Mission, in the east end of London—drew the contrast in his book *The Kitten in the Crater* (1917), which was reissued at the beginning of the Second World War, as *The Cross at the Front: A Chaplain's Memories* (Epworth Press). Serving as a chaplain on the Somme front, with Territorial Army volunteers from London, Thomas Tiplady kept a diary which captures his experiences:

Ah, me! We did not know the meaning of hymns in England. When you are far from home, with the darkness gathering round you, and the guns booming in your ears, you see again the angel faces you left behind you, and wonder if the dawn will ever break through, for you, the long night of the war, and restore them to you.

Unutterable longings come to you, and at such times you know the meanings of hymns. As we sang Newman's hymn and prayed for light, 'kindly' light, we knew something of Newman's secret. We understood something of his feelings, as with the shadows gathering over him, he sat alone on the deck of a wandering ship, far from England and home. The British army in France is cut off from its churches, as completely as if they had been destroyed. Yet the music of the church lingers in our memories.

Pictorial magazines, like the weekly 'War Budget' carried photographs of shattered churches as evidence of the barbaric behaviour of the enemy. But real life events were more dramatic than any news story, as Thomas Tiplady pointed out. In a shattered church in France, he found a young soldier playing the organ, which though damaged, was still playable.

Out of the soul of the organ came a chord sweet as the fragrance of violets at the unsealing of a maiden's letter, and dear as 'remembered kisses after death'. It was the Lost Chord of Germany. All unconsciously the English lad at the French organ was calling up the spirit of the old Germany (through the music of Mendelssohn) to witness the havoc of the new Germany in the temple of the God it had ceased to worship.

At the close of his still evocative book, Thomas Tiplady recalled a service held in a barn, not far from the front line, on Christmas morning, probably in 1915:

Two of our men had been killed, and I was asked to arrange for their burial. In the afternoon, I buried the two lads and two others beside them. A company commander, one of his lieutenants, and a number of men came to pay respect to their memory.

As we walked away, the captain asked, 'Why doesn't God stop this fearful slaughter?' I could not answer. Nor could I say why the sun was blood red as it sank a few days before. But I know the black shell cloud turned rosy because the sun was red. And I know that the world's liberties are being saved because those four lads are lying in a soldiers' cemetery. If peace were a mechanical or a political thing, God might step in and stop the war. But 'peace and goodwill towards all men' are spiritual things, and must work themselves out in the souls of men . . .

Peace is not made by politics, but by martyrdom. The lads killed in the trenches have died for more than England. They have died for all generations and all lands.

First to go to France with the expeditionary force were accredited clergymen, Anglicans, Methodists and Roman Catholics especially. As an evangelist, not ordained within any denominational structure, Gipsy found it difficult to find position, in the 'official' chaplaincy system. In any case, the authorities might have considered him 'too old' to face the rigours of life close to the front line.

Gipsy finally found his 'berth' with the Young Men's Christian Association (YMCA)—an answer probably suggested to him by a friend seeing his disappointment at being rejected for 'official' service. Writing of 'the tragic years of the war' in his early 1930s memoir, *The Beauty of Jesus*, Gipsy noted that 'often today, I meet ex service men who were in my meetings in YMCA huts in France, of which a whole volume might be written'. If he did not produce a 'volume', Gipsy did write a popular paperback, in 1917, *Your Boys* (published by Hodder and Stoughton) which related some of his experiences in 1915–16.

The Gipsy was entirely favourably disposed to the work of the YMCA, but it has to be said that at the outbreak of war in August 1914, the YMCA structure, like many of the arrangements followed by the churches, was not designed to take the strain of events. Happily, a new dynamic influence came from outside these shores, new nations coming to the aid of the 'mother country', as Britain was called in those days.

Some idea of the YMCA's problems was given in the weekly part-work, *The Great War*, published between 1914 and 1918. In Chapter CCXLVI, 'Welfare Work for the Soldiers, from Base to Battlefield', F. A. Mackenzie suggested that at the time of the war's beginning, 'the YMCA had for some time been controlled by a group of men who had not kept fully in touch with the younger generation'. But he thought that contact with younger generations was better in the USA, Australia and New Zealand, Burma and India, and in Canada, yet adding that the British

YMCA 'caught up'. As in so many Christian groups and organizations merely meaning well was no longer sufficient in facing the new 'testing by fire'. This assessment of the YMCA can help us see the problems facing the churches, as they had been defined by Free Church leaders like Rev. J. E. Rattenbury and Charles Silvester Horne. F. A. Mackenzie thought that the target audience for the YMCA, prior to the war, had been too narrowly defined, seen as 'the young shop man, and warehouse man, particularly in the drapery trade'. The same writer added that the YMCA leaders in Britain had

> carried the narrower religious practices of the middle of the nineteenth century into the twentieth century. For example, they looked on smoking with abhorrence—men who smoked were looked upon with suspicion, and it was only after a very long struggle, that they allowed smoking in certain rooms of their institutions. Some of them, though by no means all, were not too favourable to athletics. A billiards room was anathema.

The new approach was characterized by Mr J. J. Virgo, a leader of the YMCA in Australia, who came to Britain with Australian troop contingents. He was given offices in Tottenham Court Road, in London, and a new 'forward organization' for the YMCA was set up. This encouraged innovative work among young men who had never before had *any* contact with any Christian organization or church. Arthur (later Sir Arthur) K. Yapp, a young, energetic English member, was appointed National Secretary, and represented a new lively-minded generation of YMCA activists. There was no intention of abandoning the inspiration of George Williams, the organization's founder, but a sense that he would have encouraged adapting to new needs. Mr Virgo's rhetorical question— 'which is better, billiards at the YMCA, or over in the public house?'—is almost reminiscent of General William Booth's famous enquiry about music (i.e. 'Why should the devil have the best tunes?'). Arthur Yapp, a remarkable man, took up the task of directing the Emergency War Work Committee, and later, the government's National Food Economy Campaign, with drive and flair. Of course, there were other diligent men helping the growing work of the YMCA, including Sir Henry Proctor (who looked after financial matters) and Sir Thomas Sturmy Cave, who chaired the Emergency War Work Committee. Mr F. J. Chamberlain CBE, National Secretary of the YMCA, added his energies to new ideas, but of all these excellent men, none had more influence on Gipsy's ministry than Oliver McCowen, CBE, LL.B., who had been YMCA Secretary in Burma, prior to the war. He was given the somewhat awesome task of organizing YMCA facilities in France, often close to front line conditions, as Gipsy recalled in his talks. A main YMCA resource was the prefabricated wooden hut which could be quickly dismantled and re-erected without delay on a new site. Necessarily robust, and able to be adapted to a number of purposes (canteens, worship, recreation, even accommodation, etc.) the huts were subject to continuing design improvements, and eventually the marquees which had been used at the beginning of the war were phased out altogether.

F. A. Mackenzie, writing in *The Great War*, had no doubt as to the YMCA's achievement, noting that the huts were sometimes erected in the shelter of ruined buildings, even at dugout or trench level in order to avoid sniper fire from ruined buildings. Originally sited at base depots on the French coast, the YMCA's huts went 'from Dixmude to Ypres, from Ypres to Armentieres, around Loos and behind Souchez, in Arras and Albert, everywhere right up to the fighting troops'. In these YMCA centres, Mackenzie added, soldiers found 'food different from regulation rations, warmth, light, friends, books, chairs to sit on, lectures and concerts to attend, and in some camps, there were . . . *billiards tables.*.'

Gipsy Smith at times must have been reminded of the old discussions at the Free Church council meetings, as he saw how the YMCA, and other organizations, found new ways of serving and reaching young men who had lost all connection with 'formal religion'. He illustrated this point, in a story which is included in *The Beauty of Jesus*, and which, incidentally, the present writer quoted to a lady who, whilst being a church member, thought that her faith was becoming 'unreal':

Very soon after I began my work in France, in one of the huts

I saw a lady standing beside two urns—coffee and tea. She was pouring out, and there were 150 to 200 men standing around that hut waiting to get served. The fellows at the end were not pushing and crowding to get first, but waiting their turn. They were more good natured than a religious crowd waiting to get in, to hear a popular preacher.

These boys, wet and cold, were waiting for a cup of coffee, and one of those red-hot gospellers came along, and he said, 'Sister, stop a minute and put a word in for Jesus. This is a great opportunity.'

'But', she said, 'they are wet and tired. Let me give them something hot to drink.'

'Oh, but let's put in a word for Jesus', urged this chap.

Then a bright faced soldier lad called out, 'Guv'nor, she puts Jesus in the coffee.'

This is what I mean when I say that you have got to put Jesus into every bit of the day's work.

One of the projects in which he was involved had to do with the Canadian army's move from the Ypres area to the Somme sector during the summer of 1916. The move showed up the problem of getting canteen facilities to the troops, mainly because the existing YMCA (food) storage facilities were insufficient to meet the demands placed upon them. Britain, facing a food blockade from German U/boats and suffering from other shortages, could not offer help, so the Canadians arranged the shipping to France each month of some two hundred tons of 'comforts', consisting of sweets, potted and canned foods, candles, stationery and other items. By the beginning of 1917, the distribution system was running so well that any soldier calling at a YMCA hut was provided with a mug of tea at no charge, and food at nominal charges. At home in Canada, the YMCA pledged some five per cent of its gross income to army welfare, and devoted some of its best brains to the work.

The contribution of the Canadians to the welfare of the allied forces in France was at times remarkable. They were keen on sports and athletics, and brought baseball, lacrosse and other

Canadian 'specialities' to France. And it was a Canadian university professor, Dr Tory of the University of Alberta, who prepared a programme of adult education for service personnel, a model for later work, including that of the Army Bureau of Current Affairs (ABCA) during the Second World War. In 'the khaki university' project, devised by Dr Tory, building design was important, i.e. for teaching/lecturing areas. From the autumn of 1917, the Canadians constructed huts one hundred feet long, in base camps and reception areas. Among a total of some forty of these large huts, about ten were also adapted for cinema use, and at least one anticipated the days of touring drama groups, for it included a scenery workshop, costume storage and equipment for some hundred live presentations presented each week in Canadian YMCA huts.

There seems to have been a little friendly rivalry between the national YMCA organizations, for the Australian and New Zealand YMCA contingents did all they could to blaze new trails. It was said of the New Zealanders that they pushed their huts and canteens so far forward in the front line that the enemy soldiers could smell their doughnuts. The Australian YMCA had worked in army camps (in Australia) before the war started, and it is a little surprising that the authorities did not make room for YMCA workers in the troopships coming to Europe—not that is, until some fuss had been made (as only the energetic 'Aussies' could make it) so that by 1917, some one-hundred-and-forty YMCA personnel from Australia were engaged in direct war service, at least a third of them in France. Moving the work along was one of Australia's best known leaders in the YMCA movement, H. A. Wheeler, who had persuaded the Minister of Defence in Melbourne of the YMCA's great value to the war effort.

There is no doubt that Gipsy's work benefited mightily from his association with the YMCA, where, in addition to meeting old friends—like Rev. Peter Fleming who had been minister of Flinders Street Baptist Church in Adelaide, prior to his YMCA work—Gipsy made many new ones. Being in France meant that Gipsy Smith was also a missioner to the Commonwealth of Nations, to an extent that he could hardly have anticipated when he made his first visit to front-line France in 1915. It is worth noting that the work of the YMCA was non-sectarian, in the sense that it served all those who came through its local hut doors. A YMCA worker, recruited in Perth, as part of the Australian effort, was an architect and a rabbi, a man who did a great deal of first class work among Jewish service personnel. It was a new assertion of the ecumenical vision, not in the 'watering down' of one's personal conviction but in a recognition that men on the battle line were laying down their lives for friends, and for others that they had never known, of many faiths and none.

Gipsy was to challenge the churches about their failure to reach young men who had not hesitated to 'answer the call', and he echoed the comment made by F. A. Mackenzie, in his article: 'the idea of the fighting man as a rapscallion is long out of date'.

Gipsy's approach to his ministry in France was flexible, that is, he did not 'pre-arrange' matters too closely. Faced with the opportunity of speaking to units made up of Roman Catholics, for example, Gipsy did not launch into doctrinal topics, but rather told the story of his life, in which his own testimony to the purposes of God came out clearly. Often, Gipsy would lead some hymn-singing, beginning with a few well-known popular songs, around a hut piano, and add some comment of his own, when it seemed right. He wore a neat YMCA uniform, but this must have looked crumpled at times, for we know that he lived as the servicemen did. He recalled his moustache and hair being frozen to a bench on which he had been sleeping in the cold trench conditions.

Spiritual harvest

Gipsy was later to write of a remarkable spiritual harvest among the troops:

> Time and again, since the war, when I have been preaching, mothers, wives, sweethearts, and young widows have come to me, and said, 'Gipsy Smith, my boy's last letter before he died had your name in it.'

I have had mothers kiss my hand, and say, 'I want to kiss the hand of the man who led my boy to Christ.' I saw thousands upon thousands of boys turn their hearts to God during the years of the war. Those boys taught us all a lesson. They knew how to die. They knew how to suffer. They knew how to make sacrifices.

In 1918, the British Government asked Gipsy to undertake a goodwill mission to the USA, and for this, and other services, he was awarded the MBE. As he said, Gipsy treasured with pride the honour pinned to his chest by King George V, but he treasured more 'the magnificent spirit displayed by those lads'. For some, the 'great war' ended a Christian vision, and some have said, not without reason, that in 1914 most people had a kind of folk religion, blended with Christianity, in which God's purposes were thought to be synonymous with the interests of the British Empire, or even with the class system that prevailed. Easily shattered in the realities of war, this folk religion was the last vestige of what might be called a national faith. Certainly, one could meet in recent decades men who had left the churches in 1914 because 'the bishops blessed the battleships', but the issue of pacificism remains largely unresolved. Only those who faced the issues amid the bloodshed could really provide a true perspective, and one might close this chapter by recalling Rev. Thomas Tiplady's view that

Sceptics sitting at home in comfortable armchairs point to the shell ploughed fields of the Somme as the burial place of a fallen Christianity, but that is not the view of the officers and men on the spot, There, amid the evidences of man's cruel hatred and greed, they realise most fully the presence of Christ, and the Love that made Him die for them. They cannot understand the mystery of God's providence, but they are assured of His presence and love.

And like Gipsy, Thomas Tiplady could say that he was often shamed by the faith and testimony of the wounded. It is at home, and not on the battlefield, that men grow sceptical.

14
Hell-bent on pleasure—
the challenge of the 1920s

Whenever I think of America some
amazing stories leap to my mind.
(Gipsy Smith)

Elected President of the USA at the end of 1920, Warren Harding, the senator from Ohio, promised a return to 'normalcy'. Congress refused to ratify membership of the League of Nations, and the campaigner for that cause when President, Woodrow Wilson, died in 1924 after years of illness. Ironically, the affable President Harding had died months earlier, following an exhausting political tour in Alaska. Scandals surrounding members of his administration, relating to sales of oil-lands reserved for Navy use (the celebrated 'Teapot Dome' scandal) probably added to his burdens. 'Normalcy' was turning out to be rather different from the expectations of the voters in 1920, added to which the Volstead Act prohibiting the sale of liquor, generated widespread evasion, bootlegging and 'speakeasys'.

British politicians could hardly pretend that 'returning to normal' would be an easy matter, given the traumatic, long-lasting effect of the war. Even apart from the loss of manpower, markets for manufactured goods had been lost during the years when British industry had concentrated on armaments and army ordnance requirements. Depressed wages, high unemployment rates, and low morale, especially in the old industrial areas, were features of the 1920s, and only when government policy changed in the 1930s, with the advent of new light industry, did anything approaching full employment appear. In Britain as in the USA, rearming and eventual involvement in the Second World War brought prosperity to long poverty-stricken families.

Gipsy, enjoying his sixtieth birthday in 1920, hoped that he could help build up church life, which indeed had always been his aim. Most of his missions were now to be under Methodist Home Mission auspicies, though he always took his own line. The themes of repentance, the 'new birth', regaining one's spiritual bearings, were often to be found in his preaching, though, if Gipsy could be considered an old-fashioned preacher, he was also aware of the work of his fellow ministers in helping local populations in communities hard hit by unemployment and recession. During the 1930s, there appeared a substantial literature on the subject, written by ministers, *Christ in the Valley of Unemployment* being a widely selling title from Hodder and Stoughton. That Gipsy spent so much time in the USA in the 1920s, was at least partly due to the paucity of invitations from churches in Britain, many of whom had been deeply injured (in terms of lost sons and fathers) by the war. Perhaps, too, some thoughtful church leaders wondered if the population at large any longer gave much heed to the gospel. The nation, it was suggested, needed a good long rest, a retreat from anything that looked like idealism.

Gipsy's preaching

Some flavour of Gipsy's work in the USA in the early 1920s is recorded in a collection of *Evangelistic Talks* given by him at the Ryman Auditorium, Nashville, Tennessee, during a mission of February and March 1922. Rev. James Vance, a good friend of the Gipsy's, was chairman of the inter-church committee responsible for the mission, and he wrote the introduction to an interesting collection. These were impromptu addresses, given by the Gipsy immediately following the Bible reading (the choice of which was unknown to him). James Vance thought that, in delivering those talks 'off the cuff', Gipsy reached 'a height of pulpit power I have not known surpassed. To find satisfying explanation, one must go back to Pentecost'.

Published in the USA by George H. Doran, and later in Britain by Hodder and Stoughton, this collection of twenty sermonettes represents an all too rare record of Gipsy's mission addresses. It is true that some Christian papers, including *The Christian Herald*, published Gipsy's sermons, but these were often from the earlier part of the century (one may even find sermons from the NCEFC publication, *As Jesus Passed By*), though some Sunday newspapers ran sermons based on Gipsy's preaching at crusade meetings in the metropolis.

It is quite impossible to define any pattern—Gipsy, though he had his favourite topics, could have as many themes in his sermons as colours that might be found in a field of wild flowers. But here at least, are some of the many thoughts found in his 1920s preaching:

Need of the Church and Christians to live up to the Gospel of Love

There are lots of people out of the Church who would have been in, if you had looked after them, if you had spoken a good word and extended to them your friendship. There are many people all around you with broken hearts. Let them feel your love.

Assertion of Biblical teaching on the nature of man

I have seen the worst kind and the best kind of people in the world—if there be any best and worst. There can only be two kinds of sinners in the world—those who are found out and those who are not. I wonder how many people here today would be in jail if their real selves were known. I wonder if your friends would recognise you on the street, or sit beside you in church, if they knew you as you really are.

But the wonderful thing is, no matter how far you have strayed from God's commands, how greatly you have erred, the grace of God can save. This is the hope of the world.

Urging a new spirit of affection and encouragement among the churches

I receive letters every day saying, 'Why don't you preach the Gospel? Why don't you preach this and that?' These letter writers are angry because I do not emphasise their denominational differences. We have been divided long enough, and it is time that something or someone brought us together. My brethren, it is Christ that matters. Every man who loves Jesus Christ is my brother.

A call for charismatic enthusiasm—a new joyful commitment to the church

It is the extreme people who are useful, who stand out as the people of God. It is the lukewarm that are no use, they are a hindrance. Some of you are up to your knees in the church, you go to church once on Sunday and you have had enough then, and you have graced the sanctuary with your presence, and patronised the preacher, and made him feel he ought to consider himself complimented that you were there.

Poor deluded thing . . . poor half-starved thing . . . you are only up to your ankles. There are depths for you church people who are in the shallows. Go out that you may know the heights and the depths.

Gipsy did not hesitate to comment on the 'high moral tone' of people who declared that they were good enough as they were, and did not need any help from the church to be so.

Men boast of the Golden Rule. They'll never understand or be able to practice the Golden Rule until they are born again into the spirit of the nature of Him who taught it. Many really good people, anxious to do what is right, fall into all kinds of blunders and some are led astray by popular heresies which are easy to the flesh, simply because they do not read and ponder and inwardly digest the living, abiding words of the Lord.

Gipsy was not a 'progressive' in social terms—he regretted that through economic circumstances, many women had to go out to work to bring in a household income, a view that he might emphasize in our own day. But the outcome of his preaching was bound to effect social change. In the same address in which he presented woman's traditional role as mother and home-maker, he stated that the Bible was the foundation of women's rights: 'it is among the idle rich that the most liberties are being taken, the morale of women workers is on the whole, sound.' In short, Gipsy was affirming that women, more often than well-off men, were setting standards of morality, a radical message indeed in the USA of the 1920s.

Much of his preaching, as always, included aspects of his own life, and indeed his own need of fellowship. This was a refreshing change from the preachers of the time 'who hit town, took the collection, and departed', men who set themselves up as 'experts in religion'. Gipsy's impact endured, largely because of his humility, summed up in a comment he made in the series of sermons at Nashville, and already quoted:

> You know that the world is dying for want of more love. Don't be afraid of spoiling someone with love. More people die for lack of a little spoiling than for too much of it. I want more of it myself. *What we need is to be so drenched with the love of God that it would cover everybody.*
>
> If Gipsy Smith stood on this platform, and talked about any other subject in the world for days on end, you could not fill this building. It is the Gospel of the Son of God that has got hold of your heart. Christ in me means there's hope for someone else.

His war-time experiences were never far from his mind, and he devoted a chapter to those 'dreadful days' in his book, *The Beauty of Jesus*. He sometimes reminded his American audiences of the 'great sadness' abroad in Britain: 'a million of our boys were laid under the sod, there were two million more of casualties, our hospitals are filled even now with the wounded and the helpless.' Perhaps Gipsy felt that events might have been different in 1914, had the churches been more faithful to their calling and had the evangelical free churches in Britain stayed together in their original spiritual mission. There was far more to Gipsy's call to unity than what sometimes passes for 'ecumenism' today:

> Jesus prays that we may be one . . . People don't draw together enough for fear of being scratched. What religion is meant to

do, is to take the scratch out of us. Less briars, more roses, more violets, lilies of the valley and perfume to the beauty of the Lord.

A further collection of sermons, from the same publishers in the USA as in Britain, appeared in 1922, these 'Revival Sermons' being described as addresses delivered during Gipsy's recently concluded twentieth visit to the USA.

In that same year, a young Church of England curate, Rev. Frank Jennings began a work that took him onto the 'highways and byways' of Britain, for some four months every year, to share the lot of travellers, Gypsies, and the homeless. Although he became known as 'the tramps' parson', Frank Jennings was also a keen student of Gypsy life, an area of research and assistance he began in the mid 1920s. He was in terms of reaching a wide audience with narratives of Romany traditions and the life of travellers (and tramps) singularly successful, but Jennings did not pretend to take an academic approach to his subject.

Albany

Gipsy Smith—who met members of Gypsy clans, once resident in 'the old county' during his visits to the USA—sometimes conducted missions with his son. Albany, the elder of Gipsy's two sons, had for years worked as a seaman, employed on the trans-Atlantic run, but following his marriage, he settled in New York, and took up a business career. Albany had been a committed Christian since his youth, but had not considered becoming a preacher until he was thirty years of age, probably at about the time of his father's decision to leave the NCEFC. Part-time employment in a grocery store was necessary to help sustain him and his wife, while he studied at theological seminary in Philadelphia. Like his brother, Hanley, he looked more like his 'mother's side of the family'. His preaching was well measured, thoughtful, yet he shared with his father the same sweetness of spirit in evangelism and, one might add, the same ability to find a pithy phrase on the spur of the moment.

It was perhaps hardly surprising that he became known as 'Gipsy Smith Junior'—probably the 'inspiration' of some chairman of a mission, overcome with the sight of father and son on the same platform. In May 1922, Albany held a mission in Poindexter Park, Jackson, Mississippi. Frederick Sullens, the editor of *The Jackson Daily News*, wrote and published a booklet, of some twenty thousand words which included some of the addresses given by Albany, as well as some notes on the event. Mr Sullens, who was a generous supporter of Albany's work, paid for several thousand copies to be distributed free of charge to homes in the city. One finds close parallels to Gipsy Smith's speaking and writing style in that of his son: 'You cannot put business first and God second'. 'God's sun never shone on a bigger fool than the man who sins and thinks he can get away with it.'

Like his father, too, Albany was the most approachable of men. Frederick Sullens recalled that the evangelist (Albany)

> found genuine happiness in walking up and down Capitol Street, exchanging greetings with the many people he met during his memorable revival in Poindexter Park in May 1922. He loved people of all kinds, and classes with equal intensity, because it was part of the man's nature.
>
> He was never happier than when meeting and mingling with his fellow men, always in a modest and unassuming way. Just to meet him strolling down Capitol Street, to see the happy glint in his eye, the genial smile in his face, to feel his firm handclasp, to hear the magic of his husky voice, made the day happier and the sunshine brighter.

Albany's work is little recalled now, not least because he did not seek the roving ministry of his father. But Frederick Sullens might have been speaking of either preacher when he commented:

> The magnetic personality of the man was a great asset both in his preaching and in personal contacts. The glow of his winsome smile, the loving kindness of his heart and his marvellous energy, all combined to make him an outstanding figure in the pulpit, and wherever he met and mingled with either saints or sinners, for he did meet and mingle with both. He was a thorough Cosmopolitan.

Some indication of Albany's preaching style comes from the same source, for Frederick Sullens, a friend for some thirty years, said that Albany

> never muddled a sermon with theological disputation or ecclesiastical hair splitting . . . in truth his theology could be summarized in four sentences: (i) Jesus can and does save sinners; (ii) You cannot be happy without the love of Jesus in your heart; (iii) It is better to be safe than sorry; and (iv) Don't fool with your weakness.

But this was hardly a restricting approach. There was, we are told, 'subject matter of amazing variety in Gipsy Smith's (i.e. Albany's) range of sermons. He was a deep student, widely read and marvellously eloquent.'

Remembering the old Gypsy tradition about fear of vast oceans, it is interesting to note Frederick Sullens' assertion that Albany never forgot his sea-faring days, and that he found refreshment and inspiration out from the land.

> Love of the sea was with him a consuming passion. The boundless waters, the surging tides, the free blowing breezes on the sea's bosom seemed to bring him into closer communion with God.

Albany Smith died from a sudden heart attack, whilst in his boat, off shore from Passe A Grille, Florida, in August 1951. It is a strange coincidence that both father and son died whilst on the waters, Gipsy Smith in August 1947, on board the RMS 'Queen Mary'. Albany was seventy years of age. Hanley, Gipsy's younger son, was also a preacher, ordained to the Methodist ministry, holding circuit appointments in Sutton Coldfield in the industrial west Midlands, and later in Walcot, Bath.

Helpers

It was largely thanks to his visits to the USA that Gipsy Smith became one of the early religious broadcasters, and was also something of a pioneer in putting gospel songs onto widely selling gramophone (phonograph) records. He was indeed fortunate to find expert help on both sides of the Atlantic. In Britain, just after the end of the First World War, Gipsy secured the friendship of Harold Murray, a competent musician and also a journalist of no mean ability. Better known as 'H.M.'—the initials that appeared at the foot of much of his copy—Harold Murray was the son of a Congregationalist minister, and had spent some of his early life in the city of Peterborough in Cambridgeshire. At the time of his encounter with Gipsy, Harold Murray was facing the consequences of the death of his wife, and was uncertain as to his future path. Gipsy offered a happy solution: 'Why not come around with me?' Gipsy needed a reliable accompanist, and Harold's knowledge of journalism could ensure that missions were well reported, and liaison with the press done well. It must be said that for all the pages of copy devoted to Gipsy's missions in Britain and across the world, Gipsy rarely if ever thought about imposing his opinions on the final drafts. True, he did suggest that exaggerations in the American press, or on posters, be at least toned down, but he relied on Harold Murray's descriptive pen and flair, being never disappointed in the matter. There is no doubt that H. M.'s expertise on the musical side smoothed a few problems as well. An informal check on the piano at a local church, say, a day or two before Gipsy arrived, could ensure that it was in tune. Gipsy was not much pleased with out-of-tune pianos, not merely on his own account, but because he wondered as to the sense of pitch (spiritual and musical) experienced by the church using so poor an instrument.

Harold Murray's help was confined to Britain, and he did not cross the Atlantic with Gipsy, who found expertise State side in Dr E. Edwin Young, a musician who was later appointed Dean of the Fine Arts Department at Hardin Simmons University. In arranging songs, and in composition too, E. E. Young (as his name appeared on song sheets) proved a great asset to Gipsy's work. There was some advantage in the association from the musician's point of view. Accompanied by his wife, Edwin Young arrived to play for Gipsy at a mission being held in Dallas, Texas. The place was crowded out, with a good-humoured and hopeful queue outside. A doorman gazed at Edwin thoughtfully, and said, 'Unless you are Mr and Mrs Edwin Young from Abilene, there is no way you are going to get into this meeting.'

The President of Hardin Simmons University, Dr J. D. Sandefer, thought Gipsy's appeal impressive; in the USA as in Britain, Gipsy, even in his sixties, found no difficulty in communicating with students. Edwin Young's influence on Gipsy's musical ministry was no less impressive, and he helped write one of Gipsy's best-known solos, 'Not Dreaming'. The story goes that Gipsy was travelling by train to one of his scheduled missions in an American city, and, taking time to relax was sitting in the corner seat of the railcar with his eyes closed. A group of teenagers came by, en route to their own seats, and one joked, 'He's only dreaming!'

Gipsy, who had been reflecting on the ministry of Jesus, responded, mentally, at least, 'If I am dreaming, let me dream on.' He made a note of the line, added a few more words, and then showed this idea for a new song to Edwin Young, who wrote the music line, and produced an arrangement.

Gospel songs

When first presented with a demonstration of the phonograph, or gramophone, Gipsy had not been impressed with the idea of having one's voice heard, long years after that performer's death. But, persuaded otherwise, Gipsy was to use his God-given musical skills to great effect, both in recordings and radio. Like his friend, Herbert Silverwood, the young evangelist whom Gipsy met at Cliff College in the late 1920s, Gipsy was always ready to 'take down' the words of a chorus that attracted him. Two editions of the *Gipsy Smith Song Book* were published, but on balance, these seem to have been aimed at soloists rather than church congregations as a whole.

A song that became something of a theme for his work as a whole was written by Leonard Voke, 'Can others see Jesus in you?' The first chorus turned the question around, 'May others see Jesus in me?' A Columbia 78 rpm recording proved to be one of the most popular that he produced. No less popular was *The*

Beauty of Jesus, which, as has been observed earlier, was used as the title of a collection of memoirs, written by Gipsy in the early 1930s. Written by the Salvation Army leader, Lt-Commissioner Albert Orsborn, it was virtually adopted as the theme song of Gipsy's missions in the 1920s, to the point that many people thought that the evangelist had written it. Gipsy always made sure that congregations were corrected on the point. Albert Orsborn wrote the tune, after hearing a melody in a musical, 'The Pink Lady'; he did not copy the tune, but saw how a waltz rhythm on similar lines would fit his words. 'Let the beauty of Jesus be seen in me' (or, 'The Beauty of Jesus' as it was known to music publishers) was first sung by Albert Orsborn, at a Holiness Meeting held at the Salvation Army Congress Hall in Clapton, London, in 1916.

Gipsy Smith told the young gospel singer, Tom Jones, that he had hardly conducted a mission after 'adopting' the song, without teaching his congregation to sing it. Gipsy added that once, when returning to Britain from the USA on board an ocean liner, he received a radio telegram from leading bishops and ministers thanking him for using the wonderful chorus during his just concluded tour. Tom Jones, recalling some of his adventures as a gospel singer, in his *Living in the Ministry of Song*, published in the 1930s, reported that during 1934, he had received a letter from a lady in the USA, stating that she had had the words of 'The Beauty of Jesus' printed on neat cards, which were left in many places, factories, hotels, shops and offices. The impact of the song—thanks largely to Gipsy's consistent use of it—was impressive indeed, and the Moody Bible Institute radio station in Chicago (WMBI) introduced one of its programmes 'Mother Ruth's Bible Class', transmitted on Saturday afternoons, with 'The Beauty of Jesus'.

Tom Jones, following Gipsy's example, used the song to great effect during a tent mission at Bridlington, Yorkshire, in 1926, and because so many people asked for a copy, decided to publish it (with his own musical arrangement) in a leaflet, selling for a penny, which also contained some of his other choruses. When *Joyful News*, the paper associated with Cliff College, and which reported Gipsy's mission, mentioned that Tom Jones could supply words and music, he was inundated with requests.

The young gospel singer had not intended to publish his song material for wider distribution, nor had he been able to discover the origin of the words. Albert Orsborn's letter to Tom Jones, asserting his ownership of the copyright, must therefore have been something of a surprise, but Mr Orsborn was both 'gracious and generous', and the two men came to an excellent arrangement whereby the copyright was owned jointly by them. The income from the royalties went to missionary causes.

Gipsy Smith offered his best wishes on the publication of Tom Jones' book and his handwritten letter, from 'Romany Tan, Cambridge' is reproduced at the beginning of the work:

May your new and enlarged book of songs help the Church to sing. Singing is the sign of joy. The people who can sing, and do, are the happy and triumphant. The early Christians sang their way to victory. When the Church has a song in her heart, she will sing with grace to the Lord. The Word will follow.

The editor of collections of Cliff College choruses and 'sunshine songs', Tom Jones, was one of a new generation of gospel song collectors that was inspired by Gipsy's pioneering work.

Henry Beedell, a senior member of the Queen's Hall Methodist Mission in Hull, was a gospel song lyric writer, of no mean ability. One of his verses which saw the light of day as a completed song, related to a story told by Gipsy, about a mission held in Scotland. The narrative might seem a little trite, but it was true nonetheless, and Gipsy always had the time of day to listen to a youngster.

He was attempting to make his way through the crowds outside a hall, at which he was to speak, and as he politely approached the building, he realized that someone was tugging at his overcoat to attract his attention. He turned around to face a girl, who asked, 'Are you Gipsy Smith, please?'

He agreed that it was, whereupon the girl produced a bag of carefully wrapped boiled sweets and presented them to the evangelist: 'I have brought you this bag of sweets, I have got a new daddy through you.' Genuine, heartfelt conversion, Gipsy knew, made all the difference to family life, even if problems remained to be faced and solved. He accepted the bag of candies gratefully, and with obvious delight. It was, once more, evidence that God graciously blessed Gipsy's words. Mr Beedell wrote a verse based on Gipsy's story, and suggested that Tom Jones set it to music. Alas, faced with a busy schedule, Tom Jones forgot the existence of the verse, until, some months later, he came upon it, whilst going through some papers in Edinburgh. He at once set about writing a tune for it, and the subsequent song was used at women's and other meetings (Tom Jones usually told the story of how the piece came to be written).

Although Gipsy clearly believed in responding to the mood of the moment—under the guidance of the Holy Spirit—he always worked hard at his basic preparation, and spent no small amount of time in prayer. His songs came out of conviction, and common-sense; if people cannot be reached by a sound argument, well, why not try a song? Nor was Gipsy content with a song that merely sounded 'pretty' and had a sprinkling of piety. He was in his way, something of a classicist, valuing religious music as something of a spiritual discipline, as well as a means of impart-ing a genuine 'holy joy'.

As well as enjoying the influence, and guidance of Ira Sankey, Gipsy knew many hymn and song writers. In his autobiography he records:

I met Miss Fanny Crosby, the well known hymnwriter, at New York (during 1896). Many of her compositions appear in the Free Church Mission Hymnal, but her identity there is dis-guised by her married name, Mrs F. J. Van Alstyne.

Miss Crosby is seventy years of age, a very tiny woman and quite blind. At one of my meetings, sitting on the platform besides me, she heard me sing a hymn of hers:

Like a bird on the deep, far away from its nest,
    I wandered my Saviour from Thee,
But Thy dear loving voice called me home to thy breast,
    And I knew there was welcome for me.

165

When I had finished, Miss Crosby said, 'Brother Smith, I did not know there was as much in that song. You have broken me all up.'

A writer and musician who had a profound influence on Gipsy's music was undoubtedly W. H. Jude, born some eight years before Gipsy, and like the evangelist, probably as well known in Australia (from his visits and public appearances) as in his home country. Few today recall his great services to church and choral music a century or so ago yet, in these times of revived interest in the music of the baroque and early classical period, it is worth recalling that in the late nineteenth century W. H. Jude worked with some choristers to bring new attention to the works, virtually all then neglected, of Henry Purcell. The founder of the Organ School in Liverpool, teacher, concert recitalist, W. H. Jude's special legacy to the churches he so clearly loved, was the new tunes he attached to old, well-known hymns. There is perhaps unconscious point in the fact that in the same year that his hymn collection, *Music and the Higher Life* was published (1904), revival came to Wales, the land of song. Gipsy used some of W. H. Jude's arrangements, and there is at least one report of Jude acting as his accompanist. Probably the best known of the recordings that Gipsy made, was his use of W. H. Jude's tune for 'I Heard The Voice of Jesus Say'.

This background of continuing interest in music for worship, and his encounters with singers and writers, helped Gipsy develop a repertoire, which served him well in the new era of radio, though (apart from broadcasting) it does not seem that Gipsy was ever much at ease with the microphone. Harold Murray said in 1948 (in *Christian Life* magazine, January issue) that Gipsy would not use a microphone unless it was vitally necessary. 'He prided himself on his power to throw his voice to the rear of a great hall. He had a way of saying, "Listen!" that hushed a crowd.'

Even after hearing at first hand, and reading many letters relating memories of the missions conducted by Gipsy Smith between the two World Wars the aspiring biographer is bound to feel that something more than sentiment was involved. Gipsy might have had the power to make his hearers burst into tears, or laughter, but the sentiment was part of his personality; it was not used for effect. He would not have been as effective, had he not developed his flair for song, and that in itself might be inspiration for some today, remembering that the song itself was a message, more than a mere musical interlude. Rev. G. B. Mountford offers a better judgment than the present writer feels able to provide:

I was at a North London evangelistic meeting which seemed somehow very uninspiring. Suddenly, and as far as I knew, unannounced, Gipsy Smith came in, and presently began to speak. Almost at once, the atmosphere changed, the meeting was alive and spiritually thrilling.

Gipsy Smith left as suddenly as he had come, and someone asked me to take him to an Underground ('Tube') station opposite the hall. As we went, I asked Gipsy Smith why there was such a difference after he had come.

Oh, I don't know,' said Gipsy Smith. 'Maybe it's because I have never knowingly crossed God's will.' (personal letter to the author)

15
Cornelius

You may do away with your quiet Sunday,
but will you like the nation you are left with?
(***The Pioneer*** temperance journal, 1926)

Gipsy's Father, Cornelius, lived into 'wise old age', and Harold Murray recalled an especially affectionate farewell between Gipsy and his widower parent, who was now in his ninety-first year, prior to Gipsy's departure for the USA. Gipsy was never to see his father again, on this fallen planet at least, for Cornelius died during that mid 1920s tour. Cornelius had made his final home in a house next to that of Gipsy and his family, or better, extended household. A glimpse of domestic arrangements was provided by Mr S. W. Warwick-Haller (in a personal letter to the present writer) who had studied at the Leys School, Cambridge and later at Jesus College in that same city, during the 1920s.

I often went to the Gipsy's home at Cherry Hinton on Sundays. Mrs Smith was a gentle, lovable person who always welcomed me with open arms, as indeed they both did. I well remember how proud Gipsy was of the old carved mantelpiece in the sitting room, and which portrayed his old family caravan.

The importance of a soundly-based home life was a major theme of Gipsy's preaching in the years between the wars. When he spoke to his attentive congregations in the USA, he could sometimes be blunt in his comments about those who had a crowded social calendar (he would, I think, have a timely word of warning to contemporary Christians who seem to regard an over-crowded diary as evidence of saintliness). But he was often thinking of his own family life, as he readily explained, when offering 'models' for Christian parenting, a topic much in vogue in our time. Cornelius Smith was a remarkable man; that can certainly be said, but his willingness to speak to his son at times of uncertainty in the latter's life, was especially significant. In his autobiography, Gipsy recalled:

Before my conversion, while I was under deep conviction of sin, I used to pray, 'Oh, God, make me a good boy. I want to be a good boy—make me *feel* I am saved.' In my young foolishness of heart, I was keen on *feeling.*

My father had heard me pray, and had tried to meet my difficulty, but without success. However, it chanced that one afternoon, we were invited to drink tea at the house of a friend, in a village where the three brothers (i.e. Cornelius, and his brothers) were holding a mission.

Attached to the house was a beautiful large garden, containing many heavily laden cherry trees. My father was as merry and whole-hearted as a boy, and not ashamed of liking cherries, and we all went to pick the fruit.

Presently, I was amazed to observe my father gazing up steadfastly at the cherries and saying in a loud urgent voice, as he kept the inside pocket of his coat wide open, 'Cherries, come down and fill my pocket! Come down, I say. I want you!'

I watched his antics for a moment or two, not knowing what to make of this aberration. At length I said, 'Daddy, it's no use telling the cherries to come down and fill your pocket. You must pluck them off the tree.'

'My son,' said my father in pleased and earnest tones, 'that is what I want you to understand. You are making the mistake that I was making just now. God has offered you a great gift. You know what it is, and you know that you want it. But you will not reach forth your hand to take it.'

Gipsy's strategy of sometimes surprising his congregation was, as he pointed out, theologically sound, as God has his own surprises. Yet there was no doubt on Gipsy's part some following in father's footsteps, as it were, and present-day preachers can find good illustrations and examples in Gipsy's all-too-few stories of Cornelius. What a biography of his evangelist father Gipsy might have written!

Stories

My father was frequently engaged by Mr George Chamberlain of Norwich, to do evangelistic work in the vicinity. There was an exhibition of farm machinery in connection with the Agricultural Show being held in the city, and Mr Chamberlain gave my father an admission ticket, saying, 'Go and have a look around, it will interest you. I'm coming to the Show myself shortly'.

When Mr Chamberlain reached the show ground, he found my father standing on a machine, with a great crowd (to whom he was preaching the Gospel) gathered around him. Mr Chamberlain gazed upon the scene with delight and astonishment. When my father came down from this 'pulpit', Mr Chamberlain said to him, 'Well, Cornelius, what led you to address the visitors, without any previous arrangement, too, and without consulting the officials. I sent you here to see the exhibits.'

'That's all right,' said my father. 'But the fact is that I looked around at all the latest inventions, and I did not see one that even claimed to take away the guilt and the power of sin from men's hearts. I knew of something that *could* do this, and I thought these people should be told about it.'

Cornelius' enthusiasm for open-air work was clearly 'passed from father to son'. Gipsy recalled an open-air meeting at Leytonstone in east London. Cornelius was in full flow when a costermonger, i.e. an itinerant or market-trader, passed by, in his donkey-cart. 'Go on, old party, you'll get half a crown for that job!' he shouted, referring of course to the half-crown coin (two shillings and sixpence) which represented a goodly sum in those days.

Cornelius paused for a moment, looked at the costermonger, and said, 'No, young man, you are wrong. My Master never gives *half* crowns away, He gives whole ones. "Be Thou faithful unto death, and I will give Thee a crown of life."'

Although Gipsy considered his uncle, Woodlock, the 'deepest theologian' of the three brothers, he did not have the advantage of a sympathetic wife. Indeed, Gipsy stated that she had no sympathy with Woodlock's religious activity. In contrast, Bartholomew ('Uncle Barthy', as Gipsy referred to him) had married a lady who was entirely supportive of her husband's evangelistic concerns. This contrast between the domestic background of his two preacher-uncles must have added ammunition to Gipsy's preaching about family life.

When I was conducting the Simultaneous Mission campaign at the Metropolitan Tabernacle in south London, she (Barthy's wife) came to hear me. The building was crowded, and the policeman would not let her pass the door.

'Oh, but I must get in,' she said 'It's my nephew who is preaching here. I nursed him, and I'm going to hear him.' And she was not disappointed.

From this, we surmise that she acted as a foster mother (of sorts, at least) following the death of Gipsy's mother. The Simultaneous Mission at the Metropolitan Tabernacle, during Rev. Thomas Spurgeon's pastorate, in the first year of this century, is noted here, because Gipsy and his father both preached from that pulpit. One of the stories coming across the years from that memorable event has the power to stir the heart today:

My father had an alert mind, and some of the illustrations in his addresses were quaint. During my mission at the Metropolitan Tabernacle, he spoke to the people briefly. His theme was 'Christ in us, and we in Christ'.

He said, 'Some people may think that that is impossible, but it is not. The other day, I was walking by the seaside at Cromer (on the east coast) and I picked up a bottle with a cork in it. I filled the bottle with salt water, and driving in the cork, I threw the bottle into the sea, as far as my right arm could send it. Turning to my wife, I said, 'Look, the sea is in the bottle, and the bottle is in the sea. So, if we are Christ's, we are in Him, and He is in us.'

We are alas short on such 'Corneliuses' today, though given demographic trends, and the new interest in developing leadership resources among older church members, we may find at least a few. As already noted, Gipsy often referred to his father's practical encouragement and spiritual insights, during his own first two decades of preaching. 'When I was conducting a mission at Torquay, I talked to the people so much about my father, that they invited him to conduct a mission among them. Later, they wrote to me, "We love the son, but we think we love the father more."'

Notable sermons

Gipsy's reference to the close-knit, if at times impoverished, family life he had known, was effective as he preached to congregations across the world in the 1920s and 1930s. Indeed, one of his most powerful sermons had the title, 'Christ in the Home', and though he preached it first in the early 1920s, his reference to the divorce rates shows a resonance to our time. 'It is home instruction that determines what your boys and girls will be,' he declared. 'It is the home life that tells . . . the home is the sanctuary of the soul, as well as of the body.'

Sentimental as some of Gipsy's comments might seem in our day, there was a similar emphasis in the evangelistic churches in Britain. Some of the thrust earlier contained within the National Council of Evangelical Free Churches had by the 1920s moved into the temperance and anti-gambling movement. One of the more forceful avenues for these views was *The Pioneer*, a monthly magazine which was the 'official organ of the Wesleyan Methodist Temperance and Social Welfare Movement', edited by Rev. Henry Carter. There was a progressivism about the post-war movement, a sense that teaching men and women to use time well, was more important than attempting to close places of entertainment on Sundays. William J. May put it well enough in a November, 1926 article, relating to 'saving Sunday for our children':

> Are the children who grow up in a land without a Sunday likely to be a generation of which we shall be proud, or a generation who will establish the things that make for right-eousness? Will not the secularisation of Sunday mean the paganising of life?
>
> Evil is only destroyed when it is overcome with good, and that principle holds for the law of Sabbath observance. The empty hours must be filled with ways of fellowship with God. The Sabbath day is not kept holy by compelling men to be lazy.

There are after-echoes here of the revival that occurred between late 1904 and 1906. Just as the revival period had brought new interest in learning, as well as restoring family life, so in the 1920s a new spirituality sought to bring enlightenment to the mind. Men like William J. May, found in all the churches, argued that a nation that lost its Sunday would soon suffer social devastation one way or another. But a social morality based merely on pragmatism in the face of rising crime statistics was hardly likely to work.

> Dr Maltby at York, drew an unforgettable picture of the old weeknight prayer meeting, where men stood with their faces turned to the wall, and saw through the wall, and laid hold upon the world intangible and saw clearly the world invisible. But such a faith was only possible to men who remembered the Sabbath Day to keep it holy. We have lost the sense of eter-nity that lies all round our little human lives because on the Sabbath Day, we have so many interests that we forget our souls . . .
>
> Will a generation whose Sunday memories mean a succes-sion of popular songs, find the strength to fight the world, the flesh and the devil, which their fathers found in the memory of the 'Rock of Ages'? Will life have any meaning, any purpose, any satisfaction if the eternal is crowded out?

Is not Amiel true: 'There is no rest for the mind except in the Absolute, and there is no rest for the sentiment except in the Infinite, and there is no rest for the soul except in the Divine.'

The quest for a new heart-felt spirituality, for revival even, was integral to the reforming vision of church leaders, local and national, who were trying to 'pick up the pieces' after the shattering effect of the First World War. Gipsy reflected their concerns, and it was perhaps significant that his sermon, 'The Lost Christ' was often heard in his missions. Had the churches lost their first love? There seemed to be a weariness abroad in the land as if few people had any belief that good intentions were worth having. A mood, some might think, that Gipsy might equally address today. His influence as a popular preacher was hardly diminished, even though all too few churches in his native country seemed able to arrange local missions. His appearance at the Kingsway Hall, London, for a ten-day campaign in 1923, showed that 'the Gipsy' could still draw a crowd.

The place was packed every night, the people sat on every stair, and some were left standing down the sides of the hall. On one Sunday evening, we had an overflow meeting in either the Aldwych or Strand Theatre, I cannot remember which, and this the Rev. J. Ernest Rattenbury conducted.

Miss Muriel Place, in a personal letter to the present writer, recalled that she had taken her shorthand notebook to the meeting, at the suggestion of her shorthand teacher. She 'took down' the sermons, and later transcribed them.

The Gipsy spoke to me on the same day that he preached on 'The Lost Christ'. I told him that I was a member of Kingsway Hall, and was learning shorthand. He asked me to let him have a copy of my transcription, which I did. I didn't get any further comments on it, so I presumed it was passable.

There was an elderly man sitting right in the front row of the hall. He had white hair, and a very happy face. After leaving the hall, he spoke to me. He said that he had come down from the north of England, and was very deaf so that he could not hear what the Gipsy said, but had felt the wonderful effect of the service. Would I let him have a copy of the sermon (he asked) and this I did. It transpired that he was a Methodist class leader and he read the sermon to his people and spoke of the wonderful effect that the Gipsy had on him. He sent me a donation, which was the first I had ever received for the work of the Kingsway Mission.

But some church leaders and ministers inevitably wondered if Gipsy's approach, born in the hurly burly days of the 1880s, would meet the needs of a nation beginning to move into an electronic era. Gordon Wyllie, who heard Gipsy during the inter-war period, thought the Gipsy possessed 'great gifts of imagination and heart, who, with all his faults, was completely given over to Christ, and dedicated to the work of evangelism . . . an individualist who conformed to no school of thought'.

Some reason for the 'mixed feelings' of men trying to build a local church work, among many difficulties, may be gleaned from Gordon Wyllie's recollection (in a personal letter to the present writer):

Among some ministers, he was regarded with less than enthusiasm perhaps for this reason (i.e. his unconventional approach). His preaching was at times rather overcharged with emotion, but it seemed to me to arise naturally from a nature that felt strongly and could not be dispassionate and cool on matters that burned like a fire in his soul.

At times, he could be hard hitting and trenchant as on the occasion when he held a mid-day service at Grantham in the Finkin Street Methodist Church. Getting to grips with the matter of prayer and prayerlessness, I can recall as if it were yesterday, how he made the congregation squirm as he banged the pulpit and said, 'You call yourself a Christian and never pray! What a humbug you are! What a hypocrite! What a walking fraud!' And they would take it from Gipsy straight from the shoulder.

Evangelists in any generation are accused of being 'emotional', and Gipsy once compared a cool, calm and collected model of a preacher with the excitement he saw in the commodity dealing room in Chicago, where 'futures' were being bought and sold with a fervour based not on spirituality as such, but the making of money. That the place was known as 'the pit' would not have gone unnoticed. But thoughtful and scholarly men, or women perhaps, with years of ministry behind them, may well have forgotten 'life on the bottom rungs of everyday existence'. That former servicemen, met during the First World War, went to hear Gipsy was evident enough, especially when he went to Australia and New Zealand. William Macfarlane had been an officer in the army, and was persuaded, by a former comrade in arms, to go and hear Gipsy when the latter came to Glasgow in 1923.

The Gipsy's very informal approach and obvious reality arrested me, and when he sang, 'Wonderful Jesus', I was immediately impressed by the realisation that this man knew Jesus Christ as a real living person. I went home straight after that, and asked God to make Jesus real to me like that. From that time, I began reading my Bible, and learning the way of Salvation more perfectly.

Only once after that did I hear the Gipsy, when he was in Glasgow some years later. I think he was greatly used by God, and although he was accused of being too emotional, I believe his very sincerity and directness were needed at that time, as I think they are needed now.

Two remarks made by him are typical, I think. He was asked in America if he would accept a 'D.D.' and when told what the initials meant, he declined and said that his 'Divinity' did not need a 'Doctor'.

On another occasion, he asked a minister how many members he had in his church, and when the minister replied, 'Nominally six hundred', Gipsy had to look up the dictionary for the meaning of 'nominal'. He found it given as 'unreal'.

He was a very attractive personality, and I am sure has gone to a very real commendation from the Master he loved and served.

Working with Methodist Home Missions (and its beloved secretary, Rev. Dr Luke Wiseman), though eager to help all churches concerned with revival, Gipsy found it hard if not impossible to fill his year with 'bookings' from British churches. His routine thus came to be a year divided between the old world and the new.

16
Campaigns in New Zealand and Canada

He does not quarrel with pastors
and call it 'preaching the Gospel' .
(Dr John Clifford, of Gipsy Smith)

In the mid 1920s, and for some long years thereafter, churches were called to help the unemployed, and those caught up in wage disputes associated with wage cutting in the coal-mining industry. There was evangelism, but it was the evangelism of the soup kitchen, the free clothing supply, the minister journeying with hunger marchers, throughout the decade and into the 1930s. Gipsy, who had laboured among the poor in Manchester with Rev. Samuel F. Collier, continued to give priority to spiritual matters, no doubt believing that effective spirituality made men dip into their pockets to express the church's all round mission. Thus, in his early 1920s missions in the USA, he had warned that 'the spirit of the world creeps into the church' and those earnestly concerned with the effective work of the church had to stop the drift towards secular 'success' values. Indeed, he advocated a return to the pattern of the apostolic church which combined spirituality with practical aid to the poor.

I want to tell you something (else) you office holders would be doing, if you were like the members of the apostolic church. You would come to church every Sunday morning, a little earlier to meet in prayer with your minister, and that would have a mighty effect on the day's services, upon the preacher, and upon the congregation.

What a wonderful uplift your preacher would receive if he knew that every office holder in the church spent an hour in the vestry praying for him, that his message might be filled with the power of the Holy Spirit.

But it proved hard to secure such a commitment, and one might wonder if we are any better at responding to Gipsy's call.

A fine example of a combination of spirituality and aid to the poor can be seen in the Old Market Methodist Mission in Bristol, an enterprise which had much in common with the Manchester mission of Samuel Collier's day. Collier, who died in 1922, was a major inspiration to Gipsy, as to many others. He often found his sermon themes as he handed out food to the hungry, or visited the poor in their homes, to see how he might help. No doubt, Gipsy knew the city of Wesley well, and it is interesting to note that the superintendent minister for some years was Rev. J. A. Broadbelt, who succeeded to the Principalship of Cliff College following 'Sam' Chadwick's death in 1932.

One of Gipsy's best friends, Hugh Redwood (the journalist and author) came from Bristol, and began his writing career on a paper printed in Baldwin Street, close to the present city centre. In 1924, Gipsy and Rev. Dr Luke Wiseman, with another evangelist of note, Rev. Charles Hulbert, visited the Old Market Mission to join in the celebrations linked to a development scheme. The Mission eventually closed in 1984, a remarkable endeavour in which 'feeding the poor and hungry' had been expressed in both catering and preaching. Was this a pointer for other churches? Certainly, the author of *A Good Ideal: The Story of the Central Hall, Bristol*, published privately in 1974, thought it was:

At the same time (the 1930s) there seems to have been a tremendous hunger after the things of God. How much this was due to the church helping to meet the social needs of the time is difficult to assess, but the numbers flocking to the various organisations of the (Old Market) Mission were most impressive.

Gipsy spent much of 1926, the year of the general strike in Britain, on his Australian tour. It was something of a marathon for a man who, in other circumstances, might have been enjoying retirement. Between 8 February and 10 August, he preached in churches and other buildings in Australian towns and cities, some two-hundred-and-seventy-five times. After a brief respite he travelled on to New Zealand on 20 August for some hundred more preaching appointments. During these missions, an estimated 100,000 decision cards were completed. On the tour, Gipsy was accompanied by Mr and Mrs Edwin E. Young, though a mission at Dunedin in New Zealand began rather unhappily, when the Youngs and Gipsy were involved in a car collision, as they were being taken to view a local 'beauty spot'. Gipsy fell unconscious to the floor, and Mrs Young was taken to a nearby hospital, needing treatment. Edwin Young, though shaken and suffering from shock, would not hear of absenting himself from his appointment as Gipsy's accompanist, but it was, one way and another, a strange launch to the visit. This mission had been initiated by the local Congregationalist minister, Rev. C. Maitland Ellis, a former student of Cliff College, who had known Gipsy from meetings conducted prior to the First World War. Referring to the accident, Mr Ellis wrote:

> With a courage and determination that endeared them to all present, the Gipsy and Mr Young carried on right from the first night. And I will never forget that opening night when Gipsy preached his famous sermon on 'The Lost Christ'. In spite of the fact that he was in great pain, and spoke with a great deal of difficulty at times, it was the same face and voice which I remember moving audiences in the homeland (i.e. Britain) fifteen years ago.

Gipsy's enthusiasm for the work was impressive. At Auckland Town Hall, a little-publicized mission attracted crowds, some two to three thousand coming each evening of the event, with well over 5,000 decision cards being signed. Without diminishing the value of the mission, it should be noted that just over 3,600 of these were described as 're-consecration of church members', with about a third of that number (some 1,394) coming from those owning a first commitment to Jesus Christ. This balance was probably characteristic of many of the missions, but then Gipsy always considered himself to be a member of that honourable company of 'spiritual stokers', rekindling the fires of local churches.

His visit to New Zealand, and especially his encounters with the Maori (native) people, was reported in Britain, with particularly good coverage in the weekly, *Christian Herald*. Gipsy loved ceremonial 'with a bit of colour in it', and he found such occasions warming to his own personality. He not infrequently remarked that the aloofness of some congregations 'froze the pastor to death'. So we should not be surprised at the liveliness of the visit (try comparing these 1920s reports with much of our somewhat austere church life today!)

Among the Maori people

When the Maori people heard of Gipsy's impending visit to New Zealand, they urged the organizers—a council of free churches—to include a visit to the village of the Maori King (Waahi Pa) and the Faith Healer (Ratana Ba) in the arrangements. Gipsy, with Mr and Mrs Young, was happy to accept the gracious invitation, and at Waaki, an ancient welcoming ceremony was performed. As Gipsy and his companions approached, loud and expressive cries of welcome soared over the trees, soon to be accompanied by the waving aloft of green branches, and singing of welcome songs, the Waiatas. Dances of welcome, the hakas, added to the gaiety, but Gipsy and his friends well appreciated what whilst heartfelt, the ceremonial was also about etiquette and respectfulness.

The appropriate speech-making—the whai-korero—then proceeded, Gipsy's address being translated by a Maori minister, Rev. Matene Keepa. Gipsy added a song to his talk, no doubt aided by the Youngs, and then the official welcome by the Maori King was made. The serving of the meal was accompanied by hakakais, the food chants which served as a kind of benediction upon the banquet and the guests. What a memorable day it was! Gipsy was presented with a chief's cloak (horowai) by the King's mother, and then allowed the rare privilege of being photographed with members of the Royal Family.

About a week afterwards, Gipsy and his colleagues visited Ratana Pa, where 'chieftainesses with green boughs in their hands waved them into the Pa' whilst beautifully modulated calls of welcome to 'the sons of God' thrilled the party. In his address and singing, again with Mr and Mrs Young, the evangelist from England made a great impression. Then the guests were invited to view the new church building under construction, this being part of a co-operative community development to include schools, retail stores, a printing plant, restaurants and a church administration building. Of special interest to Gipsy was the collection of 'abandoned fetishes', charms and spirit-linked heirlooms, now to be found in the Museum. These were part of the old, darker aspect of folk religion, though it should be noted that the churches were keen to foster the traditions of kinship and precedence, as these sustained the community.

Gipsy was particularly interested in the sight of the many crutches and other supportive aids, abandoned by Christian folk who had claimed healing from God. Given the context, it was hardly likely that these could be dismissed as exaggerations (not least because the subsequent evidence of the healing, and the conversion lifestyle could be observed over a long period, by local people). Healing was an issue in the the churches in Britain in the 1920s, much as it has become in more recent times. Gipsy obviously thought that broken hearts could be expressed in what we would call diagnosable medical conditions, but he did not say a great deal about 'healing' *per se*. But his message in those inter-war years was surely that a community life centred on the gospel, and empowered by the Holy Spirit, was the model for any local church worthy of the name. Mere religious formality could make people ill, in the long run, if the normal tensions of fallen human relationships were allowed to run in any church or committee.

Vancouver

At the end of December Gipsy sailed for Vancouver, landing there early in 1927. This was something of a return visit—Gipsy was a great enthusiast for 'return visits' for he had missioned in Vancouver some seven years earlier. Vancouver had something of a flavour of an English county town, though it had quite a cosmopolitan population.

No one was surprised when it became necessary to utilize two church buildings for the 'overflow', after all the seats in the Empress Theatre had been occupied. Characteristically, this was an inter-church mission, though planning was undertaken in the main by the First Presbyterian Church. The local Salvation Army corps closed its citadel during the main meeting, in order that the corps band, in full uniform, could appear on the stage. A choir, drawn from members of Vancouver's churches, also 'backed up' the preacher.

Rev. J. Richmond Craig, the minister of the Presbyterian Church, acknowledged the visit of the Salvation Army contingent, and jested that he expected a good increase in the offertory, because the Salvation Army soldiers were so expert at taking up a collection.

'Indeed,' added the minister, 'that was one of the various things that so appealed to me, that I was at one time tempted to join the Army myself.'

At once, Gipsy leaped to his feet, and seized Richmond Craig's arm. 'You were tempted, were you? Well, *I did it!'* Smiling as he delivered the comment, Gipsy returned to his seat, the audience appreciating the joke.

A press report on Gipsy's appearance at Vancouver states that he looked 'scarcely any older' than on his visit some seven years earlier, 'his voice was still clear and his messages powerful'.

Thanksgiving

Gipsy's return to his home country was cause for more rejoicing, and 1927 was also the fiftieth anniversary of Gipsy's becoming a preacher. Services of thanksgiving were held in London,

Manchester, Hanley, Sheffield, and in other places especially associated with his work. In addition to the Welcome Home given at the Hills Road Wesleyan Methodist Church, the city of Cambridge honoured Gipsy by hosting a special Homecoming Meeting at The Guildhall, on 5 May, and at which Sir Robert Perks presided. Representatives of the university, and of local companies, as well as community bodies and churches, joined in the occasion, which no doubt gave Gipsy an opportunity to say a good word for Jesus. He preached at the Southport Convention in July, and further interest in his work was shown by a serialization of his life story in the 'Gold Star' page, for young people, published in *The Christian Herald*.

Gipsy's celebrated testimony lecture, 'The Story of My Life' was still in demand, and his 1901 autobiography covering the first forty years of his life remained in print until well after the First World War. Today, it is something of a classic, thanks in part to Gipsy's editorial helper, W. Grinton Berry, an employee of the Religious Tract Society, publishers of 'The Boy's Own Paper', and 'The Girl's Own Paper'. The final edition, circa 1919, was a reprint of the original with an additional chapter on Gipsy's wartime experiences and other material. That no further editions appeared was perhaps due to the flagging impetus of inter-church arrangements at national level. Gipsy, who had always laboured for co-operation in the cause of the gospel, must have realized that the early ideals seemed to have been lost, or neglected, over the years. A press report of March 1927 noted that the National Free Church Council was still far from being a 'Parliament of Free Churches', but added, somewhat cryptically, that it was hoped that the Wesleyan Methodists would soon give greater recognition to the body. One can appreciate why the Methodists were preoccupied with other priorities, as the proposed unity scheme (between the Primitive, United and Wesleyan connexions) was being earnestly discussed in 1927.

In the mid 1920s, Harold Murray produced a thirty-six-page booklet, selling for sixpence and called 'Gipsy'. It was printed in 1925, no doubt at Harold Murray's expense, by the Lincolnshire Printing Company of Lincoln, a city that he knew well. According to a brief note of introduction, the booklet was written entirely without Gipsy's knowledge:

> You see, so many people ask questions about him during his missions, and as far as I know, there is no little sketch of this sort available in handy pocket form. This is for love, and not for money. I expect most of the copies will be given away, but should anyone wish to order one, I'll deduct the postage, and the rest can go to (Methodist) Home Mission Funds.

This was characteristic of Harold Murray, or 'H.M.' as he was more often identified in print. He spent a small fortune in printing eminently useful booklets, giving them away to appreciative friends and others met at missions.

'Gipsy', as the blue card covered booklet was entitled, was the forerunner of the more detailed paperback that H.M. was to write for Marshall Morgan and Scott in Gipsy's silver jubilee year, 1937. Although it has little by way of detailed biographical or family background, the 1925 booklet is valuable for its portrait of Gipsy, as the evangelist was in his mid-sixties. Harold Murray is also interested in the media's attitude to Gipsy, and thus to the gospel in general, and there are some revealing comments for those who today struggle with these issues. But a main interest in this booklet is surely the attitude of the public at large, and of British congregations to the role of the preacher.

> Why *does* the crowd flock to hear this man? Why are there queues outside the places where he speaks?
>
> Why did I see two persons comically hitting each other with umbrellas in the struggle to get a seat in one hall?
>
> How is it that Gipsy could fill the Albert Hall in London for ten nights, which means approximately 80,000 or 90,000 people, when Lloyd George or Asquith or even a popular movie star couldn't have done it for more than two? I think I know.
>
> They are hungry for the good news. They are fed up and disillusioned and weary, and they know quite well that unless there is a spiritual revival in some form or another, things are going from bad to worse. They know that where all the

186

politicians and philosophers and educationalists fail, the Christ spirit can prevail.

Gipsy's long career, if so it might be called, and his spontaneity presented him with advantages over younger seminarians, though he had his critics, often because members of his audiences (laypeople and clergy) thought his high view of discipleship amounted to a criticism of their own considerably lesser commitment. Harold Murray thought that effective use of humour was one of Gipsy's spiritual weapons:

> People know that this romantic man presents the Gospel in an attractive way, in a direct way, in a sincere way, in a natural way. They know that he is a jolly man, who can make them laugh, who takes them by the arm to the sunny side of the street . . . I get awfully tired of reading in the newspapers that he was short and stockish, whatever that means, and swarthy, and had big magnetic eyes, and all that sort of thing.
>
> The only feature I care about is his happy smile.
>
> A preacher may be very big in every way, but if he has forgotten how to smile, he may be good for funerals, but for little else.

That Gipsy was 'what he purported to be' can hardly be questioned, for he was often reported as being 'in it for the money', though a journalist's visit to Gipsy's home in Cambridge would soon have confirmed the modesty of his lifestyle, though like most Gypsy folk he liked 'comfort'. Anticipating the careful and ethical accounting methods developed by later evangelists like Dr Billy Graham, Gipsy did not benefit from the offertories, and must have been surprised when a mission secretary in Plymouth reported a rumour that Gipsy received an extra twenty shillings for every convert that went to the enquiry room. Harold Murray recalled Gipsy being asked if he knew that two busy ministers had married rich wives.

'I hope they did!' responded Gipsy, all too aware of the pressures on preachers. His income was probably hardly more, if at times as much, as that of a nonconformist minister with a church of reasonable size, although, as one would expect, his expenses were fully covered.

Certainly, in his 1925 booklet, Harold Murray shows that Gipsy had often courteously rejected invitations to appear at functions, at which he could have secured a fat fee. Perhaps he was aware of the words of his ebullient fellow preacher, Rev. John McNeill: 'they say that money talks, but all that mine has ever said is, *Goodbye!'*

Gipsy, as we shall shortly see, was making a new impact as broadcaster, where his poetic, descriptive approach proved effective. His continuing impact into old age, however, with a message that had changed little over three or four decades, related to basic spiritual needs. For example, whilst Gipsy's recollections of country life could evoke a sense of personal identity with the created order, his life story seemed full of examples of 'guidance'. And 'guidance' was a major preoccupation, outside the churches as within them, during the inter-war period. The topic was featured in newspaper articles, readers being invited to send in their own experiences of being guided by the Almighty.

Spiritual experience is certainly an issue today, with surveys suggesting that many people who do not attend church (or indeed think that church formality could embrace their experience) have encounters with a power beyond themselves. Guidance was bound to be an issue in the 1920s, because politicians and war leaders so often seemed ineffective. If God had 'permitted' the war to happen, how sure could people be that God was benevolent, or even existed at all. For those who at the end of this century seek to discover reasons for the churches' decline, this seems a good starting point, just as an upsurge in spiritualism reflected a hunger for the 'proof of personal survival' of loved ones lost in the Great War. Guidance, then, as it was widely known, was concerned with understanding how the Almighty could shape the personal decisions to obey it.

A. J. Russell, the former Fleet Street journalist (and later, founder of the Arthur James publishing house) interviewed Gipsy Smith for the book, *One Thing I Know*, published by Hodder and Stoughton in 1933. Although other Christian leaders of the time (including Hugh Redwood) are subjects of chapters in the book, the one on Gipsy Smith is especially revealing for the evangelist's view on guidance. Some of A. J. Russell's questions were clearly searching ones, but the answers show how clearly Gipsy was committed to the biblical concept of guidance.

The Holy Spirit, for Gipsy, was the 'Pentecostal power which still achieves results', but to be led by God's Holy Spirit presupposed that those who called themselves 'Christians' continued in private prayer, Bible reading and witnessing to others. The object was the building up of the Church, not personal fortunes.

By the time Gipsy became a regular visitor to the Cliff College of Evangelism (at Calver, near Sheffield) in the late 1920s, he could offer instruction in almost any topic, apart from the biblical languages, for he was a student and exponent of gospel singing, broadcaster, writer, counsellor, as well as preacher, and from his early days, had necessarily gained considerable experience in leadership and planning. But he would never have adopted that tempting title of 'expert'. One can imagine him talking to an appreciative group of young people, hoping to serve God in evangelism, along the following lines:

I used to make clothes pegs [Gipsy would probably show the old knife he kept as a souvenir] and I learned how to do so from my father. If people were to accept these clothes pegs, they had to serve well, and stand up to all weathers. It would be no use making clothes pegs that only held the washing on a calm day with no wind. My father didn't read any big books about clothes-pegs . . . he couldn't read . . . and I don't remember him ever going to hear a lecture from someone who had great new theories on clothes pegs, and how they evolved.

No, it was a matter of picking the right wood for the job, taking time to shape the wood, to make it firm with a support, and to try it out. I think preaching is a bit like that. You can learn from others, but most important from our Father, and make sure you offer a faith which holds on windy days, when lots of other things are flying away, because they cannot stand up. It's *that* which brings people to my meetings, and sometimes they bring clothes pegs they bought from me years ago, and which still hold. What they say to me is, 'Gipsy, you were right, it kept its grip.' And, do you know, I'm not sure whether they are talking about the old pegs or their faith in God.

One of the students that Gipsy met, and who later laboured with him in mission work was a sturdy Yorkshireman, Herbert Silverwood. And Herbert long used one of Gipsy's good pieces of advice, 'you catch more wasps with treacle than by throwing bricks at them'.

17
Gipsy and the microphone

You may make a mark on time that will
not be erased in eternity.
(Gipsy Smith)

Among parallels between the 1920s and our own day, is the way that communications technology seemed to offer new possibilities to the churches. There was no doubt as to the possibilities of the new medium of radio, even before the setting up of the British Broadcasting Corporation on 1 January 1927. Rev. 'Dick' Sheppard, who had by then handed the work at St Martin's in the Fields to his successor, Rev. 'Pat' McCormack, said in April 1927 that whenever he made a broadcast from his London church, he had received between one thousand and four thousand letters. He remains something of a model to Christian communicators, and at the time of his death in 1937, a popular radio interest weekly offered a salute which had been well earned:

> It is true to say that Dick Sheppard, more than any other person, was responsible for the religious revival brought about by broadcasting. In these days of emptying churches, the BBCs religious broadcasts command a tremendous following, and among our wireless preachers, Dick Sheppard was unsurpassed.
>
> What was the secret of his popularity? It was his gift of happiness, which made him love telling humorous anecdotes, even in his sermons. And it was his great sympathy for his fellow men particularly in his work for the down-and-outs (i.e. the homeless) whom he welcomed to the crypt of St Martin's in the Fields.

Origins of religious broadcasting

It seems that John Reith, the General Manager of the British Broadcasting Company, and who was son of a Scots minister (and friend of Gipsy) proposed the idea of religious broadcasting to Dick Sheppard over tea at the Savoy Hotel in London. Eager to see this opportunity taken up, Dick Sheppard thought that listeners (then a small but growing number) would be most interested in hearing services from the major churches of the metropolis, and eventually other cities. He hardly expected the rebuffs he received, even from those then in charge of St Paul's Cathedral. That St Martin's in the Fields became for many the 'church of the airwaves' was not a deliberate strategy of Dick Sheppard, but rather a 'fall back' position given the discouragements he faced elsewhere. Health problems prevented him from pushing forward the cause of religious broadcasting to the extent that he might have wished, yet the editor of 'Radio Pictorial' was right to credit him, more than any other person, with the upsurge in national regard for Christian values and family worship.

John Reith had a direct cable line, from his London home to the studios at Savoy Hill, so he would listen in to the broadcasts in 'near perfect conditions'. Guests were invited to share in this 'novelty', some in the early 1920s only having the vaguest idea of 'what radio was all about'. One of these guests, in the spring of 1923, was the then Archbishop of Canterbury, Dr Randall Davidson. Dr Davidson decided to invite various church leaders to his suite in the House of Lords, in order to discuss the kind of input the churches could have into religious broadcasting.

Radio had already been developing in the USA, and some of Gipsy's early broadcasting ventures were being undertaken there. When Percy W. Harris, a well known journalist and writer on science topics, wrote *ABC of Wireless* in 1922, he included in the paperback, a full-page photograph of a Presbyterian church in the USA, where 'sermons and church services are regularly sent out by American wireless broadcasting stations'. A recent (1994) history of Christian broadcasting in the USA (*Air of Salvation* by Mark Ward, published by Baker Book House / National Religious

Broadcasters) shows how ready the churches in the USA were to seize on the new medium of radio. Religious broadcasters who had come to the USA from Britain were valued, and when in the mid 1920s Gipsy's friend Rev. John McNeill, the Scot was invited to accept the pastorate of Church of the Open Door, Los Angeles, it was noted that the church 'already broadcast services to Honolulu, California, British Columbia, Arizona, and New Mexico'.

Stuart Hibberd, who had many years experience as a news announcer, was presenter of a BBC radio programme, 'Silver Lining', which combined music, testimony, personal greetings and a little basic Bible teaching. In an interesting personal retrospect, *This is London* (published by Macdonald and Evans in 1950) Stuart Hibberd stated that the first broadcast religious service was transmitted from the top floor 'attic studio' of Marconi House, in the Strand, London. The format for the Christmas Eve, 1922, broadcast was a short service of carols, this being conducted by Rev. John Mayo, rector of St Mary's Church, Whitechapel, one of London's oldest churches, which was alas destroyed in the bombing of London during the Second World War. In the 1930s, however, this church was used by the BBC for Christmas Eve services, and John Mayo must have taken a keen and knowledgeable interest— important given the uncertain acoustics of some church buildings—for he made good friends at the BBC, including the director of The Wireless Singers, Stanford Robinson (who became a well known broadcaster in musical programming, later). Having received so many letters of appreciation for the Christmas Eve service, the British Broadcasting Company arranged a New Year's meditation by Dr Fleming of the Pont Street Presbyterian Church, London, and one assumes that the same 'attic studio' was used. Studios were small, almost cupboard-like affairs in the early days, with no room to 'swing a cat'. When Rev. John Mayo was invited to add more broadcast work to his already busy parish schedule, he found that the British Broadcasting Company left a great deal to the broadcaster's initiative:

There was a request from the studio for hymns, so I supplied the music books, and chose a couple of hymns for Sundays. Later, a Nonconformist minister ventured on a prayer, and I on a short Scripture passage. I then suggested that Anglicans and Nonconformists alternate, i.e. in arranging the services, and this was done. This was the genesis of the broadcast service.

John Beasley, a south London Methodist and historian, has described (in his *Who Was Who in Peckham*, published by Chener Books, London, in 1985) the initiative of Dr James E. Boon, who could probably claim to be the first man in Britain to deliver a sermon by radio. Dr Doris Boon recalled, in a cyclostyled leaflet produced about a quarter of a century ago, how her father had broadcast his 1922 sermon from the Burdette Aerial Works in south east London, a company which, as a manufacturer of radio equipment, held a licence permitting transmissions.

Gipsy and radio

Gipsy's involvement with the new medium was almost inevitable. He was after all the foremost popular preacher of his time, and his three-and-a-half-years war service with the YMCA had brought him into contact with many young men, who were now husbands and taking an interest in the new hobby of radio, or 'wireless' (after 'wireless telegraphy' as it was known in Britain). The first broadcast made by Gipsy was in connection with his mission at the Albert Hall, London in 1924, and he seems to have used the attic studio encountered by other religious broadcasting pioneers. Harold Murray noted this early experience with the microphone in his sixpenny, *Gipsy*, booklet issued in 1925:

What is his message to the world? It may be stated in a few words. The first time Gipsy broadcasted, he went on a Sunday night to the top of Marconi House in The Strand (London) and it was really comical, as he had addressed 10,000 people that day, to see how cleverly he got through the ordeal of standing in a weirdly silent studio, and pouring his soul into an unresponsive little microphone. The next time was at the Glasgow station, where he was backed up by a few friends from the mission who sang a chorus. The third time was the best. The Albert Hall service was broadcasted. It seemed to me all the mixed gravity and gaiety of London was portrayed in the wireless programme that day . . . The items included: Some Voices at the Zoo; Children's Corner; Service conducted by Gipsy Smith; De Groot and the Piccadilly Orchestra; Weather, and the News!

The results were extraordinary. For weeks afterwards, Gipsy was busy replying to a thousand letters from listeners. Some wrote that they were in public houses and put down their beer, leaving it untouched after the service. A friend at Cotgrave in Nottinghamshire, wrote that in 1880, he heard the Gipsy's sister (Tilly) address a thousand people in the middle of the village, many turning to Christ. He little thought that her brother, forty-four years later would be speaking to a vast audience in the Albert Hall in London, and would be distinctly heard in the same village.

The village postmaster, a very enterprising man, fixed a loudspeaker in his doorway, and the singing and the sermon were heard as distinctly by a little crowd, as if the latter had been in the Hall.

The message delivered by the Gipsy—a talk lasting perhaps seven to ten minutes, to which was added his singing of 'Wonderful Jesus'—can be found in Harold Murray's 1925 booklet. Its colourful language and direct appeal would perhaps be unlikely to be permitted by the broadcasting establishment today. Whilst Gipsy assured his listeners that 'God sees possibilities in every one of you that are tremendous' he thought that the world, as it sought for new thrills and new pleasures, was 'bankrupt, a social swindle, having nothing new to offer.' And one might imagine the tingling phone lines and faxes to the BBC or other networks today if it permitted a preacher to declare, as Gipsy did, that 'if you have no time, no service, no money for Jesus, then I say emphatically you cannot be a good man or a good woman.'

Even John (later Sir John, and Lord) Reith seemed at times a little unsure as to Gipsy's off-the-cuff comments on air. Harold

Murray, recalling Gipsy's early broadcasting experiences in 1937, in his *Sixty Years an Evangelist*, suggests that the evangelist thought his initial encounter with the microphone a total disaster:

When in that luxurious little studio, he had to stand on a chalk line, and talk into the cold and unresponsive microphone, he felt miserable. He missed the crowd, their laughter and their song. He was worried by the silence, the necessity of watching the clock, all those queer sensations that must afflict every man who has to talk to the great unseen audience from this place.

Just before he began, the courteous young announcer said sweetly that Sir John Reith would prefer that Gipsy should not mention his name in any way. Gipsy had not intended to do so, but the request was understandable, because one of Gipsy's favourite stories is about his friendship for the Reith family up in Scotland many years ago.

But Gipsy learned from his broadcasting experiences, and making his final broadcast from London, as he neared the end of his life—and just before the made his final journey to the USA—his sincerity and appeal were evident enough. Dick Sheppard had helped create training opportunities for clergy who were interested in using radio, but you cannot impart the 'natural oratory' which Gipsy possessed. Further, Dick Sheppard seems to have learned from Gipsy's use of radio, in association with the Albert Hall mission, to relate major evangelistic occasions to everyday Christian commitment. *The Radio Times* in 1925 admitted that there were some in religious circles who saw in the decision to allow religious broadcasting, 'the death blow to the already declining habit of church attendance'. Yet it added that 'when Rev. H. R. L. (Dick) Sheppard of St Martins in the Fields asked listeners to meet him in the Albert Hall on a certain date, the great building was full to overflowing . . . the broadcasting of great religious meetings such as those of Gipsy Smith had increased the audience from thousands to millions, and had not diminished the numbers going to church.'

On radio Gipsy was primarily involved in preaching the gospel, enjoying opportunities which probably reflected his national popularity rather than 1930s official policy (on religious broadcasting) at the BBCs new 'battleship building' in Portland Place, London. His effectiveness as a broadcaster is undeniable:

> I am eternally grateful to this messenger of God.
>
> On a Sunday evening in 1933, my fiance and I heard him speak in a BBC (radio) service, and his message on John, Chapter 3, verse 16, brought spiritual stirrings that led to my loved one's conversion soon afterwards. I had been praying for this—knowing that I could never face an 'unequal yoke'. A radiant Christian, my husband gave his life early in the Second World War (1940) and the knowledge that he is with the Lord, together with the wonderful grace of God, has enabled me to keep going until we see Him face to face. Just one testimony, I am sure, to Gipsy Smith's gift of communicating the Gospel by the power of the Holy Spirit and with simplicity. (Mrs Winifred Hibbins, letter to the author)

Gipsy clearly took the line that if Christians were to use radio, they had to ally a necessary sensitivity (and imagination) to expectation of some outcome. An interesting example of this comes from Gipsy's visit to Australia—his second—in the mid nineteen-twenties. When he held meetings at the Sydney Hippodrome, he met at least forty people (seated close to his podium) who had been converted during his campaign in the city some thirty years earlier. Rev. Geoffrey Hope Hume, who describes the evangelist as 'tall' and 'big' (in his letter to the present writer) states that Gipsy announced the hymns from the songbook, 'Wonderful Jesus and other songs'.

> When Gipsy Smith read the opening lines of the hymns, and called on the people to sing, with a sweeping movement of his raised right arm, there was a resounding response all around that large stadium. He created an uplifting atmosphere of praise and prayer. I had made a public decision for Christ at a Sunday School mission campaign conducted by Mr Cumming, the Scottish evangelist, in Sydney several years previously. This

was followed later by a deep spiritual experience of the meaning of 'love' to God.

Something more was needed. Gipsy Smith's meetings provided the inspiration. It was as if I were walking on air as I left the meeting one night, with the words ringing in my ears, 'Believe on the Lord Jesus Christ and thou shalt be saved'.

Since my ordination to the Christian ministry in 1934, I have mentioned Gipsy Smith many times in my sermons. (Rev. Geoffrey Hope Hume, Gilberton, South Australia)

In addition to the four thousand or so who crowded the main meetings, there were special seminars for businessmen, held at the City Hall. Showing a keen awareness of the potential of radio, the sponsoring churches arranged that outlying churches could share in the Sydney mission, via the broadcasts. Local ministers were given guidance on how to 'use' this long distance ministry. One of the ministers taking up the opportunity, Rev. William G. Taylor, had no doubts as to the programme's impact:

Distant? No! A voice right there in our midst, with all its vibrant power.

Aye, and with far more than that, for indeed, God was in that voice. Think of it!

The Holy Spirit coming to us through the wireless, reaching and moving the congregation as never before we have seen it moved.

I preached the first service here at Lindfield thirty years ago. Through all those intervening years, never have there been witnessed in this church such scenes as last Sunday night, as it was our great joy to rejoice in.

Congregations many miles from the Sydney Mission were caught up in the spirit of the occasion, and ministers in many places must have become suddenly aware of the possibilities of radio, for the cause of the gospel. Rev. A. F. Walker reported that local publicity in his area had attracted many people to his church at Newtown. As the people arrived, the singing of choruses and hymns, no doubt those associated with Gipsy, was enjoyed until the time came for the broadcast to be heard. When, at the end of his radio address, Gipsy made his appeal, and the people at the Sydney Hippodrome began to go forward (to the enquiry room for counselling) Rev. A. F. Walker reduced the level of the radio signal, and then made his own appeal. Two-thirds of the congregation rose to their feet, to re-dedicate themselves to the cause of Christ, and to show their intention of becoming believers. The minister, quoted in Gipsy's 1932 collection of 'memories and reflections' (*The Beauty of Jesus*, published by Epworth Press/Edgar G. Barton) added that 'a wave of divine power seemed to grip our hearts'.

Gipsy did not draw any contrasts between his broadcasting experiences in Britain and in other countries, more friendly to what might be called 'Gospel broadcasting'. When the young child of Charles Lindbergh, the famous American aviator, was kidnapped in March 1932, Gipsy did not hesitate to link his radio broadcast from an American station, to the event which seemed to have shaken the nation.

> I said, 'God is speaking from an empty cradle. Once He spoke from a full cradle. He is speaking again now. Will you listen?'
> (*Beauty of Jesus*, page 132)

Gipsy, in his 1930s missions in the USA, was not short of radio opportunities, and there are tantalizing references to his missions being reported in cinema newsreels. This seems to have been the case at Brooklyn, New York, in early 1932, when Gipsy was invited to join Rev. Dr Parkes Cadman. This was presumably the 'National Radio Pulpit' programme, sponsored by the National Council of Churches. According to Dr Cadman, whose own radio experience covered some ten years' ministry, Gipsy's message, on 'The need of the heart' reached some fifteen million listeners.

In the early 1930s, Gipsy 'found the Americans made serious by their financial losses and crises, and ready to think and pray. That mood was my opportunity.' Gipsy in his American missions seemed to find time for some telephone counselling too—not an opportunity readily available in Britain, which had far less telephone ownership per capita. A reporter interviewing Gipsy commented that

> our brief conversation was several times interrupted by the ringing of the phone. Hundreds of people seemed eager and waiting to ask the advice of the evangelist in matters relating to their soul's welfare, or to thank him for the new spirit of Christianity brought into their lives. A number of long-distance calls were received from outlying towns . . .

> Gipsy Smith, hanging up the receiver for perhaps the tenth time within a space of fifteen minutes said, 'The man I was just talking to has been a drunkard for thirty years. In my meeting yesterday afternoon, he got converted and has promised God never to touch alcohol again . . . He went home and said grace at his own table for the first time for many years.

For those who look for the 'secret' of Gipsy's ministry, one answer might be 'accessibility'. Strangers felt that Gipsy would listen to them, and that he understood their problems. Also, Gipsy did not tread on toes that did not need to be trodden on. It may be surprising to health-conscious people today that Gipsy did not attack smoking, or the sale of tobacco, seeing that he spent so much time promoting temperance. But Gipsy did not see tobacco as destroying lives and domestic happiness as alcohol clearly did. His mission at Winston-Salem, North Carolina, was held in a tobacco warehouse, seating six thousand people. Here again, radio greatly extended the audience, and members of the remote radio audience requested decision cards. Gipsy thought the campaign, the best organized that he had encountered. But two especially significant expressions of Gipsy's sensitivity can be recorded.

First, he was careful not to do anything to offend the local Lutheran minister, who had been 'antagonised and alienated' by actions of other so-called evangelists, and before the mission was over, 'the Lutheran was with us, body and soul'.

A second fact was his general refusal to preach to segregated audiences. He said quite plainly in his 1930s sermons and writings, 'Religion is the only thing that can deal with the problem of the colour line (i.e. racial/ethnic prejudice). Religion is the only thing that can save the world from revolution.'

Gipsy's attitude to radio, as to much else, is reflected in a story told by Harold Murray in his 1925 booklet:

> Once, when he was over-strained and his nerves were on edge, Gipsy was recommended by a doctor to go fishing. He went down to the pier one summer's morning, and fished for two hours—and caught nothing but a cold.
>
> Then an old fisherman came along and said, 'Mester Smith, try this other bait!'
>
> Gipsy tried this 'other bait' and he had a bucket filled in a few minutes.
>
> Later, Gipsy said, 'if you cannot catch folks with one bait, try another'.

If people would not, or could not come to church, radio represented 'another bait'. Coupled to this enterprising approach from a man long past his sixtieth birthday was a continuing reference to the need for revival, a fresh breath of the Holy Spirit, in generous measure, upon churches who often worked hard but had little genuine joy in their worship. There is something contemporary in Gipsy's warning that rounds of meetings and committee work might be a waste of time, unless conversions and the building up of the church resulted.

> You may be content with the ordinary jog trot round—dead, cold and formal—yes, and you may have a graveyard and peace, but it is the peace of death.
>
> I want a Revival that will make businessmen less keen about saving money and more keen on saving the City. I want a Revival that will make husbands go home and talk to their wife as lovingly as they did when they were courting.
>
> I want a Revival that will encourage people to pay their debts, a Revival that will make people good to live with, that will make you work honestly, and write that letter that needs

to be written, and forgive that old injury, and discover that your employees have souls. I'm not out for emotion and excitement. I don't care a hang for it. I am here, without any tricks, for sanity, truth, righteousness, beauty, harmony and . . . *Jesus*.

Gipsy broadcast from Wesley's Chapel in City Road, London, during the mid 1930s and during the service, his friend, Rev. George McNeal, related his own conversion, through Gipsy's ministry, some forty years earlier. Such outspoken personal testimony was not always to be encouraged by the BBC; religious broadcasting, even some ten years after the opening of the first stations, remained a controversial topic. As 'The BBC Year Book for 1933' points out, there were complaints about 'the quality and force of many of the religious broadcasts'. But the same publication notes that Gipsy Smith 'was certainly able to project his smouldering fires across the ether especially to those thousands who knew his voice and appearance of old'. Reassurance of a sort was offered by the enigmatic comment that 'thunderbolts are rare from the broadcast pulpit'.

'Romany'

The year 1932 saw the first broadcasts by 'Romany', Rev. G. Bramwell Evens (known in family circles as 'Bram') and a lively work for good that has hardly been equalled. That 'Romany's books—originally published from the late 1920s to the early 1940s—are still sought via the collectors' magazines today, says something for their enduring quality. His truly merry yet reflective writing and radio work are recalled in magazine articles, books and, some thirteen years ago in a BBC North East television programme, presented by Eric Robson. Gipsy appears to have hoped that, as he (Gipsy) withdrew from evangelical work, his nephew might take up the challenge. But 'Bram' was not an evangelist in the sense that his 'Uncle Rodney' was. His great work was in sharing of the wonders of the natural world with young people especially, and with showing of the order that had been ordained by the Almighty.

A fine biography, written by his widow, Eunice Evens, appeared in February 1946, soon after Romany's death (*Through the Years With Romany*, University of London Press). They had married at a Congregationalist Church in east London in August 1911, only a few years after Romany's ordination into the Wesleyan Methodist Church, and coincidentally with his studies for a divinity degree, as an external student of the University of London. He must have made an impressive figure, for Eunice tells us that he had raven black hair, 'thick and glossy, worn rather long, and inclined to curl. His dark hazel eyes were deep set and sparkling, and changed with every mood. He had heavy eyebrows, a dark moustache, a strong nose and chin, and the high cheek bones typical of the Gipsy race . . . He could not have been called handsome in the usual sense of the word, but when he smiled, he was irresistible.' Incidentally, the moustache must have departed soon after the marriage, for there is no sign of it in the photographs of the writer found in his books, often with a briar pipe between his teeth.

Romany's early ministry in east London (Dalston) was close to places well known to the family, generally, he and Eunice sometimes 'taking walks in Epping Forest . . . the only place within easy reach of Dalston where (we) could get away from the din of traffic to the quiet of the woods and fields.' But his writing was really shaped by his subsequent work in Goole and Carlisle, where he built up the congregation at the Methodist Central Hall, also guiding a major development scheme. He ended his work at Carlisle in 1926, the same year in which Gipsy undertook his second mission in Australia and Zealand.

At the time, he was identified as 'The Tramp' rather than 'Romany' in his writings, which originally appeared in provincial papers and the Methodist press. Indeed, one could say that the bounty of books fall into two main areas—the first, including *A Romany in the Fields* (Epworth Press 1929) combining nature lore with adventures of his friends, and the second, the later titles, being almost entirely about birds and animals, accompanied by good black and white photographs. No doubt, the latter were proposed by publishers aware of their potential as Sunday school prizes and presents for children generally, for their author under-took many Sunday school anniversary chores in the last decade of his life.

But the first titles are, from a modern point of view, far more interesting, for they capture a way of life, a philosophy of living even, and the characters are clearly based on people that 'Romany' knew and loved. There was also the companion, 'Raq'—the spaniel which the writer thought 'the most lovable and sensible thing on four legs'. The spaniel was always a 'star' at the Sunday school anniversaries addressed by this most knowledgable and friendly of Methodist ministers.

Included in the stories are John Fell, the game keeper; Jerry, the poacher; Alan and Joe, farmers; Ned, the village postman, Sally Stordy, and John Rubb, the angler. The philosophy contained in these delighting books was stated in the first paragraph of *A Romany in the Fields* (by G. Bramwell Evens, *The Tramp*, 1929):

I ought to say at once that I am a 'tramp' by choice and not of necessity. Lingering in the city either to gaze at shop windows, or to be regularly amused by some 'show' is not my highest form of bliss. I prefer to loiter in green meadows, to explore the fringes of quiet pools and the margins of laughing streams, to muse under shadowed hedges—in a word to potter about where the wild bird sings or where the trout rises to the fly.

Illustrated with neat inset line drawings, as well as photography, the early books combine humour, nature lore, philosophy of life and at times shafts of insight befitting a preacher. There is, for example, in the 1929 book, a foreshadowing of a similar insight 'Romany' recorded in the early days of the Second World War, a glimpse of eternal verities transcending the follies of men:

As I entered the town that evening, all the sights I saw gathered themselves round the dominant theme of the day.

Paper-boys were selling the latest edition to eager buyers.

Groups of listeners gathered round the shops' loudspeakers, as they circulated the doings of the larger world. In the streets were small gatherings of neighbours gossiping about the life of their acquaintances and friends. All were eager for news.

Then I had a vision of half empty churches, bored listeners, listless congregations, and I wondered whether the messages delivered there, had the quality of news—the 'Good News'. I heard too another Voice saying, 'It is like a sower—like leaven—like a merchant seeking goodly pearls'.

The famous 'vardo'—or gipsy caravan—in which 'Romany' did much of his writing, is photographed for the 1929 book, and was much mentioned in the BBC 'Children's Hour' broadcasts. Restored in its original dark green and white livery, through the generosity of the Macclesfield Borough Council, the caravan can be seen by visitors to Wilmslow, Cheshire, the community in which 'Romany' (after various other circuit work, as in Huddersfield and Halifax) spent his final years. It is a graceful reminder of a man who, whilst advising many to take a more reflective view of life, did not turn away from 'much hard work'. There is indeed, no lack of counsel for those who have become over-stressed victims of the so-called progress of our times. One could escape, with 'Romany' into a world which might be as close as the nearest river or stream, meadow or woods. Here, promises 'Romany', 'will I introduce you to my companions of the stillness'.

The 1930s now seem something of a golden decade for children's broadcasting and in recent years, there has been careful attention to its influence (see for example, *Goodnight Children Everywhere* by Ian Hartley, published by Midas Books, 1984, and *2ZY to NBH: An informal history of the BBC in Manchester* by the same author, Willow Books, 1987). In the latter work, Ian Hartley recalls that the invitation to Romany to audition at the BBC's Northern Regional studios came from Olive Schill, programme organizer at Manchester, and who had heard of 'Romany's talks to school children in the area.

The format of the programme was simple enough, a walk in the fields, or 'ramble' conducted by 'Romany' for his two young friends (Muriel Levy and Doris Gambell) and accompanied by

'Raq'. Stated baldly, there seemed nothing out of the usual, but the combination of 'Romany's spontaneous approach, and the remarkable production quality, with innovative use of sound effects etc., made the 'Out with Romany' programmes outstanding. Devoted listeners *really felt* that they had been 'out with Romany' and, on the whole, one could find no greater compliment to any broadcaster. Surprisingly, only one of the programmes has ever been recorded.

He had his moments of humour. There was a reference to the new vacuum cleaner arriving in the Evens household, and prompting a suggestion that the principle might be adapted to church collections. A vacuum device at the end of every pew could be operated at a given time in the service, and 'suck' up any loose change that was in the worshippers' pockets. There are fragments of domestic bliss, as when he describes the chores of seeing that his son is well prepared for his return to school for the new term, a business calling for marking this and that:

> Personally, I think that matters would be simplified if, for the last week of the holidays, a boy were kept in bed. All mending, washing, darning, adjusting, could then be carried out at leisure.

But amidst all the merriment, and the finely-drawn descriptions of rural life, 'Romany' rarely strayed from his first love, being a minister of the gospel. Faced with ever-increasing demands on his time, he offered his resignation to the circuit, simply because he felt he was unable to fulfil his pastoral responsibilities. It says much for the wise outlook of those involved, that they affirmed 'Romany' in what he was doing. They saw, as perhaps he did not, that he was showing that in essence the task of the church is—as his 'Uncle Rodney' so often put it—to bring the beauty of Jesus into our lives and to show it in relationships. So it is that in Romany's books, we find the occasional shaft that can help the present-day communicator of the gospel:

> What a sense of reality would be imparted to our Church prayers if instead of thanking God for 'mercies received' and 'blessings enjoyed', we were to say,

'We thank Thee for the green fields and clover blossom, for marigolds glowing like the sun, and for violets hidden in the hedgerows'.

And, finally, also from the 1929 book, *A Romany in the Fields* a word that applies cuttingly to much of our experience in our over-busy lives:

I rather fancy that many modern residences are merely private hotels—roosts for the dark hours, but not homes.

And as I entered my own dwelling, there were two verses which hovered about my thoughts, 'Abide in Me'—therein is the permanent nest. And, as a background to it, 'As a bird that wandereth from her nest, so is a man who wandereth from his place'.

In 1940, Romany ended one of his talks with a reference to 'the things that last, that which cannot be destroyed, the precious possession of the love of nature, its healing effect. In all these things, we need to go apart sometimes, and let nature do its work'.

Both Gipsy Smith and Bramwell Evens ('Romany') reminded their contemporaries of man's God-given stewardship of this remarkable, vulnerable planet. Their emphasis is even more needful today when rain forests are being destroyed and the atmosphere polluted by man-made agents.

18
Good Companions—
the car tours

Opportunity goes round disguised as hard work.
(Elbert Hubbard)

A mong the many listeners influenced by the new medium of radio, Hugh Redwood wrote of an experience which 'came out of the blue' one Sunday evening in 1927. Like many enthusiasts of the time he had been assembling a new 'set' and, after some initial problems, found that the reception was better than any apparatus he had owned previously. It was in this 'knob twiddling' test of the set's potential that Hugh Redwood tuned into a broadcast service from Folkestone in Kent, conducted by Rev. W. H. Elliott, the Church of England clergyman destined to become one of the most influential religious broadcasters and writers of the 1930s and 1940s. Describing the experience in his book, *God in the Shadows*, and referring to it in his 1948 title, *Bristol Fashion* (published by Latimer House) Hugh Redwood showed how the radio signal became the voice of Jesus Christ, speaking personally to him. For the Bristol journalist, the Folkestone preacher had receded, as it were: 'it was another voice to which I was listening, a voice which spoke to my mind and my heart'. The essence of the message was the reality of prayer, and the experience changed the journalist's life. Two other aspects of the experience were significant to him. Inevitably, he was frustrated by the sense which he could not explain, and yet felt that something important would happen in his forty-fourth year: 'What I had half expected was that at forty-four I should die, or be killed; what actually occurred was that at forty-four I began to live.'

The broadcast from Folkestone had occurred shortly after Hugh Redwood's forty-fourth birthday, and thrust him into a new work for God. A second aspect was that the experience occurred in a room, in which, a year earlier, he had sensed the presence of evil. There was a sense that some kind of spiritual battle of awesome dimensions was 'in the background', and, as the present writer (like many others), has had a not dissimilar experience, one can see that there are revelations beyond conventional religious observances.

Declining support

Probably the most influential layman of his time—and the first full-time religious correspondent for a national newspaper, *The News Chronicle*—Hugh Redwood knew Gipsy well, and on at least one occasion, spoke from the same platform. *Bristol Fashion*, the autobiographical book written by Hugh Redwood just after the Second World War, gives a perspective on the last decade of Gipsy's labours. Not that Gipsy spent as much time as he would have wished in the Britain of the 1930s, and though he worked especially with the Methodist Home Missions Department, even the persuasive powers of its secretary, the beloved Rev. Dr Luke Wiseman, seemed unable to enlist the support of some churches for evangelistic missions. Indeed, by 1932, when the three main Methodist connexions came together in the Methodist Union, the day of the lay evangelist seemed to be all but over. Gipsy would never have felt like the metaphorical 'fish out of water', but there must have been times when he believed that securing active involvement in evangelism, by local churches, was like swimming against a very powerful stream.

As Hugh Redwood observed some half century ago, there were a number of church leaders who in the early 1930s thought that the nation needed to be called back to God, but there was a notable absence of any action to follow up the pleas of such men as the saintly Sir Evan Spicer.

Archbishop Lang sought to do it. The National Free Church

Council, as it then was, might actually have done it had it been less afraid of giving offence to Free Church ministers . . . The old man (Sir Evan Spicer) who was well in his eighties, saw plainly the storms into which we were heading, but dreamed of a Britain regaining her faith and giving the world a Christian lead. He hoped the young men would share the vision, and first of all the young men in the ministry. He realised that an awakening in the Church was an indispensable prerequisite and he urged the (Free Church) council to sound the reveille by sending to every one of its ministers an immediate summons to prayer and action.

Whereupon the Council appointed a sub-committee, as it probably would have done had the call been 'the Bridegroom cometh!'—and the sub-committee wasted the best part of a year in discussing drafts and gentling them down until at last it produced a document incapable of disturbing the rest of the lightest sleeper. It was too late by then; the high time of awakening had passed.

There is clear evidence in the religious press of the time that the great aspirations which had launched the Simultaneous Mission of 1900–01, and which had so enthused Gipsy and his comrades, W. R. Lane, Rev. J. Tolfree Parr and Rev. Thomas Law, had all but gone. Hugh Redwood's analysis, coming from the mind of one well trained to observe and report, suggests that the decline came with the First World War. Over the thirty-year period representing the span of Hugh Redwood's 1948 retrospect, there had been no sign of a 'thaw' in the 'freezing up' of church life. A lack of interest from the population at large had been accompanied, to borrow Hugh Redwood's phrase, 'by a deadly apathy of a great majority within the churches'. The size of that majority might be as high as ninety per cent of church members at that time. And, as Gipsy Smith had long warned, indifferent, aloof churches— relying on tradition, privilege, or even their own theological correctness alone—made for poor nations. Given the modern tendency to think of the late 1940s as a period of renewal and new hope, Hugh Redwood's view comes as a shock:

If God and His claims are treated today (1948) with contempt in almost every department of our national life, the chief responsibility lies upon them (i.e. the great majority in the churches) for by their silence and inactivity they have repeatedly allowed the government, the press, the drink trade, and the gambling interests, together with atheistic (philosophy) to get away with things against which they should have fought with every ounce of their power, and all the added grace that God would have given them.

At the heart of our people there is a core of real faith, possibly a ten per cent core, which is fluid and active and with which God may do mighty things. It is finding new unity under pressure, it is impatient of old separations and denominational jealousies. It is looking to God for a lead, and I believe it will not look long in vain.

Harold Murray, in his 1937 portrait of Gipsy (*Sixty Years an Evangelist*, published by Marshall, Morgan and Scott) seems to write for our times as well as his own, for he asked if the churches are really prepared for revival. How well would present-day church members 'cope' if asked to counsel enquirers, to help seekers find Christ, or indeed help newcomers overcome problems in their own lives. As a Baptist pastor, engaged in church growth in the south of England put it recently, 'the people come in, but they bring their dirty washing with them', that is, problems needing practical input from the churches, as well as from the Welfare State (assuming that the help of the latter is available). No man did more to encourage ministers and overworked church leaders than did Gipsy—and he did not 'count the cost', in terms of his own time and energy, of aiding such diligent people. But he had to warn churches where membership had become a sort of religious club, and where, even worse, there was no concern or training to meet opportunities just over the church threshold. Harold Murray wrote in 1937:

I never in my life saw Gipsy more disturbed than when he was in a certain church in the north of England, and could not find one single (church) officer or worker who would go into the enquiry room with those who were seeking salvation. Some of the most learned and cultured men he has known have done it. He cannot understand how it is that prominent workers in any church should so often confess their inability to do it.

Until they are born again, he urges, there can be no revival. They may be 'fussy' (as he calls it) in all sorts of good works, in socials, bazaars, entertainments. The real work of the Church will never be done until they sink their pride, become truly converted, seek the lost and tenderly lead them into the fold.

Gipsy's message changed little in the 1930s, and when Sunday newspapers printed his sermons we find familiar themes and subjects. He did not pronounce on international events, for example, or on the economic and social problems facing a great number of families in the land. However, he would have been aware of them, not least because writers like Hugh Redwood were drawing attention to them, and also through the kind of 'practical ministry' being offered by churches in hard-pressed areas.

An aid to mobility was the car (automobile) that some of his friends in the USA presented to Gipsy at about the time of his seventieth birthday. Given the four-wheeled approach to church-going that sees all too few people *walking* to church, it is perhaps something of a surprise to learn that the advent of the car provoked as much controversy as the arrival of radio, among religious people. Writing in *The Quiver*, a family magazine, in the early months of 1907, Rev. J. D. Jones, MA, one of the foremost preachers of his day, urged that 'the King's business requires haste' and pointed to General William Booth's initiative, a year or so earlier, in organizing his 'white car crusade' which took him through Britain as far north as Glasgow, no mean achievement for a man in venerable old age. Paul the Apostle would surely have used a car, had such gadgetry been available in his day, 'to reach the regions beyond and to preach the Gospel to those who had not heard it'.

Mobile ministry

As Gipsy's friend from NCEFC days, Rev. F. B. Meyer was a member of the party of 'motor tours' reported in the 1907 article, he

(Gipsy) was clearly aware of the possibilities. Rev. J. D. Jones explained how he and that other Free Church Council stalwart, Rev. C. Silvester Horne, with other friends, were able to get away from their demanding pulpits for a few days here and there, and thanks to the judicious use of the car (driven by volunteers) they were able to make brief calls to rural churches that might never otherwise have had the opportunity to hear these prominent preachers.

Gipsy followed this 1907 example in 'the Good Companions Tours', which took him to many parts of the country. In 1931, for example, Dr Wiseman and Gipsy managed a 'lightning tour' between Wellingborough in Northamptonshire, and Beverley in Yorkshire. Will Sizer, a member of Gipsy's household, and a local preacher was 'official chauffeur'. Held during the summer months, as and when other commitments permitted, the 'Good Companions' (motor) tours had a delightful informality, and one can see Harold Murray's point when he wrote that, but for his age, Gipsy might well have done more—by gipsy caravan rather than a car!

He revelled in the opportunity of visiting many villages in Devon, Cornwall, Yorkshire, Westmorland, Cumberland and other counties. It was with sheer delight that he would arrive in some small rural place at eleven o'clock in the morning, and find an over-crowded little chapel waiting for him. A hurried lunch, then off some forty miles or more to an afternoon service and so on. These tours (still being arranged in 1937) were tiring because of the long distances covered by car, and the holding of more than three services a day. They were extraordinarily fruitful.

They appealed to one as a great, much advertised mission could never do. The evangelist in the heart of the country was just what he laughingly says he feels—a Boy Scout. On a north country moor, he would jump out of a car and begin an impromptu prayer meeting. In a rural lane, he would stay for a little while, peering in the hedges and trees for nests. On village greens, he would start the singing of a Gospel chorus while the wondering villagers gathered around. (*Sixty Years an Evangelist*, by Harold Murray, 1937)

In one sense, the motor tours showed how evangelists might stir up churches that had otherwise abandoned any ideas of local evangelism though, of course, Gipsy was eager to encourage and to cheer as well. As clearly indicated by Harold Murray's comment much of the work and encouragement was done out of doors, as well as within small churches and chapels. Sometimes farm buildings were brought into use, like the Dutch Barn at Skillington, a small village near Grantham, Lincolnshire, in 1932, for a meeting arranged by the Grantham Methodist Circuit. An entire haystack had been moved out of this 'cathedral with a corrugated iron roof' (as one described it) though not all of the original poultry inhabitants. A piano, in good tune, stood on a platform made of planks, and a microphone/public address system had been installed, in anticipation of a large crowd. Indeed, some fifteen hundred people crowded into the Dutch Barn, many more stood outside.

Gipsy placed his trilby hat over the microphone (he usually preferred to sing without such aids) and as one would expect, won over many by his winsome, optimistic approach. The choice of song was 'Lean on His arms, trusting in His Love', and the 'ecumenical' spirit of the occasion is clearly seen in the presence of two local Anglican clergy, one of whom cheerfully announced that tea was available at Skillington Vicarage for all who wanted it.

The 'Good Companions' were there in force; in addition to Will Sizer and Gipsy, there were Rev. J. A. Broadbelt, Rev. Charles Hulbert, Rev. A. S. Hullah, and Rev. J. Day, all well known for sturdy and reliable work in evangelism. There is a pre-echo of Hugh Redwood's 1948 comment, quoted above, in Gipsy's challenge made at Skillington, some sixteen years before *Bristol Fashion* was published. Gipsy said, in 1932, 'In the name of God, I ask you—have you done anything specifically to bring Jesus Christ to the people? You may get very fussy and excited over an entertainment, festival, social, bazaar or circuit gathering. But do you ever get tired out in trying to secure conversions?'

Gipsy's unexpected challenges were often made in the context of an address or sermon which, at first, might seem aimed 'at someone else'.

During one of the meetings he held at Watford in 1934, the Gipsy was holding the audience spell-bound so that one could have heard a pin drop. Suddenly, there was a disturbance in a corner, and he begged everyone to be quiet and not to disturb the atmosphere. Unfortunately, one of the water pipes had developed a leak, and those nearby were being soaked, and were not able to move!

At another meeting, he was talking about the value of prayer and prayer meetings. He turned to the minister and asked him on which day of the week the Church Prayer Meeting was being held. Quickly, the minister replied, '"There is a special one tomorrow night, Gipsy!' Of course, there had not been any prayer meeting planned at the Church. (Mrs Kathleen Spence, personal letter to the present writer)

Gipsy was hardly 'hoodwinked' by such responses to his questions, and he was surely making a point, as he did at the close of one mission, when he asked the audience if they would meet regularly for prayer, if he came back to hold another campaign. As one would expect, the response was a loud 'Yes!'

'Then, if you would do it for me, why don't you do it for your minister and your church?' he asked.

Cliff College addresses

Some of the motor tours surely called in at Cliff College of Evangelism, and to see old friends including the beloved Rev. Samuel Chadwick. A Cliff College report of the early 1930s has a photograph of Gipsy and Harold Murray, with pleasant but concentrated expressions on their faces; they were presumably about to lecture students. Gipsy's addresses to the young people at Cliff must at times have been unforgettable, though not always close to the kind of seminar one might expect at seminary today. Rev. C. Johns recalled:

I remember him addressing students at Cliff College as long ago as 1930, and he said that, as a boy, he used to watch the

216

clouds chasing one another like ivory chariots across the canopy of heaven. He also referred to how he used to go into the fields and watch rabbits at play. I recall a particularly outstanding talk he gave to us students on the subject of Soul Winning. He concluded by saying that he sometimes wrestled with God in prayer, especially when he thought he was not getting as many souls for God as he should have been. He would say, 'Lord, if you don't give me more souls, I shall die!' and ended his talk with the question, 'Have you ever prayed like that?'

At Southport, Gipsy conducted a special service for the High Schools and the Girl Guides. When he came to make his appeal for converts, he said with tears in his eyes, 'Oh, you beautiful young women, all in the prime of life, what can I do for you? I would lay myself prostrate on the floor of this church all through the night to see you converted.' How they responded— they queued up to reach the Communion rail. (personal letter to the present writer)

'Sam' Chadwick, the principal of Cliff College, who had known Gipsy from the days of the National Council of Evangelical Free Churches (NCEFC) was a man who shared the same spiritual heart-beat. His work in Leeds, during the period of revival (1904–06) was such that the church hardly closed, and he was able to report to the 1905 NCEFC Congress: 'I rejoice that in my church (Brunswick Methodist Church, Leeds) and in the whole of the churches in Leeds, we have had a wonderful year of blessing and saving power. I believe it all began with the League of Intercession with which we opened the year 1904. Hundreds of people banded themselves together daily to call upon God in secret, without fail, and to wait upon Him for a renewal of His Work and the outpouring of the Holy Spirit. Immediately, there was a rise in temperature.' It was a combination of the prayerful, the pentecostal and the practical, happily combined, that brought this remarkable saint to Cliff College, and he is remembered still, more than sixty years after his death, not least thanks to his excellent book, *The Path to Pentecost*.

Gipsy drew great inspiration from his visits to Cliff College:

I do not know that I address during the year any gathering more remarkable than that on the lawn after tea at the Cliff College Anniversary. By means of loudspeakers, five thousand people in the open-air, crowded in front of us, and behind us on the terrace, and listening at open windows are reached. Many a time, I have sung here with Rev. F. L. Wiseman at the piano. (*The Beauty of Jesus*, 1932)

This first-hand report suggests that at Cliff at least the veteran preacher overcame his disdain for microphones and amplifiers.

Back to his roots

One day in 1934, an improvised stage was erected at 'the Dell' near Baldock, the country lane in which Gipsy's mother Polly had died more than seventy years earlier. The event was note-worthy for the fact that Gipsy and his older brother Ezekiel (also a preacher) spoke from the same platform, as also did his sisters. In June 1935, a service was held close to Gipsy's birthplace, 'in the parish of Wanstead, not far from the Green Man', though the Epping Forest Commissioners understandably laid down some rules, including the prohibition of any collection.

Hugh Redwood was also present and spoke to the crowd. A memorable event, as Harold Murray affirmed:

Anyone could find the meeting place by following the crowd, but many who had to stand at the back among the trees could not hear the whole of the service. Some of Gipsy's relatives brought a real gipsy van, and from this, with his wife and daughter sitting inside, Gipsy gave an address. It may be imagined with what emotion he referred to the strange beginnings of his eventful life.

This emphasis on family links with the area probably helped a church project at Letchworth, the 'garden city' created by Ebenezer Howard and his friends. The Letchworth Methodist Circuit, in the mid 1930s, consisted of two churches, In view of the growing population, it was decided that new church facilities were required at Norton Village. Mr Charles Cooper, the secretary of the church, thought it would be appropriate to dedicate the new building to the memory of Gipsy Smith's parents, a proposal warmly supported by the members, as indeed it was to be by Gipsy himself. Gipsy helped raise funds for the development, which was opened in 1934 as Norton Methodist Mission, now known as the North Avenue Methodist Church, Letchworth Garden City.

An inscription in the church reads: 'To The Glory of God, and in memory of the beloved parents of Gipsy Smith'.

It was a source of great satisfaction to the evangelist, to know that the graves of his parents were only a relatively short distance away from this pleasant and welcoming church. Gipsy Smith was in the USA when the mission was officially opened by his daughter, Zillah, and her husband, Mr J. T. Lean. Later, however, Gipsy and his brother Ezekiel conducted evangelistic meetings in the building, and the church has had a continuing interest in the Gipsy's ministry. The pulpit is shaped in a caravan style, and the history of the church, and Gipsy's links with it, was written and produced privately some years ago by the late Keith Sell. Exhibitions linked to the Gipsy's work have been held, together with other events, but vandalism followed by a fire in December 1996 has presented the church with a bill of approximately £100,000: details from Peter Cannell, 3 Cashio Lane, Letchworth 5GG 1AY.

Gipsy's power in preaching was at least partly due to his 'freshness'. He was perhaps the closest Britain has come in this century to having its own 'Francis of Assisi'. Visiting the lane in which his mother had died, now the road which runs from Baldock to Letchworth Garden City, Gipsy prised an old root from the grassy bank, took it back to Cambridge, and planted it in his garden beneath a pear tree. Away from home on a mission, he heard from his wife that the 'dirty old root' had produced a lovely bunch of primroses. It was a typical sermon illustration for Gipsy: 'The flowers were in the root all along. They only wanted the sunshine and the atmosphere. Many a man does not know what is in him. It is our business to bring out the beautiful, the noble and the true.'

19
The final
peace-time missions

There is no age in love.
(Gipsy Smith)

Gipsy Smith was not overly interested in political or economic affairs, though he knew politicians and statesmen on both sides of the Atlantic, and for that matter in Australia and other countries. This prompted David Lloyd George's remark that if he were ever lost in the desert lands of western America or in the Australian bush—'where they have never heard of British politicians'—he would simply find his way to the nearest habitation and announce that he was a friend of Gipsy Smith. A somewhat mercurial individual, and a hard-working one, David Lloyd George welcomed Gipsy to his official home (10 Downing Street, Westminster, London) during his premiership. His familiarity with the fervour and power of the Welsh Nonconformist tradition must have become part of the dinner-table conversation:

He [Lloyd George] never made any secret of the fact that he believed with all his heart England needed a great spiritual revival, and asked me to tell him about some of the wonderful conversions I had seen. He talked with enthusiasm, of hymn singing—which he loved. (*The Beauty of Jesus*, Epworth Press, 1932)

But the prime minister would have found Gipsy unforthcoming on subjects outside of his own interests, for as Gipsy wrote in his 1932 recollection:

I am not a politician. I have never tried to shine in any political argument. It is not my sphere. I try to keep abreast of political affairs intelligently. In my work, I acknowledge no 'party, creed or faction'. If I can bring men to Christ, I can trust them to vote according to their conscience.

Here, then, we see why his sermons remained biblical and generally free of comment on current affairs, at least as far as political decision-making was concerned. But there must have been times when he was tempted to make one or two points in that direction. Awarded the MBE (Member of the British Empire) for his services to the nation during the First World War, which included his mission to the USA proposed by 'official circles', Gipsy liked to think that the royal family retained an interest in his work. It seems that they did, for King George V read a report about Gipsy's visit to Tulsa, Oklahoma, in the early months of 1934. At the beginning of the mission, Gipsy commended the showing of a large 'Stars and Stripes' flag on the platform, but wondered if a Union Jack flag might be shown also. His comment was in the nature of a genial comment, not a formal request, but before the meeting concluded, a beaming man rushed in with the British flag, and before the veteran evangelist knew what was happening, the flag was draped around his shoulders. At once, the congregation rose to sing, 'God Save The King', and then the American anthem, which used the same traditional melody, 'My Country 'Tis of Thee'. When the cheering subsided, and Gipsy could make himself heard, he said that he had always sought to create bonds of friendship between the two nations.

A message of greeting from King George V arrived at Binghampton some time after the Tulsa mission, and in good time for the opening of the mission at a local theatre, in this New York community. In the message, the monarch showed that he had read about the flag episode and had appreciated the sentiment. When all the exaggerations of press and public relations are allowed for, it might be said that Gipsy appreciated the burdens of kingship, and may well have preached on the issue. There were seemingly unending demands on one's time and energy, long journeys away from home to be made (and for which all the comforts in the world could make only modest recompense) and Gipsy knew well enough the stresses of being always in the public eye.

Missions at Elizabeth

Among the last great missions in the USA in the 1930s, that at Elizabeth, New Jersey in 1936 might be rated with that in Dallas, Texas 1934, as especially newsworthy. At Elizabeth, a chorus, 'Sixty Years of Service', was written as a tribute to Gipsy's long service as an evangelist, and performed by the choir, which numbered around four hundred, drawn from local churches (but also including some who had travelled from Britain to support the Gipsy's work on this memorable occasion). Using the word 'revival' in the American sense of 'lively evangelism', the newspapers gave Gipsy far more publicity than preachers in Britain, now or then, were ever likely to enjoy. True to type, the mission was arranged by the local Council of Churches, the ministers' association and the YMCA. Gipsy often tried to extend the bonds of inter-church co-operation and mutual regard through his missions, and probably regarded this aspect of his ministry as vitally important.

For five minutes, on every evening of the mission, all the churches in Elizabeth rang their bells, in order to remind local citizens that the meeting at the Armory, a large auditorium, would soon be beginning. Some flavour of the Gipsy's preaching in his mid-seventies is provided by the local press reports.

The *Elizabeth Daily Journal* reported that Gipsy said that he wants 'revived churches, stronger Christian sentiment and attitude in the homes . . . honesty and straightforward dealing with God and with man. He emphasized the point that church membership alone is not sufficient, saying that the primary need is for persons to be converted. Every time you drink, you help the devil (Gipsy told a women's rally of two thousand). But although Gipsy told his hearers that the greatest need of America was 'godly mothers' not fashion plates, he was only drawing moral judgments in an inspirational sense. At Elizabeth, as elsewhere in his last decade of active preaching, he urged his congregations not to be satisfied with a little Christianity, but to 'get all you can'.

The local press reported that Gipsy's lecture on his experiences during the First World War drew a capacity crowd. Like his testimony lecture on his early life, Gipsy knew that an attractive 'lecture theme' and title, could attract people who were not much interested in the formal religious meeting. In his lecture:

> Gipsy flayed the prudishness of the church and condemned the clergymen who believe that one cannot be a follower of God unless he (or she) has a Bible in one hand, and a 'hail Jehovah' on the lips. Gipsy said that one of the biggest things that most people could do for their church was to leave the church service, *smiling*.

The impact of the mission was remarkable, greater than anything seen in the missions held in Britain during that decade. Hundreds of decision cards were signed during the Elizabeth mission, and there is no doubt that churches throughout the community were encouraged and strengthened. Fifteen thousand copies of the *Gipsy Smith Hymn Book* were sold or given away during the two weeks of the event, and not a single copy of Gipsy's autobiography remained on the bookstall. The warmth of feeling towards the old evangelist was reflected in the basket of sixty roses presented to Gipsy on the sixtieth anniversary of his conversion. The choir, not wishing to be left out of the celebrations, presented Gipsy with a handsome umbrella to 'combat the rains of England'. The festive atmosphere was enhanced by the choir's singing of 'He is Mine', said to be 'Gipsy's favorite song'.

Some indication of the strengthening of the churches is shown by the words of a local minister, Dr S. N. Reeves,

> The coming of Gipsy Smith to Elizabeth is a distinct and clear challenge to the spirit of Christian unity in our midst. The call of Christ is heard now with commanding impressiveness, 'All ye are brethren'. Are we?

The opportunity is ours to demonstrate that we are, by the united way in which we give God's messenger the right of way in our lives during these fifteen days.

Given the vital importance of America's friendship, and support of Britain in the Second World War, (e.g., through Lend Lease) before the USA itself entered the conflict, Gipsy was unknowingly performing another great service to his nation as he forged links between believers in his own country and those in many cities across the States.

Missions in Britain

But Gipsy was eager to do what he could for churches in Britain, despite a generally unpromising spiritual climate. Family links with Hull were recalled when he held a mission at Queen's Hall, then the headquarters of the Hull Methodist Circuit. Mr William Branton, ARCO, organist at the Hall, for some twenty years, from 1933 to 1953, provides a good description of Gipsy in the mid 1930s:

> A rather stocky man, swarthy of appearance, with a full moustache, he preached for the conversion of souls and his audience approach was emotional. Looking rather like a prosperous business man, energetic and full of vitality, he quipped about the fact that he used to be 'in the timber trade'—selling clothes pegs!
>
> At one particular meeting, he stumbled up the platform stairs (the canvas being very worn in places) thus causing the trustees to carry out necessary repairs within the week. After the meeting had got under way, he pulled at my jacket—he was seated just beneath the organ console—and asked me if I would play for him when he sang. Of course I agreed—how could I do otherwise? In front of two thousand people he rubbed both my cheeks vigorously between his hands and whispered, 'Mind you play in tune, boy, it's for Him!'
>
> Gipsy's singing voice was in the tenor range, powerful and clear in tone, albeit the appeal was to the emotions. On this

225

occasion, he sang 'Wonderful Jesus'. To accompany him as he sang it, as only he could, and then to play it for a two thousand congregation was something I have never quite forgotten.

I recall that he altered the last line of the chorus the last time from 'in the heart' to 'in *thy* heart'. (personal letter to the present writer)

Long years before it became fashionable to describe some especially fervent believers as 'charismatic', Gipsy hammered home the message that a transformed life was the only evidence of true commitment. Yieldedness to the Holy Spirit was one of the dominant themes of Gipsy's preaching, as a former student of Cliff College, Gordon Wyllie (1934–5), records. He had been invited by Rev. J. A. Broadbelt, the College principal, to enjoy the weekend of the Cliff College Anniversary as a guest of the College:

I had tea with the Gipsy. In the evening, he preached with great power to the crowd on the lawn. I can remember how he held them as he cried, with the tears running down his cheeks, 'Don't you dare to thwart the Holy Spirit! If He is calling you, don't stand in His way.'

It was also in 1936—a busy year for the preacher—that Gipsy came to Leeds, to hold a mission at the Oxford Place Chapel, which enjoyed full congregations every Sunday. The Oxford Place mission was held at the suggestion of Rev. Dr Luke Wiseman who, as Home Missions Secretary of the Methodist Churches, had to create occasional opportunities for the Gipsy's work. There were almost certainly examples of churches who were invited to hold missions, but felt themselves unable to do so. But the effectiveness, and lack of formality, in the Gipsy's approach was undeniable. Of the 1936 event, Rev. J. T. Hodgson, MBE, TD, wrote (in a personal letter):

I met Gipsy Smith at the Central Station, Leeds. In five minutes, he was talking to the porter who was carrying his bag, inviting him to the special service that night. He was an ideal guest, and had a wonderful influence in the home, especially over our maid. She thought he was 'super'. Others will refer to his evangelism, but I speak of him as a welcome guest in the home. He held us spellbound as he talked about the birds of the forest and beauties of woodland, and the little animals of the forest.

Before going to sleep, he usually read *The Three Musketeers*, and delighted to talk about his reading.

Every night of the five day mission, the church was packed. The stewards estimated that about three thousand people came each night to hear him sing and speak. His messages were most challenging. His searching sermons were shot through with reason and emotion, and thousands of people registered the intention to dedicate their lives to Christ, and the work of His Church. All kinds of people attended these meetings, college professors, students from Headingly College and Leeds University, business men and young people sat side by side.

After an exhausting evening, he would return to our home, and immediately sit on a stool with his back to the fire. I asked him why he did this.

'Always after a meeting when I am hot, I find this habit an excellent thing to do,' he said. 'It prevents me getting a cold or any rheumatic pains.'

My wife and I count it a high privilege to have had the opportunity of acting as host when Gipsy Smith came to Leeds.

Sixty years an evangelist

Looking back, 1936 was a year in which Gipsy—and indeed those earnest believers looking for revival—might reflect on 'what God hath wrought', for in that year two other fine preachers, Rev. Dinsdale T. Young and Rev. Dr G. Campbell Morgan celebrated their diamond anniversaries. Only Gipsy, of the three, was to live into the post war era. Harold Murray, whose reporting of preachers and missions had enlivened the pages of various papers over the years, was commissioned to write books on all three men, and they appeared in 1937, from Marshall, Morgan and Scott's publishing house.

A celebratory meeting was arranged at Westminster, to rejoice in Gipsy's long years of service, and David Lloyd George was invited to say a few words, if only 'a *few* words' might be expected of this memorable orator. A beautiful silver model of a gipsy caravan, designed by the Gipsy's grandson, Rodney James Lean, and also serving as a biscuit barrel, was presented to the evangelist. The outcome of that event, and the 1937 publications from Harold Murray's pen, it could be argued, was a new bonding of the itinerant evangelist and the local church congregation. For Gipsy, evangelism in a local church was not some 'little bit extra', an option to be taken up now and then, but a reminder to Christians who they were, and what was their inheritance. Gipsy did not speak about lack of zeal, so much as lack of joy, in the churches.

His spiritual exuberance was well captured by Harold Murray in his book which was so well received that it had to be reprinted within a couple of months of publication. *Sixty Years An Evangelist—An Intimate Study of Gipsy Smith* is more a sketch book than a true biography. Its one hundred-and-forty pages are the work of a journalist, not a scholar, who served his friend (and later researchers) well by capturing Gipsy as he was in his seventy-sixth year. Gipsy's old friend from NCEFC days, Rev. J. E. Rattenbury, who was in 1936 President of the National Free Church Council, compared Gipsy's influence to that of John Wesley and General William Booth. Old friends were not in short supply in the later life of Gipsy, and his 1932 collection of 'memories and recollections' (*The Beauty of Jesus*) abounds with such references.

Perhaps the most interesting comment made by Harold Murray is that, as Gipsy grew older, he found memories of the old Gypsy days becoming clearer and sharper. He loved to talk about them, Harold Murray added, and Gipsy was ever ready to discuss the origins and traditions of his (Romany) people. Older people (and, in terms of personal experience, the present writer's mother) have spoken of the clarity of their childhood memories, coming through in later life: 'God gives back your memories in old age.' In speaking of his own early life, Gipsy undoubtedly helped older members of his congregations to reflect on their own life's journey, which in itself could lead to a new commitment to Christian purposes.

There is no doubt that Gipsy loved his own people, and their ancient traditions, but he was aware, as Harold Murray was, that times were changing. When Harold Murray accompanied Gipsy around Bideford Fair, in North Devon, in a mid 1930s visit, Gipsy was impressed with the range of facilities found in the new travelling caravans, used for the most part by showmen. Fitted with radio, electric lighting, fitted furniture and the like as they were, 'none of them were true gipsy wagons', according to Harold Murray's account. At Bideford as elsewhere at the time, there were 'gipsy fortune tellers', and at Blackpool, Harold Murray had even seen a palmist advertised as the 'Original Gipsy Smith'. It was hardly surprising that Gipsy found so few evidences of his people's traditions, for there had been a continuing departure from Britain of the old, true Romany clans, looking for better opportunities in the new world and elsewhere. And it had to be said that the government in Britain, not to mention ever expanding use of the car (now threatening to strangle many communities) had discouraged the old ways of life, as indeed had that bundle of mixed blessings usually identified as 'progress'.

Gipsy's wife, Annie, died, at the age of seventy-nine in the early spring of 1937, shortly after the original publication of *Sixty Years an Evangelist*. Gipsy was conducting missions in the USA when the news came, and there was no shortage of tributes to this gentle lady who had decided to 'look after the home', whilst Gipsy travelled on his missions. Harold Murray gently suggested some difference of opinion in regard to the 1930s mission, that is, after Gipsy had passed his seventieth birthday:

Annie was not anxious that her husband should go to America in later years, saying 'Old England is good enough for me'. But she never put any obstacle in the way when Gipsy felt he could not refuse a call (i.e. to conduct a mission) that came to him.

Indeed, Harold Murray, who knew Gipsy better than most, seems to think that Gipsy was an incorrigible traveller. Yet, with that sense of timing that Gipsy often seems to have possessed, it might have been that Gipsy saw that the new world would again have to come to the rescue of the old. For the USA was to send much aid to Britain even before Pearl Harbour brought it into the war in December 1941. Important too was the Marshall Plan which. in the late 1940s, brought aid to a devastated and hungry Europe, including Britain.

Mary Alice

Annie's death was bound to present major questions to Gipsy, and he solved them, in part at least, by marrying a lady considerably younger than himself, Mary Alice Shaw. A university graduate in English Literature, and only twenty-seven years of age, Mary Alice became Gipsy's second wife, in a church ceremony held in California on 2 July 1938. To describe the reports as 'controversial', as they arrived in the homes of ministers and church activists, might be a modest understatement, but looking back, from our times, when relationships take far more forms than ever was the case sixty years ago, we can see that Gipsy had little choice. He needed someone to look after him, and as Mary Alice was already supportive of his work as his secretary, and knew what was involved, marriage was a better arrangement than a merely informal relationship which would equally have invited criticism. Perhaps few people realized that Gipsy was following Romany tradition, for in patriarchal societies, it was not uncommon for widowed men, still active and able to serve, to take a 'new' younger wife. Indeed, this must have been common enough among the peoples of Old Testament times. There was of course a bond of affection between the ageing preacher and the young woman, but as Gipsy pointed out, 'there is no age in love'. Some critics no doubt suggested that Gipsy might have waited a little longer before marrying again, but it is hard to see how this would have improved matters. Gipsy and Annie (Pennock) had long years of affectionate, mutually supportive marriage, but as the Bible clearly shows, relationships on this planet are limited to this earthly order. In heaven, infinitely better ones are to be found.

As it was, Mary Alice was able to look after Gipsy for the last nine years or so of his life, and enabled him to continue his ministry, affected as it increasingly was by health problems. Harold Murray considered Mary Alice, 'a capable, highly educated and practical Christian'; she sang at some of the mission meetings, and helped Gipsy in secretarial and other chores. Dr Oswald Smith of the People's Church in Toronto, was no less certain that Gipsy's decision had been wise, for he considered Mary Alice, 'a great comfort to him during the later years of his life'. In relatively recent times, until her death in the 1980s, Mary Alice lived in London, and sometimes spoke and sang at meetings, recalling the 'old days'. She is remembered as a pleasant and helpful lady, able to carry on teaching the message that Gipsy had preached. So the 'story of the gipsy tent' endured into our own times.

Gipsy seems to have decided to spend most of his time in the USA, and on the suggestion of his son, Albany (who lived in the southern states of the USA), sold 'Romany Tan', the family house in Cambridge. It later became the home of a local businessman, but as recently as the late 1980s it was featured in the Cambridge press for its associations with the evangelist.

Had Gipsy been presented with more opportunities for evangelistic work in his home country during the 1930s he would surely have taken them, but economic depression and disillusionment following the end of the First World War (not to mention manpower losses in that conflict) had caused a malaise which affected many churches and communities. Some have suggested that Britain continued its grieving over the loss of so many fine young men, from 1919 well into the 1930s. The USA, which had suffered far less in that war, did not appreciate the extent of Britain's trauma, and Gipsy performed a great service in telling his audiences 'what it was really like'.

Unable to return to Britain, as he would probably have wished, Gipsy spent the years of the Second World War in the USA. Eighty years of age in March 1940, Gipsy kept in touch with his daughter Zillah (Mrs Zillah Lean) by correspondence, and related some of the missions in which he was involved. Some of these, held before the USA entered the war in December 1941, were held in churches in New York, Chicago, Los Angeles and Augusta. Then, as the USA mobilized, Gipsy talked to groups of servicemen, some of these meetings no doubt arranged by officers and chaplains who had worked with Gipsy in peace-time missions. There is reference to Gipsy relating the 'story of the gipsy tent', so that one has the impression that Gipsy's approach was more by way of personal testimony and recollection than formal preaching. At Marion, Ohio, in 1944, an air-raid practice and blackout was postponed, so that the Gipsy Smith meetings would not suffer by way of unnecessary distraction. Backed by some fifty ministers and their churches, the Marion mission was one of the last to be led by Gipsy. Diminution of energy and stamina necessitated longer periods of rest, as well as an acceptance of fewer invitations. Thus, proposed missions at Philadelphia and Massachusetts were cancelle, in order to permit more rest for the tired, but still hopeful warrior. In all these final labours, Gipsy was sustained and cared for by Mary Alice.

20
Coming home

I face a new spring
(Gipsy Smith)

Although thousands of miles from his old 'stamping grounds' in Britain, Gipsy managed to keep in touch with some of his old friends. One of his letters to his daughter, Zillah, mentions the death of Rev. Dr F. Luke Wiseman in 1944, who had been Gipsy's colleague in the missions arranged by Methodist Home Missions between the wars. Dr Wiseman was a talented man, a biographer of Charles Wesley, the hymn-writer, and one of the best musicians found in British churches this century. Yet, for all his scholarship, he might have easily been found helping some (seaside) beach mission, playing a portable harmonium for a group of youthful preachers, as discovered in some majestic pulpit. Gipsy's hearing of his old friend's passing prompted some comments in his letter: 'I begin to feel somehow the shadows of the night seem to be coming nearer. I have lived through the spring time, the rainbow hues of summer, the beauty and the glory, the satisfying golden harvests, the rigours of winter. I now face a new spring, the dawn which shall be eternal. I shall see them all—all who have gone before—and I shall see Him whom I have served and loved and tried to lift up and preach, the Sinner's Friend and Saviour and Lord . . . see Him face to face, and tell the story saved by grace.'

Return to Britain

The reasons for Gipsy's returning to Britain in 1945—now in his mid-eighties—have to be surmised rather than analysed. Given the heavy bombing of Britain and the near bankruptcy of its economy, Gipsy must have felt the nation needed a little help, even from so old a preacher. There was that 'homing instinct' too, reflected in his subsequent visit to his birthplace in Epping Forest, and which was reported in the 'utility issue' religious papers. Gipsy must have been deeply saddened by the bomb sites in London, many of which remained derelict for many years. These debris-strewn sites, some almost taken over by wild plants and weeds, remained mute memorials to the bombing which London, like other cities, had suffered, and although the British people were urged to maintain that stoicism—'Britain Can Take It'—which had helped secure the victory, the years immediately following the war were marked by emotional let-down. Far from securing evident fruits of victory, the 'dollar crisis' of 1947, and the bleak winter of that year, meant cut-backs in food, fuel and energy. For those who lived through the war, and that seemingly unending time of austerity (as the present writer did) which followed it, the period seems one which had little cause for rejoicing.

Yet there was a sense, as there had not been in 1919 and 1920, that the churches could make an impact even if they would need help from outside Britain (as it came, especially, in the shape of Billy Graham and his fellow crusade organizers). Within the churches in Britain, strategies like the Christian Commando Campaigns were being planned, with ideas that would have delighted Gipsy, though whether all free churchmen today would approve of a minister giving an impromptu testimony on top of a double-decker bus is another matter. Gipsy preached in London and also paid a visit to Hanley, where his roving ministry really began. People were truly surprised to see him—some had thought he had left Britain permanently, or had died! Some of his former friends, like Dr Wiseman, were no longer alive, and Gipsy must have realized that there was little for him to do, in terms of play-ing a part in the slow, and at times half-frozen, efforts to stir up the Christian cause in Britain.

Mary Alice and Gipsy lived in a small apartment in London, and here they were able to greet friends, including Dr Oswald

Smith of Toronto, who visited London in January 1947. Two years earlier, Gipsy had written an introduction to Dr Smith's book, *The Spirit at Work*; the two men had been friends for a long time. Indeed, Gipsy had stayed with Dr Smith's family, and had preached at the People's Church in Toronto. The old evangelist had been captured on colour 'home movies' whilst taking a rest at the Churchill Farm at Buffalo, possibly at Dr Smith's suggestion. It was strange indeed that Dr Smith decided to write an article about Gipsy in *The People's Magazine* (his church's publication) this appearing just after Gipsy's death in August 1947. Dr Smith heard the news just as the magazine was being published.

Someone at the BBC decided it would be a good idea to invite Gipsy into the studio to make a short (i.e. three-to-five-minute) devotional talk, and this final broadcast must have ben retained on disc, for it has been re-broadcast in more recent times. The essence of this brief yet evocative talk is to be found in his 1932 book, *The Beauty of Jesus*, in which (on pages 203-4) Gipsy recalls the prayer of an old West Countryman, a farmer, who in Gipsy's early ministry, prayed fervently, 'Keep him low, Lord! Keep thy young servant low. Keep him low!' In the broadcast, though not in the book, Gipsy adds the prophecy of the old fellow who saw that the young preacher would have an influential life's work, but that prayerful humility had to be at the heart of it. 'In the most exalted moments of my life, and before five kings and queens, I have heard that old man say, Keep him low.'

Gipsy's health began to falter, and he was taken into hospital, where he was visited by old friends, including Herbert Silverwood, now known as the 'Yorkshire Firebrand'. An ebullient, spiritual preacher, whose fund of good stories delighted crowds at Cliff College anniversaries, Herbert Silverwood had been converted through the ministry of a layman with the appropriate name of William Challenger. Thanks to a businessman, who heard Herbert preaching at an open-air meeting at Keswick in the mid-1920s, the young firebrand was despatched to Cliff College, in the days of 'Sam' Chadwick's supervision. Thereafter, and following Rev. Samuel Chadwick's death in 1932, Herbert kept the old flame of cheerful spirituality alive, and incidentally showed the potential to be found in working men, with few advantages of formal education.

Last journey

Gipsy and Mary Alice left London for Torquay, in search of better health in the 'English Riviera', but for all the benefits to be found in Devon (an area which he knew well) Gipsy did not make much headway and it was decided at last to return to the USA. There, he might find warm sunshine and specialist attention, plus plenty of good food. In late July 1947, an ambulance took him to Southampton, and the liner that would take him once more to the new world.

RMS 'Queen Mary'—one of the most famous liners to cross the Atlantic—was still in wartime livery on this first post-war run to the USA. She had served as a troopship during the war, but, given the dollar shortage and Britain's need to recapture some of its passenger traffic business, it had been decided to show as soon as possible that the 'Queen Mary' was around once more.

Mrs E. M. Miller, who was on board the ship, has written (to the present author): 'We were on deck and saw the ambulance draw up to the gangway, but we did not then know that the patient brought on board was Gipsy Smith.'

Gipsy and Mary Alice travelled in first-class accommodation and had the best of attention from the ship's medical personnel, but the great heart was failing.

Just after six o'clock on the morning of Tuesday 5th August [1947] many passengers were on deck, gazing up the Hudson River. It was a most beautiful morning.

The sun was not fully up and every boat as we went up the river blew their sirens or played their fire hoses. Planes flew low overhead. Then the word passed from one passenger to another that Gipsy Smith had died as we entered the Hudson. It was said that it was his wish to go back to America before the Lord took him, and I am sure that he had a good reception in Heaven. (Mrs E. M. Miller, personal communication)

The death of this influential preacher received only limited coverage in the press, and passing references on radio. But given the problems facing people in 1947, in Britain especially, with emergency cutbacks in food rations, and bad news from the world of finance and economics, there was much to report in newspapers running only four- or six-page editions (because of newsprint shortages and possible fuel cuts). In time, however, a more enduring memorial was proposed, which took the form of a rugged boulder of Cornish granite some four feet high placed at Mill Plain in Epping Forest, and close to Gipsy's birthplace. The Treasurer for the Memorial Fund, Colonel S. S. Mallinson CBE, DSO, MC, had a special interest in the undertaking, for his father had been Gipsy Smith's Sunday School teacher. Mary Alice dedicated the memorial stone at a ceremony held on Saturday 2 July 1949. Among speakers and old comrades present were Rev. E. Benson Perkins, President of the Methodist Conference that year, and Rev. Dr Walter O. Lewis of Missouri, the assistant secretary of the Baptist World Alliance. Gipsy would have been delighted at the presence of the Ilford Salvation Army Band and, among much else, there was a sense that a new spirit of mutual regard, long advocated by Gipsy, was growing. It was reminiscent of Gipsy's comment, 'what we need is to be so drenched by the love of God that it would cover everybody'.

The inscription on the stone, which bears the emblem of a horse-drawn gipsy caravan is:

> Gipsy Rodney Smith, MBE
> who preached the Gospel to thousands
> on five continents, for 70 years
> was born here March 31st 1860
> and called home, journeying to America
> August 4th 1947.
> WHAT HATH GOD WROUGHT.

Today, people from various parts of the world pass that way, some especially paying a kind of pilgrimage to the memorial stone. Although there were press reports of some kind of pagan ceremonial using the stone, during the 1980s, the block of Cornish granite does not of course have any powers of its own. In fact, knowing Gipsy's hesitations about publicity, he might have his reservations about its existence, being happier by far with the memorabilia, associated with his work, to be found at the Museum of Methodism at Wesley's Chapel in London.

Many enjoying the gentle environment, albeit sometimes disturbed by the noise of modern civilization, will be unaware of Gipsy's long service to God and his country. He seems to some a Victorian figure, so it comes as something of a surprise to discover that Gipsy Smith lived into the era of nuclear fission and television. Whilst it is perhaps a reckless task for anyone to suggest his influence on the evangelical scene—and preachers—in the second half of this century, some pointers deserve attention.

Gipsy avoided religious jargon and spoke of beauty rather than traditions. Since the essence of his preaching style did not change over the generations, we can derive a sense of consistency, though he did not often prepare his sermons as detailed manuscripts. But this spontaneity was based on wide reading, deep study and an awareness of the needs of congregations. Gipsy would never have approved of preachers who excuse lack of preparation, on the basis that the Holy Spirit will tell them what to say when they get into the pulpit. Gipsy was well prepared, and, as we have seen in his work with the YMCA during the First World War, he tailored his message carefully to his audience.

A clue to his approach to preaching is surely found in his youthful ambition to be a fairground 'billy' or 'barker' who, standing outside a side show or fairground attraction, urged those passing by 'to come in'. No enthusiasm has to be spared, the 'right words' have to be found, and there may be no supper for all involved if the potential audience is not convinced. Translating this into terms of evangelism, Gipsy became a kind of 'barker' for the churches. Even if no one with a bell or bugle stood outside the church, just before evensong or the six o'clock service, warmly inviting strangers to come in, there was a sense in which every church member was saying something to the world by his or her life, and the kind of community that the church seemed to be. One may find the great doctrines in Gipsy's preaching—sanctification especially—but he used the language of ordinary people, and did not give a great deal of weight to religious tradition. The fairground barker or billy does not talk of the great roles and arrangements of distant forebears, but declares what is on offer now.

It hardly needs saying that Gipsy's evocative description of the natural scene, the birds, wild animals, trees and flowers which he knew so well, attracted many and gave a 'breath of fresh air' to the sermon. He appealed to the imagination, as well as to the heart. True, some thought Gipsy an emotional preacher, but there was never any suggestion that he was 'boring'.

Gipsy saw beyond denominational loyalties to a universal kinship in Christ.

Gipsy Smith's perception that brotherly love was the key to successful (church based) evangelism was remarkable, seeing that he was so young a man when he came to that conviction. Some of us struggle our way to that enlightenment only in old age; worse, some assume that in heaven, there are special front seats for members of this or that specially enlightened group or persuasion. Because the Second World War represented such a watershed in the experience of those alive at the time, Gipsy was all but forgotten as part of a vanished peacetime world. Certainly, the opportunities facing Gipsy Smith in the 1930s, in Britain especially, were fewer than he would have wished. But he kept the torch of mission evangelism burning at a time when too many would have reached for the fire extinguisher. His missions at the Albert Hall, Kingsway Hall and other meeting places, prepared the way for the post-war missions conducted by other evangelists. The more one looks at Gipsy's work, the more one sees how well he prepared the way for the young Billy Graham. For Dr Graham too looked to inter-church support, for co-operation of churches in evangelism which Gipsy had supported some forty or fifty years earlier. Gipsy would have known about the at times competing arguments of Calvinists, Arminians and the like, the diverse ideas on ecclesiastical arrangements, but he was ready to work with anyone committed to evangelism. He also pioneered inter-racial missions. During one of his missions, in a racially divided community, Gipsy Smith was asked if Christians would be 'black' or 'white' when they got to heaven. 'I can't tell you that', said Gipsy. 'But I *can* tell you that we will be like Him!' Change 'black' to 'white' to denominational descriptions, or even to other labels like 'charismatic', 'traditionalist' and the like, and you will get the point.

Gipsy was approachable and went out of his way to talk to people.
This may well have been one of the most important aspects of his ministry, and today, when Christians rush by breathing, 'haven't got time to stop', we might take a leaf out of his book. Many people today feel that they are on a sort of treadmill, and that what used to be called 'fellowship' has to be 'market tested'; we are not so much 'ships that pass in the night', as 'saints that whiz by on the pavement or sidewalk'. Yet, the kindly word spoken on the street may do as much good in God's grace as finely polished sermons, honed by many hours' (aloof) work in the study. A characteristic illustration from Gipsy's life serves to illustrate the point:

> I know a woman who said to me once, 'My husband used to know the Gipsy, but hadn't seen him for twenty years and hadn't been to church anywhere. He came to the chapel, and almost as soon as Gipsy came into the pulpit, he (Gipsy) spotted my husband and called out, 'Hello, Bill, I'm pleased to see you.'
>
> The people all laughed, but my Bill said, 'Well, can you beat that? *That's* what I call Real Religion.'
>
> He was one of the first that day to go to the front and be converted.

Rev. Derrick Greaves, a former superintendent minister of the Central Hall in Westminster, recalled some personal memories of Gipsy for *Nornues*, the magazine of the North Avenue Methodist Church, Letchworth, in November 1984.

The last time I saw Gipsy was in the large branch of Boots Cash Chemists in Cambridge. I looked across to the medicine counter and saw three white-coated dispensers (pharmacists), spellbound and oblivious to their duties or waiting customers.

They were listening with total concentration, as though they could do nothing else, to a shortish man in a top coat, who was addressing them. It was the Gipsy, magnetic as always. Was he intriguing them with an account of some Romany herbal remedy learned in the Epping Forest woods? Or was he giving a testimony? One thing is sure. There would be some reference to Jesus—the first and last theme of his life.

Gipsy was a charismatic preacher who looked for deep religious experience.
Rev. Derrick Greeves spoke at the Jubilee Reunion at the North Avenue Methodist Church, Letchworth church in November 1984 as did Mrs Kathryn Crouch, who had known Gipsy during her residence at Cherry Hinton, Cambridge, the community in which the evangelist made his home for so many years. Descriptions of Gipsy are surprisingly diverse, even accounting for changes brought about by maturity and advancing years. Some have described Gipsy as 'big', others as 'small', and no doubt a psychologist might say that perception was shaped by the impact of the message. Gipsy was certainly a charismatic preacher with 'presence'.

Rev. Derrick Greaves was only ten years old when he first heard the Gipsy:

I had heard of his power with a crowd. But that power was due to a personal magnetism which made its impact on an individual just as much as on a crowd.

My father came home from one of the Gipsy's meeting, having sat near him on the platform, and told the family about Gipsy's skill as a preacher, and how gracefully he moved as he spoke—like a dancer, my father said, with his shoulders back, gliding and shifting his weight from one leg to another.

So it was with excitement one evening that my sister and I

were told to stay awake, because the Gipsy would be coming to our house after the rally at Bolton Central Hall. Fortunately, we did not then know what he had said to my father, 'Give me a child for a quarter of an hour, and I'll tell you what sort of parents he has!'

All our nervousness disappeared when he came round our bedroom door. Imagine a not very tall, but broad-shouldered man with a swarthy, almost Indian complexion, a shining skin and glistening black hair, and with a military waxed moustache, and fragrant with scent (a gipsy characteristic). His prominent, penetrating brown eyes held your attention, but they were full of love. They were like tiger's eye stones.

He sat on our bed and quietly talked—what about I cannot recall—but I remember clearly his gentle, deep-toned, slightly mesmeric voice. We had no hesitation in handing him our autograph album; what he wrote has been a challenge ever since: 'Gipsy Smith—Saved to Serve'.

Let no-one think that his evangelism was just a matter of oratorical technique, with emotional pressure on the listener. For one thing, like Billy Graham, he would never visit a town unless there was a period of thorough preparation and a determination to follow up results. Emotion there was, but it was all very controlled and intellectually rational.

Gipsy would not have preached the kind of message sometimes sensed in affluent times—that 'a good religion' is a useful prop to sustain self-confidence, family life, prosperity. This would have amounted to a sort of idolatry with a religious veneer. As for the 'prosperity gospel', which at its most blatant seems to suggest that material possessions represent a sign of God's favour, Gipsy would have pointed to the relative poverty of his own early life, and the disadvantages of his father and uncles, yet who, as 'the three converted brothers' did a great work for the gospel. Of course, he did not preach 'social Calvinism' which may have accounted for so much drift from the churches in the nineteenth century: if a man was poor that was what God had meant him to be. It was this attitude that prevented the established Church especially, in the first half of the century. from supporting the new self-help movements which had a new sense of grassroots morality (nevertheless based on Christian revelation).

As the Pentecostal movement of the early twentieth century found expression in new denominations, Elim and the Assemblies of God especially, the churches as a whole needed a reminder of the message that the Pentecostalists preached—that Christian living is not merely an ethical stance but a new life empowered by the Holy Spirit. Gipsy was a kind of bridge between the traditionalists and the Pentecostalists. He did not seek to prioritize spiritual gifts and he would never had become involved in arguments about the necessity of 'speaking in tongues'. As Rev. Derrick Greeves put it, more than ten years ago, 'The main impression I retain of his speaking is of a man who was desperately and lovingly serious in telling us that there is a Saviour, an effective, living Saviour, whose precious name is Jesus.'

In the years since Gipsy Smith's passing, there has been a steadily growing interest in environmental matters and the ways in which men and women (and children) need to feel a kinship with creation if they are to be whole or happy individuals. We truly live in a marvellous world, if a fallen one, although greed and materialism seem destined to curtail the variety of species and inevitably our own stay on this planet. As this manuscript is being prepared, there is continuing argument about local authority provision of suitable sites for Gypsies—an issue which has been debated for years now. Whatever our feelings about the kind of encampments shown on television news programmes, and in which so-called 'New Age travellers' seem to be a target, we have to take care lest we oppose the biblical teaching about caring for the 'stranger in our gates'.

There is also a growing interest too in the old Romany lifestyle and traditions, so often described graphically by the Gipsy and outlined in his 1901 autobiography. During the spring of 1987, the best known portrait of Gipsy Smith, that by A. J. Nowell, RA which was completed towards the close of Gipsy's life, was hung in the Radnor Hall at Wesley's Chapel in London. It was a reproduction of this portrait which was used for the cover of the Order of Service at the dedication of the memorial stone in Epping Forest in 1949. In 1987, too, *The Cambridge Evening News* published two 'Looking Back' features, recalling Gipsy's links with the university city. Recollections included those from the former garden boy at Gipsy's home, whilst a local hairdresser remembered Gipsy's 'dignified bearing and quiet suave manner'. An eighty-eight year old Salvation Army officer reported, 'a tremendous power in his message that I have never seen equalled'.

References to Gipsy's singing, and phonograph (gramophone) records were included, the highlight of the material being Pauline Hunt's interview, on behalf of the newspaper, with Zillah (Mrs Zillah Palfreman) the Gipsy's grand-daughter.

There were other evangelists during this century, and closer to our own time, men like Tom Rees and Tom Allan (of the 'Tell Scotland' campaign) who were contemporaries of Gipsy Smith, though of course considerably younger. With a new interest in evangelism proclaimed by the churches at the beginning of the 1990s, although sometimes with little of the precision that Gipsy would have wanted, we can gain from reflection on those who grappled with such issues as industrialization and the mass media. Gipsy Smith is an outstanding example of a man who started with no privileges, and who responded to people 'where they were'. I think today he would invite us to leave the lecture hall, the study, even the well furnished church or chapel, and come with him to the forest. As we stand there, beneath the bright green canopy, Gipsy would raise a finger to his lips. 'Listen . . .'

Appendix A

The contemporary revival
among Gypsies

The voice of Gipsy Smith—the subject of this book—was heard by listeners to the BBC Radio 2 programme, 'Silent Revival', on 26 November 1996. A BBC recording of Gipsy had been used in an earlier BBC Radio series, presented by Dr Colin Morris, 'Glory Days', which especially focused on the lively traditions of nonconformity. Given that the BBC's Religious Programming Department is now based in Manchester—a city in which Gipsy Smith served with Rev. Samuel Francis Collier, at the City Mission—there was a certain geographical resonance to this interesting programme. More recently, the fifty-minute 'Silent Revival' programme was aptly described, for the conversion and renewal of Romany people across Europe—and indeed across the world—has gone almost unnoticed by the wider Christian community in Britain. Gipsy Smith would surely see many parallels to his own day, for example, the link to adult literacy initiatives (as Romany people, hitherto unable to read, now seek to study the Bible). Similarly, the seeking of Christian marriage services, to supersede the traditional betrothal arrangements, well known in Gipsy's day, is now seen in our own.

The revival among the Romany people in Europe seems to have been begun in the 1950s, notably in France, then moving south into Spain, the ancient Romany tongue crossing conventional linguistic barriers. France has long had its Romany population, and Gypsies have had a significant role in the musical and artistic community of that country. Through family and kinship networks, the converted Romany in France is in a position to influence many others—as in Gipsy's earlier years—as clan heads or patriarchs gather their families to hear their testimony. Pastor le Cossec has been especially associated with the ministry to the Romany people in France, the work calling for the kind of mobility and flexibility —in physical presence and mental attitude—that does not always come easily to well-established churches. It may be exaggeration to speak of a 'Romany church' or a readily identifiable Gypsy denomination, but the revival movement has clearly brought out leaders and pastors from the encampments, calling for input from Bible colleges and other Christian organisations able to train future teachers and pastors in this area of work.

In Britain, the revival, if so it may be described, has developed from the 1970s, and whatever else may be said of (or for) the charismatic movement, the sense of openness (to spiritual experience and the blessings of the gospel) has helped the cause. A ministry attractive to the Romany clans calls for its own style and emphasis. For example, the patriarchal traditions within some Romany clans are so strong that any evidence of women in church leadership would seem a major affront. Whether or not women should keep silent in all churches, in all generations, is a contentious issue, but were the Apostle Paul here today he would probably advise us that our own considerations, either way, should not be a stumbling-block to others hearing and thereby accepting the gospel. The attitude within the Romany community may vary, not least as matriarchs no less than patriarchs are found. The 'wise woman', handing on the family traditions and deserving of respect, is a model which might at times by recommended within 'gorgio' (mainstream) society.

Further, when a patriarch, however dominant, receives Christ, he is quickly advised by his kith and kin, that he must now love his wife, even as Christ loves his Church. Paul's counsel to the church at Corinth—which seems to have been a mobile community in a get-rich-quick society—is double edged. It is not about male assertion in leadership so much as directed to the local community of Christians acting as a Christ-centred (extended) family.

Among worship networks meeting the needs of Romany people in Britain, the *Light and Life* churches are best known, there being at the time of writing (late 1996) some sixteen of these congregations or assemblies. Tom Wilson, one of the leaders of this movement, broadcast in the late 1996 BBC radio programme, 'Silent Revival'. It is suggested that of the around fifty thousand Romany folk in Britain and Ireland, a fifth are converted (this figure may be out of date by the time this book is published, though there is at least some sense that the revival period is coming to its close). Further, this figure may be under-estimated.* According to the criteria used, there may be as many as one hundred thousand or more, who could be identified as of true Romany (Romani) stock and

---

* Local authority estimates (1995) were that over 10,000 Gypsy families lived in England and Wales, but that there were only 6,200 'pitches' on legal, officially recognised sites, half of this total owned by Gypsies themselves. The survey was described as a 'massive undercount' of the Gypsy population.

lineage. As in Gipsy Smith's day, conversion has often brought challenges to one's way of life, and the earning of a living. Fortune-telling, for example, was often attacked by Gipsy, as exploiting the gullibility of people who ought to know better, and could not be followed by anyone calling himself (or herself) a Christian. Our own age is at least as superstitious as that of Victorian Britain, as a Church of England report, *Search for Faith and Witness of the Church*, reminded its readers in late 1996. *The Times* (11 November 1996) aptly produced a headline, 'Faith in horoscopes is a sign of moral decay, say churches'. True, but for the Gypsy woman who has made a living, or contributed a major portion to family income, by telling fortunes the challenge is more than merely an academic one. Christians and congregations who 'see no harm' in horoscopes are thus observed as watering down the teaching of Scripture, as far as converted Gypsies are concerned.

Post-modernism, and what is sometimes termed a post-Christian society, were little discussed until a decade or so ago. Christian witness has to be effected not merely within a secular society, one of many faiths and no few cults, but also in relation to a view of the world which seemingly has no 'laws', natural or theological. Thus, the Romany preacher of the contemporary world may—like Gipsy Smith—more ably speak to the broader Christian community, in a way close to the itinerants of the apostolic church or later times of revival. He (or she) may be especially able to speak of the conversion experience.

There is a sense of moving into light from gloom, where secular experience tends to think ideas of revelation and conversion 'out of date', even without meaning. A Romany preacher armed with such a testimony might well disturb some in spiritually self-contained assemblies.

Many travellers today are not Gypsies, though they may be described so by aggrieved householders troubled by the sudden arrival of a convoy of motor caravans and coaches. Some of these wanderers cannot cope with the kind of society that we are creating; similar attitudes in an industrialising nineteenth century saw an explosion of community living, especially in the USA, but land was more plentiful then, and it was possible to find a place to rest. The pressures of urbanizing life, as well as stricter legislation affecting trespass, make it increasingly difficult for Romany people to follow their old ways of life. They are moving into residential camp sites, where these are available, or buying houses. In the process, though, they are able to establish chapels or churches, or worship groups. One analogy might be to compare them to the Railway Missions of the last century or so, in which travelling workers came together, though their employment on the railways (railroads) and creating their own centres of worship (like the prefabricated iron chapel then available).

This departure from an itinerant lifestyle may help meet some of the problems of educating the children within travelling families, an issue close to Gipsy's heart, and focus of the research of George Smith of Coalville, Leicestershire,who also worked with canal boat families. *The Education of Travelling Children*, published by the Office for Standards in Education (OFSTED), c/o Publications Centre, PO Box 6927, London E3 3NZ is a recent survey of the task facing educators working within travelling communities. Gypsies—the largest grouping within these communities—were recognized as a minority ethnic group within the remit of the 1976 Race Relations Act. But the problems of educating travellers' children had been considered some years earlier, not least by the Plowden Report of 1967. Lady Plowden DBE was invited to become president of ACERT (Advisory Council for the Education of Romany and Other Travellers) which published a useful policy document in October 1995, available from ACERT, Moot House, The Stow, Harlow, Essex CM20 2AG. On a wider, European basis, EFECOT (European Federation for the Education of Children of Occupation Travellers) is a federation of national groups working in this area (Address EFECOT, rue Guimard 17, B-1040, Brussels, Belgium). A useful A4 booklet, *Roma/Gypsies — A European Minority* is available at £5.40 including postage (UK) from the Minority Rights Group, 379 Brixton Road, London SW9 7DE. Especially useful is the well detailed booklet, compiled by David Cannon, *Contacts, Publications and Other Resources for work with Adult Travellers*, from STEP (Traveller Education Project, 2 Davey Street, London SE15 6LF). Details of specific local or county based work is provided, together with details of literature, organisations, universities, etc.

Universities are involved in this area of work, as they are in recording oral history and other folk traditions. A pioneer in this field was Dr John Sampson, librarian at the University of Liverpool between 1892 and 1928, who was a fluent speaker of the Romany tongue. Dr Sampson was especially interested in the Gypsy clans of Wales, and shared this interest with one of his colleagues, Dr Dora Yates, whose fine book, *My Gipsy Days*, recalls some of their experiences. Among recent and well informed publications, *The Gypsy and the State* by Derek Hawes and Barbara Perez, includes discussion of research in Avon, and the broad implications of legislation and official policy (Policy Press, University of Bristol, Rodney Lodge, Grange Road, Bristol BS8 4EA). *On The Verge:*

The Gipsies of England by Donald Kenrick and Sian Bakewell was originally published by the Runnymede Trust to aid local councillors, educational and social workers *et al*. Following the passage of the Criminal Justice and Public Order Acts of 1994, local authorities are no longer required to provide permanent caravan sites for Gypsies. Other problems arising from the legislation are also examined in this useful A5 paperback (University of Hertfordshire Press, College Lane, Hatfield, Herts AL10 9AB).

The University of Greenwich specializes in Romani Studies—the relevant department assisting in the compilation of this chapter—and has links with the Centre for Gypsy Research at the University of Paris V. The estimated population of Romany people in Western Europe is some two million, with between six and seven million in Eastern Europe. Details of the University of Greenwich's work can be obtained from Dr T. A. Acton, Reader in Romani Studies, Bronte Hall, Avery Hill Road, London SE9 2HB. A book list can also be requested.

Active in Romani evangelism in Europe are Sonnie Gibbard and his wife. They have a ministry (a registered charity) called 'Gypsies for Christ', which is based at 32 Ashford Road, South Woodford, London E18 1JZ. Sonnie's own life story will be told in another book one day, I am sure, for he shows a lively perception of the problems and possibilities. At the beginning of the Decade of Evangelism, Sonnie and Rosemary purchased a trailer which they called 'the Romani Gospel Waggon' in recollection of Gipsy Smith's vardo (caravan). In 1995, they visited Belarus, and in 1996, Romania and Slovakia, working with locally based churches and/or helping to found them among Gypsy communities. Sonnie and Rosemary have that practical approach to work among the Romany people which has long been most effective, since the days of Rev. James Crabbe's work in Southampton in the early nineteenth century.

Literature in the Romany tongue is of course a major concern. In 1994, Sonnie and Rosemary worked with the Scripture Gift Mission to produce a booklet, in English and Romany, called *The Drom* ('The Way') which relates the story of the Prodigal Son and provides a clear gospel message. 'Byways—The Romani Prayer Bulletin' (linked to the Gibbards' work) is available from 'Byways', 15 Hamilton House, Amherst Road, Tunbridge Wells, Kent TN4 9LQ and gives up-to-date information on the Gypsy evangelism scene. Launched in the winter of 1996–7, the Bulletin also refers to the work of Christian broadcasters, using appropriate dialect/language for broadcasts to Gypsy populations in Eastern Europe and elsewhere. Let there be no doubt that the Romany people will have much to teach urban, sophisticated Christians (and others) also in their revived community and family life. That might remind us of some of the comments made by Gipsy Smith of his own origins, when speaking to the churches of his time.

Others working in this field include the Co-operative Baptist Fellowship, which is working on the translation and production of Bibles and other books in the Romany tongue, primarily for work in Europe. At another level of interest, museums and craft centres are recalling the old Romany traditions, in relation to an alas vanishing countryside. The Wheelwrights and Romany Museum at Webbington, Loxton, near Ambridge in Somerset, BS26 2HX is one centre, though some visitors will have reservations about the fortune-telling facility. In conclusion, one could not omit reference to the Romany Society, recently launched to commemorate the fine work of Rev. G. Bramwell Evens—Gipsy Smith's nephew—whose broadcasts on 'Children's Hour' (1933–43) delighted many, including grown-ups. 'Romany's grandson, Rev. Roly Bain, an Anglican minister, is an accredited and trained clown, who uses comedy, mime and story to convey the gospel. His book *Fools Rush In*, was published by Marshall Pickering in 1993, and is recommended. The Romany Society, supported by the Macclesfield Borough Council, can be contacted via John Thorpe, its secretary, 46 Andrew Street, Bury BL9 7HB. For those wishing to undertake more detailed research into Romany traditions, an occasional catalogue of out of print books is published by Jennifer Boyd Cropley, Cottage Books, Gelsmoor, Coleorton, Leicestershire LE67 8HQ. My own booklets on *Preachers and Gipsies* and *Gipsy Smith Souvenir* may also help researchers.

For further reading
and book hunting

As virtually all books by or about Gipsy Smith (and Romany) are out of print, one often sees requests or advertisements for them in the book collecting magazines. Second-hand booksellers can often list wants in the weekly *Bookdealer* magazine, which is certainly a good way of tracking down out of print books. *New Christian Herald* also publishes a 'Give and Take' column whereby readers may request or offer books, usually for the cost of postage or a modest gift. Apart from these approaches, reading the Methodist (or other) catalogues issues by Gage Postal Books (PO Box 105, Westcliff on Sea, Essex SSO 9EQ) is recommended. Laurie Gage, who died recently (1994) was a lifelong Methodist, who became a bookseller, specializing in out of print books across all the denominations. Simon Routh has taken on the business, and the catalogues list hundreds of books at modest prices.

A little more scholarly, but worth seeing is the catalogue of Gypsy Books issued a few times a year by Cottage Books, Gelsmoor, Coleorton, Leics. LE6 4HQ, and which gives details of a really amazing number of long out of print titles on this area.

As a guide to the main sources of information, the following list is offered, though the compiler has not seen all these titles for himself.

▲ Books by Gipsy Smith ▲

A MISSION OF PEACE: The South African Tour of 1904 (NCEFC, with green tint photographs, including some of Gipsy, his wife and daughter).

AS JESUS PASSED BY (sermons, published 1905 by NCEFC) A neatly produced book of which some of the contents seem to have been reprinted by Christian papers for some years afterwards.

EVANGELISTIC TALKS (1922, Hodder and Stoughton; in the USA, published by George H. Doran)

GIPSY SMITH, HIS LIFE AND WORK (National Council of Evangelical Free Churches, hereafter shown as NCEFC, 1901, published in the USA by Fleming H. Revell). Several editions in different colour boards were published until about the 1920s, and include photographs of Gipsy and members of his family. The book was updated from its first edition from time to time but not to any great extent.

Note: A paperback reprint was issued in 1995 by ambassador Productions, Belfast, though without the illustrations of the original 1901 edition.

GIPSY SMITH'S FAVOURITE SOLOS (and)

NEW SOLOS BY GIPSY SMITH

Slim, green cloth bound collections of the famous songs, in print from around 1905 to the 1920s.

HINTS TO NEW CONVERTS (NCEFC, a neat little item, described as 'an attractive souvenir booklet of friendly counsels that should be placed in the hands of every new convert'. In its twelve pages, it offers wise advice, and the cover has a photograph of Gipsy in sepia on cream paper—this suggests that the booklet was in use over some years, as the picture in my copy indicates a middle-aged preacher).

REAL RELIGION (1922, Hodder and Stoughton; in the USA published by George H. Doran).

THE BEAUTY OF JESUS: Memories and Reflections (1932, Epworth Press, red cloth boards and a most readable book, full of good stories, from the Gipsy; one is bound to regret that he did not write a sequel later in the 1930s).

THE GIPSY SMITH BIRTHDAY BOOK (not seen by this writer, but apparently a collection of Gipsy's comments and advice; NCEFC, circa 1901/2)

YOUR BOYS (Gipsy's narrative of his wartime experiences in France, published by Hodder and Stoughton, circa 1918, some of this material being also in his 1932 title, *THE BEAUTY OF JESUS*). The sixpenny paperback of Gipsy's wartime work with the YMCA was published by Hodder and Stoughton.

▲ Other sources ▲

BRITISH POSTCARD COLLECTORS MAGAZINE (Issue 49, Winter 1993) included an illustrated article, 'Remember Romany' linked to a new full colour postcard of Romany's 'vardo' (caravan) at Wilmslow. The magazine, £1.25 plus postage, is available from Ron Griffiths, 47 Long Arrotts, Hemel Hempstead, Herts HP1 3EX.

CAMBRIDGE EVENING NEWS (April 30th 1987). Pauline Hunt's 'Looking Back' feature is based on Gipsy Smith's residence, and work, including a good photograph and contributions from those who knew him.

FAMILY TREE MAGAZINE (monthly) carries articles on gipsy themes from time to time, see for example February 1992 issue. Whenever I write on gipsy topics, I am usually engulfed by letters asking for more information on gipsy origins etc.

FOR THE GLORY OF GOD: The Story of North Avenue Methodist Church, Letchworth, and Gipsy Smikth's associations with the ministry. The late Keith Sell's excellent research now published as a paperback, details from Peter Cannell, 3 Cashio Lane, Letchworth, Herts 5GG 1AY.

FROM THE FOREST I CAME by David Lazell (Concordia 1970, Moody Press USA, 1972). Based on the 1901 autobiography (above) as well as various personal memories and other material sent to the present writer, this paperback soon went out of print. It did not do a great deal to set Gipsy into any kind of context, and bears almost no similarity, apart from some personal memories, to this present title. But it had some interesting photographs, and those new to Gipsy's work would find it a useful acquisition.

GIPSY SMITH by H. M. (sixpenny booklet, printed 1925 to 1933, and probably given away more often than actually sold).

GIPSY SMITH SOUVENIR 1989 (homespun paperback, giving details of books etc. about Gipsy, designed to send out to people who wrote to the author for information on titles, etc. The 300 plus print run has long since gone, and the present writer, who gave copies away, has been interested to see a copy on sale recently for more than a few pounds.)

GOODNIGHT CHILDREN EVERYWHERE (Midas Books, 1983, out of print) by Ian Hartley, covers aspects of children's broadcasting, including 'Romany's work for 'Children's Hour' broadcast from Manchester. In some ways even more useful for material on 'Romany' is the same author's paperback about the origins of broadcasting in Manchester, i.e., the Northern Region of the BBC, 'From 2ZY to NBH' (the initials stand for New Broadcasting House, 2ZY was the original call sign of the Manchester station). Ian, who lives in Wythenshawe, Manchester, is a keen and knowledgeable radio historian and has been campaigning for a radio museum and historical research centre in Manchester.

HERBERT SILVERWOOD. The Yorkshire Firebrand (Foundation Publications 1972). By the present writer, and published by Vic Ramsey, this neat paperback was based on interviews with Herbert, who was then living just outside Bristol. Long since out of print, the remaining modest stock disappeared rapidly after Herbert's death in the early 1980s. Given his long work in lay evangelism, and his friendships with Gipsy Smith, 'Sam' Chadwick and other leading evangelists of the inter-war period, the book has much useful material not found elsewhere.

ONE THING I KNOW by A. J. Russell (Hodder and Stoughton, 1933). A very readable book, and something of a best seller in its day, this easily recognizable title (orange cloth boards) includes a long chapter on Gipsy, in relation to the author's interest in Guidance, an issue much in public focus at the time.

PREACHERS ONLY by Harol Murray (privately published), no date, probably late 1920s / early 1930s).

RESS, PULPIT AND PEW by Harold Murray (Marshall Morgan and Scott 1936, one of HMs many recollections, always well worth reading).

ROMANY RETURNS by Guy Loveridge. Foreword by Romany Watt and Terry Waite. 1995 tribute including biography, stories etc. (Douglas Loveridge Publications 1995, details from 124 Lower gate, Paddock, Huddersfield HD3 4EP)

SIXTY YEARS AN EVANGELIST: AN INTIMATE STUDY OF GIPSY SMITH by Harold Murray (Marshall Morgan and Scott 1937).

STORIES OF GREAT REVIVALS by Henry Johnson (Religious Tract Society, 1906). This was published in connection with the 1904–05 Revival in South Wales, though also with material on work of Gipsy Smith, who wrote the preface to the book.

Some good work on the revival period of 1904–06 and its aftermath has been done in recent years, and useful titles are in print. Rev. Brynmor Pierce Jones, of Pontypool has been especially diligent in this field, and his book, **THE KING'S CHAMPIONS**—*Revival and Reaction 1905–1935* looks at the revival and its aftermath. Though it does not go into the ministry of Gipsy Smith, this substantial work (a paperback) offers a clear idea of the tasks that revival set the church, a timely reminder! Privately published by the author.

THE BEST I REMEMBER by Arthur Porritt (the author was editor of *The Christian World*, a well known paper in its day, and this 1922 title from Cassell well captures the personalities and preachers of the preceding twenty or thirty years).

THE FLAME (January / February 1988 issue) has an article on Gipsy Smith, and *BAPTIST TIMES* (27th February 1992) includes an article on Evan Roberts, the preacher of the Welsh Revival. On Evan Roberts, the 1906 book by Rev. D. M. Phillips is a collectors' item now, and rarely seen, but a new study of the young Welsh revivalist by Brynmor Pierce Jones was published in 1995. (*An Instrument of*

Revival—The Complete Life of Evan Roberts, 1878–1951, Bridge Publishing, South Plainfield, NJ.)

THE FREE CHURCH CHRONICLE (Autumn 1995) has a useful article on Rev. Thomas Law and his work for NCEFC missions.

Free Church Year Books from the mid 1890s to mid 1900s are worth finding, as they usually detail activities of the NCEFC staff evangelists, etc.

THE WHITE LIFE—*not* by Gipsy Smith, but his fellow worker in NCEFC work, Rev. J. Tolfree Parr.

THROUGH THE YEARS WITH ROMANY by Eunice Evens (University of London Press, 1946) is a well-detailed and interesting biography of Rev. G. Bramwell Evens, whose mother, Tilly, was Gipsy's sister. There are references to Gipsy, as well as a good photograph of the two men. One is bound to think that the book would be worth reprinting.

WHAT'S ON THE WIRELESS by David Lazell (Evergreen Books, PO Box 52, Cheltenham, Glos GL50 1YQ) is a neat, illustrated book about the early days of radio. There is an interesting chapter on Gypsy Broadcasters (including Romany and Gipsy Petulengro) but a better article on Romany with plenty of pictures, from the same address, is found in *The Storytellers,* published in 1991. The chapter is based on an article that originally appeared in *This England,* and the book's dust wrapper has a find original full colour portrait of Romany by Colin Carr.

Gipsy's links with the Cliff College of Evangelism were well known to students and supporters, though somewhat surprisingly, Gipsy was omitted from the series of excellent booklets issued to celebrate the centenary of *Joyful News* in 1983. The three eminently useful booklets were on Thomas Champness (by Thomas Meadley), Thomas Cook (by A. Skevington Wood) and Samuel Chadwick (by David H. Howarth). Norman Dunning's 1933 biography of Samuel Chadwick (Hodder and Stoughton) is a substantial hardcover, but not often seen these days. The three titles were published on behalf of Cliff by Moorley's Bookshop Ltd., 23 Park Road, Ilkeston, Derbyshire DE7 5DA.

Two other titles must be mentioned—**COLLIER OF MANCHESTER** by George Jackson (Hodder and Stoughton, 1922) is an affectionate portrait of a truly great man, and who was surely an inspiration to the young Gipsy Smith. **BRISTOL FASHION,** the autobiographical title by Hugh Redwood in 1947 (Latimer House) offered a perspective on the spiritual state of the nation, and was of course published in the year of Gipsy's death. Hugh Redwood's many books on urban evangelism, and the harsh conditions faced by many working people, are today sought via the book collecting magazines. The present author hopes to tackle the topic of Christian Journalism, as it developed from the 1880s to the 1950s or thereabouts, and will (if this materializes) write further on Harold Murray, Hugh Redwood and others who sought to present the gospel in print media.

As this list ends, a new title from Baker Book House in the USA, and published in association with National Religious Broadcasters (USA) looks at the development at the development of religious broadcasting in the USA. **AIR OF SALVATION**—The Story of Christian Broadcasting, is written by Mark Ward Sr., and traces the impact of Christian output from its origins in 1921 (prior to the launch of broadcasting in Britain). The 1994 title is useful not least in showing the kind of radio opportunities available to Gipsy in the USA, though not nearly so in Britain.

Index